The Psychology of Ageing

An Introduction

2nd edition

KT-514-940

of related interest

Gerontology: Responding to an Ageing Society
Edited by Kevin Morgan and Christopher W. Smith
ISBN 1 85302 117 2

The Abuse of Elderly People: a Handbook for Professionals
Jacki Pritchard
ISBN 1 85302 122 9

The Science and Practice of Gerontology:
A Multi-Disciplinary Approach
Edited by Nancy Osgood and Ann H. L. Sontz
ISBN 1 85302 044 3

Ageing, Independence and the Life Course
Edited by Sara Arber and Maria Evandrou
ISBN 1 85302 180 6

Psychogeriatrics: a Practical Handbook
Donald A. Wasylenki et al.
ISBN 1 85302 037 0

Dementia: Case Studies of Community Care
Mary Marshall and Katrina Myers
ISBN 1 85302 142 3

The Psychology of Ageing

An Introduction

2nd edition

Ian Stuart-Hamilton

Jessica Kingsley Publishers
London and Bristol, Pennsylvania

First published in the United Kingdom in 1994 by
Jessica Kingsley Publishers Ltd
116 Pentonville Road
London N1 9JB, England
and
1900 Frost Road, Suite 101
Bristol, PA 19007, U S A

Library of Congress Cataloguing-in-Publication Data
Stuart-Hamilton, Ian.
The psychology of ageing: an introduction / Ian Stuart-Hamilton.
-- 2n ed.
p. cm.
Includes bibliography references and index.
ISBN 1-85302-233-0
1. Aged--Psychology. 2. Aging--Psychological aspects. I. Title.
BF724.8.S78   1994
155.87--dc20

British Library Cataloguing in Publication Data
Stuart-Hamilton, Ian
Psychology of Ageing: Introduction. -
2Rev.ed
I.Title
155.67

ISBN 1-85302-233-0

Printed and Bound in Great Britain by
Biddles Ltd., Guildford and King's Lynn

To Mark

A new edition

Acknowledgements

Not necessarily in order of gratitude, I would like to thank the following for their kind help and assistance in the preparation of this book. To Sheila Kerr who persuaded me to go to the conference where I met the publisher's representative who asked if I was interested in writing a book on ageing. Also to Sheila for making comments on the early drafts of some of the chapters. To Dr Elizabeth Maylor, for her supportive and helpful comments on a later draft (and who very kindly did not make a fuss about the number of split infinitives). To Professor Pat Rabbitt, most especially for first firing my enthusiasm for gerontology (for which I will always be heavily indebted), but also for his constant support and amazing patience with my dull wits. To my colleagues in the Department of Life Sciences, University of Buckingham, for providing such a conducive atmosphere in which to work, and to my students, who continue to amaze me. To the University library for ordering all the works I requested in researching for this book and being kind to my eccentricities. This book is *not* dedicated to the piece of detritus who introduced a computer virus onto my word processor and wiped my files, thus delaying submission of the manuscript. However, I would like to express warm thanks to Jessica Kingsley for being so patient during that delay. I would also like to thank my parents, not only for dogsitting whilst I typed this book, but also for their constant support and love. Finally, I would like to thank my wife, who read through the manuscripts many times and yet managed to remain sane and provide many helpful suggestions.

Contents

Introduction

This book is intended as a layperson's introduction to the psychology of ageing. As such, it has been made as jargon-free as possible, and, it is hoped, provides readers with the essence of current thinking on the subject. For this reason, the book will also be useful to psychologists looking for a primer or a revision aid.

Psychological and other specialist terms are explained in the body of the text and are denoted by bold type. The same terms, and some others which readers may encounter in their further reading in gerontology, are included in a Glossary. The text also contains plentiful references. As far as possible I have included readable and not too specialised texts as well as more esoteric primary sources. By a judicious scanning of the reference list, readers can select further items appropriate to their level of interest and/or background knowledge.

Although the book is primarily designed to be read sequentially, chapters can be read in isolation, with a minimum of cross reference to other sections.

The second edition has been expanded for several reasons. The first and most pressing was to include some key pieces of research which have appeared in print since the first edition went to press. A second reason was to accommodate new topics not covered in the first edition. In some cases, this was because at the time of writing the original work, the theories were too speculative or lacked sufficient evidence to be included in a general textbook. Three years on, they have gained sufficient weight and support to be worthy of inclusion. In other instances, I have deliberately included topics not within the rigid bounds of psychology, because psychologists are making research forays into these areas, and the topics have a significant (if indirect) bearing on psychological changes in old age. A third reason was to expand the glossary. Reviews of the first edition were gratifyingly (if bafflingly) generous, and one cause for favourable comment was the glossary of technical terms. I have increased its size quite considerably, to include what I hope is a representative selection of the common (and less common) terms currently in use in gerontological psychology. The area has expanded considerably over the last decade, and with it has come a plethora of neologisms which the reader should be prepared for.

In spite of these changes, I hope that I have honoured my original intention of providing an introduction to the subject which is accessible to non-psychologists as well as providing a primer for psychology students. I have included a greater number of 'advanced' references in this new edition, largely to accommodate the latter group of readers. This should not in any way detract from the non-psychologist's enjoyment of the book. I have also intentionally kept the chapters relatively short. My belief is that an introductory text should be just that – it should introduce the reader to the topics, leaving him or her with a picture of the basic issues, findings, and theories. I have accordingly not included details of every last study or every last alternative permutation of a theory. In trying to get to grips with a new subject, the last thing one needs is irrelevant detail. For a similar reason, the book remains devoid of pictures of 'cute' pensioners, cartoons, and so forth.

Ian Stuart-Hamilton
Worcester College of Higher Education
September 1993

CHAPTER 1

What Is Ageing?

The greying population

Ageing is not unique to modern times, but it is only in the last 100 years that it has become a commonplace experience in westernised societies. One estimate is that, in prehistoric times, no-one survived into old age, and even up to the seventeenth century, probably only about one per cent of the population was over 65. By the nineteenth century this figure had risen to approximately four per cent (Cowgill 1970). Today about 12 per cent of the western population is elderly. This proportion is expected to rise to around 15 per cent by the turn of the next century, and to 20 per cent by 2030 (Bromley 1988, Kermis 1983, OECD 1988). To take another perspective, about 70 per cent of people living in a westernised nation can expect to live past the age of 65, and 30–40 per cent past 80. In 1900, only about 25 per cent of the populace could hope to reach even their 65th birthday (Brody 1988). The modern westernised population has been described as a **rectangular society**. Since there are roughly equal numbers of people alive in each age decade (i.e., equal numbers of 0–9-year-olds, 10–19-year-olds, etc), a histogram plotting numbers against age decade appears (with a little artistic licence) like a rectangle. A graph for 1900, however, would reveal a **pyramidal society**, with a large base of young age decades, but with much smaller groups of older age decades.

This 'greying' of the population has its problems, not least of which is how westernised societies will cope with it. An increase in the proportion of elderly people means a decrease in the proportion of younger adults. This in turn means that a smaller fraction of the population is working and hence paying income tax, National Insurance contributions (or equivalent) and so forth, to help maintain pensions and social and medical care for the elderly. One way of expressing this is the **old age dependency ratio**, which is the number of people aged 60 and over divided by the number aged 20–64. This currently stands at about one fifth for most westernised nations, but is likely to rise to one third or more before the middle of the next century. The so-called 'demographic timebomb' means that a greying population will place a major (and potentially catastrophic) financial burden on the economies of the twenty-first century. However, it is worth putting this into perspective. These discussions only apply to industrialised countries – for underdeveloped nations, the 1900 figures are more appropriate. It is a sobering thought that, on a global scale, most people on this planet die before their fifth birthday (McHale *et al.* 1979).

It must also be noted that old age is principally an experience of women. In peaceful societies, until the age of about 45 years, men and women form roughly equal proportions of the population (in a society at war, the women tend to outnumber the men because of a sex difference in casualties). Thereafter, men die at a faster rate than women, with the result that by the age of 70 there are roughly six women for every five men and, by the age of 80+, the ratio has moved to approximately 4:1. Many reasons for this have been suggested. A popular conception in western societies is that it is because men have traditionally led more physically demanding lives. However, this seems to be at best a marginal explanation, since in societies where the majority of women have physically demanding occupations, the sex difference in life expectancy remains. Indeed, the difference applies across many species (Shock 1977). This suggests that it is explicable by differences in chromosomal and physical makeup, rather than environmental factors.

A more dramatic way of presenting statistics on ageing is to note that, in 1900, the average life expectancy at birth was 47–55 years (figures vary according to the country concerned). It is estimated that for people born in 1991, life expectancy will be 76 years for males, and 80.8 years for females (OPCS 1991). However, without appropriate caveats, these figures are misleading. To the casual reader the statement that, in 1900, life expectancy was in the mid fifties implies that everyone died before they reached 60, which is palpable nonsense. **Life expectancy** refers to the age by which 50 per cent of an age group has died. In other words, half the members of an age group live longer than their life expectancy figure (the so-called **survivors**). The reason for the lower 1900 figure can largely be attributed to the much higher rates of infant mortality (i.e., a lot of the 50 per cent had died in childhood, not all in their fifties). If the life expectancy of young adults living in 1900 is compared with that of young adults living today, the difference is the much lower figure of seven years. Comparing the figures for those aged 70 or 80 in 1900 and today, the difference is still less, being about 3–4 years, and for centegenerians, the difference is a matter of months (Bromley 1988, Kermis 1983). In other words, the longer one lives, the less modern society can prolong the remaining life beyond what would have been experienced in earlier times. An interesting comment on this is made by Wilkins & Adams's (1983) study, which, had an octogenarian of 1900 known about it, might have given him or her a distinct feeling of schadenfreude. Working from Canadian actuarial tables, Wilkins & Adams calculated that, of this extra 3–4 years of life, approximately 75 per cent of it is spent suffering from one or more disabilities and hence discomfort. This gives rise to the concept of **active life expectancy** (i.e., the average number of years remaining in which members of an age group can expect to lead an active life). Thus the life expectancy figures are something of a chimera – the so-called 'greying population' is due more to childhood illnesses no longer being the killers they once were, rather than to an 'improvement' in the way people age.

However, allowing for these comments, ageing is now an experience of the majority rather than the minority, and it is projected that the size of the majority will increase in the future. Looking still further ahead, some commentators have predicted that, eventually, currently fatal diseases will have been conquered, and that people will die when they have attained their **lifespan** (the maximum age to which a member of a species can live). It is further argued that the lifespan is approximately the same for all individuals. If a graph is drawn plotting mortality rate (on the vertical axis) against age (on the horizontal axis) for such a group of people, then there will be a practically straight vertical line going from left to right, which will then plunge vertically downwards when the lifespan age is reached. Because of its shape, the graph is called the **rectangular survival curve** (hence the society experiencing this has been called a **rectangular society** – note that the same term is used to express a different, though related concept above). There are obvious criticisms of such a theory (e.g. it is doubtful that people share the same 'natural' lifespan), but it is reasonable to assume that as medical care improves, **survival curves** (plots of numbers of survivors in an age group against age) will tend towards a rectangular shape, which can be seen as an ideal towards which medical care should aspire.

Individual differences in life expectancy

It is worth noting that there are considerable differences between individuals in the rate at which they age. This in part can be explained by environmental factors (e.g. poor diet and hygiene), which are a principal cause of, for example, the much lower life expectancy figures for third world countries when compared with the West. Researchers have, not unreasonably, been interested in finding the optimal environment for long life, and the search led some to make extravagant claims for remote rural populations in various parts of the world. The best known of these were a group of people in Georgia (in what was the USSR), where a disproportionate number of centegenerians were found. Various explanations were offered (mostly involving health foods and abstinence), but the prosaic truth is that there were no centegenerians. The old people, to avoid conscription into the Soviet army, had used their parents' birth certificates, thereby adding twenty or thirty years to their real ages. This draft dodging technique had backfired, because in later years the Soviet authorities had seized upon the 'well-pre-served' old people, and had used them as a tourist attraction and propaganda vehicle. Subsequent detailed medical examinations debunked the story. Other cases of 'well-preserved' groups in Pakistan and Ecuador are ex-plained by the simpler reason that the societies involved were illiterate and/or had poor population records, so recollections of ages were fraught with errors (see Schaie & Willis 1991, Chapter 13). Some commentators still accept that these elderly people are indeed very old, but the majority of evidence points to there being no 'magical' society in which people live significantly longer than in westernised nations.

Indeed, for anyone looking for the elixir of life, the answer would appear to be the Ancient Greek adage of 'moderation in all things'. Studies of the old elderly usually show that such individuals have fairly adaptable personalities and tend to be moderate in consumption and exercise (see Schaie & Willis 1991). Smoking of any amount, and heavy drinking and eating can reduce life expectancy by a decade or more (indeed, in animal studies, reducing calorific intake increases the lifespan of many species – Masoro 1988). However, it is worth noting that environmental and lifestyle factors alone are probably not the full explanation. Since longer-lived individuals tend to produce longer-living offspring (Murphy 1978), there is evidence of a genetic component determining the rate of ageing.

Definitions of ageing

There are a variety of ways in which ageing may be defined. One is to consider the causes of the characteristics found in an elderly subject. These can be divided into features which are attributable to relatively distant events (e.g. lacking mobility because of childhood polio), known as **distal ageing effects**, and those which are attributable to more immediate causes (e.g. lacking mobility because of a broken leg), known as **proximal ageing effects**. Again, characteristics can be regarded in terms of the probability that other elderly people share them. **Universal ageing** features are those which all elderly people share (e.g. wrinkled skin), whilst **probabilistic**

ageing features are a likely but not universal feature (e.g. arthritis). These terms may be contrasted with the similar concepts of **primary ageing** (age changes to the body) and **secondary ageing** (changes which occur with greater frequency in old age, but are not a necessary accompaniment). Some commentators add a third term – **tertiary ageing** – to refer to the rapid and marked physical deterioration immediately prior to death.

Another method of measuring ageing is to examine how and when the features of young adulthood transform into the features of later adulthood. Ageing is the final phase of human development, and must be seen as part of a continual process of change. However, precisely because it is part of a continuous process of change, it is difficult to find a satisfactory definition of the point where middle age ends and old age begins. This is a manifestation of a familiar problem in science – how does one divide a continuum into sub-groups? For example, if we consider the colour spectrum, it is obvious that there are bands of orange and red. However, looked at closely, one can see that the red gradually blends into the orange. At what point does the colour become orange and cease to be red? Similarly, and despite the popular phrase, people do not become old overnight. Over several years one can see people's physical and psychological characteristics change from what one considers to be stereotypically middle-aged to stereotypically elderly, but one would be hard pressed to judge the definitive time when a person 'becomes' old. Researchers are well aware of this problem, and have tried a number of methods to create an objective measure of old age. The commonest gauge of ageing is **chronological age** (simply, how old a person is). This in itself is uninformative, since it is essentially an arbitrary measure. How often the earth has circled the sun since a person was born tells one nothing about him or her unless this passage of time is correlated with other, more functional changes. As shall be demonstrated, chronological age *does* correlate with other measures, but the degree of correlation can at times be quite low. For example, age correlates relatively poorly with physical changes. One can think of 70-year-olds who look like stereotypical old people (grey hair, wrinkled skin, etc). However, one can also recall 'well preserved' individuals who lack these features (**agerasia**), and younger people who possess them early in life and are said to be 'prematurely aged' (though this should not be confused with **progeria**, a disease in which the patients appear to age at an abnormally fast rate, usually dying in their early teens). Thus, chronological age is not an infallible predictor of someone's state of being; the best it can do is indicate the condition of the average person.

Another commonly used measure is **social age**. This refers to societal expectations of how people should behave at particular chronological ages.

Thus, western culture expects the over-sixties to behave in an essentially sedate fashion, and not surprisingly, therefore, the onset of old age is often indicated by retirement from full-time employment. In some other, 'primitive' societies, old age is believed to be a reward for a pious life. Every civilisation has created myths and theories of old age and expectations of it (Gruman 1966). Two of the commonest have been classified as the **antediluvian ageing myth** and the **hyperborean ageing myth** – the myths that in ancient times or in a far distant lands, respectively, there was/is a race of people with incredibly long lifespans. The reasons for longevity are usually ascribed to piety and/or a diet of sheep's yogurt (or some equally delightful diet). Disregarding the myths, most societies hold the belief that old age marks a change in social status. However, the chronological age at which this is felt to occur varies from one society to another, with the age of onset ranging from 50 to 70 (Decker 1980). In most western countries, an age of between 60 and 65 (roughly contiguous with compulsory retirement) is a traditional choice. Most **gerontologists** (people who study ageing) tend similarly to select a figure of 60 or 65 to denote the onset of old age, or the **threshold age** (e.g. Bromley 1988, Decker 1980, Kermis 1983, Rebok 1987, Ward 1984). This is not just to fit in with western stereotypes, but also because at around the threshold age there are demonstrable physical and psychological changes, as will be seen. In this book the threshold age will be defined loosely as being between 60 and 65. This rule of thumb is intentionally vague to reiterate the caveats made earlier that:

(a) there is not a single point at which a person becomes old, and

(b) chronological age is in any case an arbitrary and not very accurate measure, so the use of a single figure for the threshold would give it a speciously objective status.

Nonetheless, at some time during the 'floating threshold' of 60–65 years, most people begin to show signs of ageing. Some commentators further categorise older people into the **young elderly**, aged 65–75, and the **old elderly**, aged 75 and over (though note commentators sometimes differ over the precise threshold ages – e.g. some believe that the old elderly are 80 and over). A variant on this theme by Burnside *et al.* (1979) suggests categories of 'young old' (60–69), 'middle-aged old' (70–79) and 'old-old' (80–89), and 'very old-old' (90–99). This seems simply to introduce new and unnecessary synonyms for 'sixties', 'seventies', 'eighties' and 'nineties'. Another method divides the over-65s into the **third age** and the **fourth age**. The 'third age' refers to active and independent living in old age, and the 'fourth age' to a period of dependence on others for basic welfare in old age. The terms have met with some favour, since they do not have the pejorative overtones which some people perceive in words such as 'old' and 'elderly'. However, this is a moot point, since terms such as 'third age' in effect classify older people in terms of how much help they need from others. It should also be noted at this point that the terms used by gerontologists are not necessarily the ones employed (and by implication, liked) by older people. Midwinter's (1991) survey found that the majority (72%) of elderly people sampled preferred the terms 'senior citizen' or 'retired', with only five per cent preferring 'elderly' and four per cent 'older people' (though these terms were used by 61% of younger people). There are sound reasons why researchers use terms such as 'elderly' and 'old'; they have an objectivity which is lacking in terms such as 'retired' (which can in any case be misleading, since people often retire before they reach 65). However, there are equally sound reasons why older people in everyday life prefer the terms stated above, and in non-technical communications, such sensitivities should be borne in mind.

Regardless of how they are labelled, signs of ageing can be both physical and mental, and are measured on scales of **biological age** and **psychological age** respectively. As the rest of this book is primarily about psychological ageing, no further mention will be made of it here. However, biological ageing cannot be passed over without some consideration, as many changes which occur to the human body (particularly the senses and the central nervous system) directly impinge on the ageing brain.

Biological ageing

The term 'biological age' refers to the body's state of physical development/degeneration. Generally, the term is used fairly loosely to refer to the general state of the person's body. However, several more specific examples of biological age are sometimes used. These include **anatomical age** (the relatively gross state of bone structure, body build, etc); **carpal age** (the state of wrist (carpal) bones); and **physiological age** (the state of the body's physiological processes, such as metabolic rate). In the instances cited below, the general term is usually implied.

Ageing is the final stage of development which every healthy and accident-free individual experiences. However, one must be careful not to over-extend the word 'development' to imply that ageing necessarily involves an improvement. Indeed, one commentator emphasises this point by classifying old age as being **post-developmental**:

> all the latent capacities for development have been actualized, leaving only late-acting potentialities for harm. (Bromley (1988) p.30)

The body's cells are not immortal – over a period of about seven years they all die and are replaced by new cells (the cells of the central nervous system are an exception to this rule – when they die, they are not replaced). However, there is a limit on the number of times a cell can be replaced. Hayflick found that living cells taken from a body and raise in vitro will only reduplicate themselves a limited number of times before they die, and the older the animal from which the cells are taken, the fewer the duplications before death occurs. This finding is called the **Hayflick phenomenon**, after its discoverer, and the number of times a cell can reduplicate before dying is known as the **Hayflick limit**. Another theory – the **somatic mutation theory of ageing** – argues that the problem is compounded because replacement cells are not exact replicas, and contain genetic 'errors' (a permutation of this – the **error catastrophe theory** – pins the blame on faulty protein replication). Further suggestions for causes of physical degeneration include environmental pollutants, incorrect diet, the theory that the body's autoimmune systems begins to attack the body's own cells (the **autoimmune theory of ageing**) and that degeneration is caused by free radicals (charged atomic particles produced by some normal physiological processes). The final theory, advocated amongst others by Linus Pauling (twice Nobel laureate) argues that, *inter alia*, vitamin C in large doses may help counteract this. This **free radical theory** has not been without its critics, however. Other commentators have observed that, beside free radicals, cells tend to produce a wide range of waste products – including a substance known as lipofuscin – which remain in the cells, and are possible pollutants (the **cellular garbage theory**). However, the correlation between presence of waste products such as lipofuscin and the degree of 'agedness' have been found to be tentative (Sanadi 1977).

One must bear in mind that the loss does not begin in old age, but in early adulthood, with most bodily systems showing a decline of 0.8–1 per cent per year after the age of 30 (Hayflick 1977). The course of this loss is very slow, and as most bodily systems have an over-capacity built into them, it is only in about the sixth decade of life that the change is first apparent to the casual observer. Botwinick (1977) notes that the decline is greater in complex than in simple bodily functions. This is probably because the simpler functions have each only declined slightly but, when used together in a more complex action, the total decline is greater than the sum of the loss of the individual components. As shall be seen, this disproportionate loss of complex over simple functions manifests itself repeatedly in both the ageing body and the ageing mind.

Another consideration is that many changes observed in the elderly may be due to disease rather than to ageing *per se*. It is virtually unheard-of for people to go through life without succumbing to any illness at all, and it is thus difficult to exclude the possibility that age changes are at least in part due to the cumulative effects of infections contracted earlier in life. The effect of even minor decrements in health is shown by Birren *et al.* (1963) in the so-called 'forty-seven healthy old men' study. The researchers took 27 completely healthy old men, and 20 men who appeared healthy, but who had slight evidence of potentially serious illness when given an extremely rigorous examination. This latter group showed a decline on a range of measures of mental functioning, such as comprehension, memory, and even brain wave rhythms. Birren *et al.* and subsequent commentators (e.g. Botwinick 1977, Kermis 1983) have argued that this shows that the decline was because of disease rather than ageing, and other studies have recorded similar findings. However, the argument, pushed a little further, is ultimately circular – are some elderly people healthy because they have never contracted a disease, or have they never contracted a disease because they are healthy?

Succumbing to illness may be a function of ageing (for example, a decline in the immune system would clearly have serious repercussions). Indeed, there are theories of evolution which argue that the body 'chooses' to age in this way (**programmed senescence**). Several methods by which this could occur have been suggested, including theories that the decline in the autoimmune system (mentioned above) and/or a reduction in the efficiency of the hormonal system are genetically pre-ordained. Why should evolutionary pressure force the body to self-destruct? Perhaps the best-known explanation is that bodies have an inbuilt programme to decay and die in order to make way for younger members of the species, and thus prevent the problem of overcrowding. This argument is accepted uncritically by many gerontologists, but it is undermined by one simple fact: very few animals in their natural habitat reach old age. Accordingly, because the elderly are so rare 'in the wild', it is unlikely that evolutionary pressure has created a method of 'self culling' a species – predators, disease and accident do a satisfactory job in themselves (Kirkwood 1988, Medawar 1952). A more compelling explanation is provided by the **disposable soma theory** (Kirkwood 1988). Modern evolutionary theory argues that an organism is driven to reproduce as much as possible, and this takes precedence over the organism's personal survival. What matters is that the genes the organism carries survive – which body they are in is of secondary importance. Thus, by this theory, it would be better for a man to die at 20, having sired 30 children, than to die childless at 100 (see Dawkins 1976). This principle, it is argued, shapes ageing as follows. Body cells die and have to be replaced constantly. If they are not replaced, then the body parts concerned decline in mass and efficiency. The disposable soma theory argues that the body allocates resources to maintaining reproductive fitness, at the expense of maintaining the somatic (non-reproductive) body parts. Accordingly, the more energy is invested in reproduction, the greater the rate of bodily decay. Taken to extremes, this theory sounds like a Victorian homily but, at a subtler level, the argument is persuasive, and Kirkwood (1988) provides strong supporting proof, which is too lengthy to review in the confines of this text.

The ageing body

The general picture of changes to the ageing body is not an attractive one. For example, at the tissue level, tissues such as the skin and muscles become less elastic (the **cross-linking theory of ageing**); at the cellular level, there is a loss in the efficiency of the mitochondria (which generate energy within the cell); and at a molecular level, the somatic mutation theory of ageing has already been mentioned. Not surprisingly, these changes have a deleterious effect upon the functioning of bodily systems. For example, the urinary system becomes slower and less efficient at excreting toxins and other waste products. The gastrointestinal system is less efficient at extracting nutrients. There is a decline in muscle mass and the strength of the muscle which remains. The respiratory system can take in less oxygen. The cardiovascular system suffers a double blow – the heart decreases in strength while simultaneously a hardening and shrinking of the arteries makes pumping blood around the body more energy-consuming. The result is that the average 75-year-old's cardiac output is approximately 70 per cent of the average 30-year-old's (Aiken 1989, Kart 1981, Kermis 1983). Many of these changes *may* be lessened by appropriate diet and exercise (DeVries 1975, Fries & Crapo 1981), although note that the experimental methods used to support this argument have been criticised (Thornton 1984).

These changes have a disadvantageous effect on the functioning of the brain, and hence on psychological performance. For example, a decline in the efficiency of the respiratory and cardiovascular systems will restrict oxygen supply and thus the energy supply available for the brain to operate. Birren *et al.* (1980) suggest that the slowing of reaction times, even in apparently healthy old people, may be due to a restriction in blood supply. Cardiovascular disease in addition to normal senescent decline will also have a detrimental effect on cortical function (Kermis 1983). The most notable example of this is the **stroke**, where blood supply to a section of the brain is interrupted, causing the death of brain tissue. At a less severe level, for some elderly people the oxygen supply may be so constricted that they fall asleep after meals because the energy required by the digestive processes deprives the brain of sufficient oxygen to remain conscious. Changes in other systems may have subtler effects. For example, a decline in the urinary system may mean a high level of toxins accrues in the body. This may in turn affect the efficiency of neural functioning. If an elderly person is receiving a drug therapy, then failure to excrete drugs may lead to overdosing problems, including **acute confusional state**, or delirium (see Chapter 6). A decline in the gastrointestinal system can have similarly far-reaching psychological consequences. If the decline has the effect of lowering the elderly person's interest in food, then malnutrition can result. This is especially serious from a psychological viewpoint if the person develops a deficiency of vitamin B12, since this can trigger a delirious state (see Chapter 6).

Another effect of the ageing body is that it can cause a person to reevaluate their state of being. This is usually not serious. Being aware that bones are becoming more brittle and muscles are less strong teaches most elderly people a sensible degree of caution. However, in others these physical signs can lead to depression (Raskin 1979). This is usually a pessimistic reaction. Weg (1983) argues that the majority of elderly people still have ample *capacity* to deal with the demands of everyday life. Whether they do, however, is another matter.

The ageing sensory systems

The senses are the brain's means of contact with the surrounding environment and, accordingly, any decline in the former directly impinges on the workings of the latter. Age-related declines in perception deprive the brain of a full experience of the world, but it would be unrealistic to assume that such loss begins in old age. Like many other declines in bodily functions, the changes often start in early adulthood, and it is important to bear this caveat in mind in when reading the sections below.

VISION

It is a frequent complaint of the elderly that their sight 'isn't what it used to be'. This is usually true. A frequent complaint is the decline in **accommodation** (the ability to focus at different distances), leading to **presbyopia** ('long-sightedness'). This is probably due to the aged lens losing some of its elasticity, and hence its focusing power. The most serious visual handicap most old people suffer is loss of **acuity** (variously defined as 'ability to see objects clearly at a distance' or 'ability to focus on detail'). Bromley (1988) estimates that about 75 per cent of the elderly need spectacles, and many will not have full vision even with this aid. Corso (1981), in his excellent review of the literature, observes a marked decline in acuity with age, though he notes that the problem can be somewhat alleviated if the visual displays have a high contrast in luminance (e.g. black on white rather than black on grey). This is borne out by studies of **contrast sensitivity function** (CSF). Experimental subjects are shown patterns of alternating light and dark parallel lines. The thickness of the lines can be varied, as can their luminance. Obviously, broader lines which vary strongly in luminance are the easiest to see. By reducing the thickness of the lines and/or the contrast in luminance between them, it is possible to make the pattern 'disappear': the observer sees a homogeneous grey surface, because s/he can no longer distinguish the lines, and they blur into one. The CSF is a formula which expresses the smallest difference in luminance for a given thickness of line which the subject can still see as a pattern rather than as a grey splodge. The less the difference in luminance, the more sensitive the subject's visual system is. Sekuler *et al.* (1982) found that the CSF declines in old age. For relatively broad patterns (measured in cycles/degree, 0.5 and 1 c/deg) there was no significant age difference. However, as the lines got narrower (2 c/deg), the contrast in brightness between lines had to be significantly greater before elderly subjects could see the pattern. A further complicating factor is that for some line thicknesses, younger subjects' performances can be improved if the visual display is moving. However, no such advantage is conferred on the elderly subjects by this procedure (Sekuler *et al.* 1980).

Another example of poor CSF performance by the elderly is that they are severely disadvantaged at recognising and matching pictures of faces when the contrast in luminance of the pictures has been reduced. Such findings bode ill for the everyday visual performance of the elderly. Sekuler & Owsley (1982) comment that most studies of acuity are conducted in optimal lighting conditions. However, in real life, many items are dimly lit, visual displays rarely provide a strong contrast in luminance and, has been seen, the elderly are especially disadvantaged in these conditions. Thus, standard measures of visual acuity may underestimate the degree of handicap the elderly suffer. This argument is further strengthened by the finding that old people's loss of acuity is appreciably worse when they are asked to focus on a moving rather than a stationary display (Fozard *et al.* 1979).

Perception of light intensities is also affected by age. The visual threshold (the dimmest light that can be seen) *increases* with age – in other words, the elderly can see *less* dim lights (Elias *et al.* 1977, McFarland & Fisher 1955). This is probably due to a variety of factors, including a diminution in the maximum expanse of the pupil, and poorer metabolism of receptor cells (Pitts 1982). Similarly, the rate at which people can adjust to low level lighting conditions (dark adaptation) decreases with age (Domey *et al.* 1960). The converse – ability to recover from glare – is also reduced, sometimes by several hundred per cent (Carter 1982). This clearly has practical implications (e.g. for the elderly's ability to drive at night). Another important consideration is the change in colour perception: elderly people perceive the visual world as being yellower. Colours at the yellow end of the spectrum (red, orange and yellow) are identified reasonably well, but greens, blues and purples become harder to discriminate between (note that this problem does not usually arise until the eighties). Many commentators have argued that this is due to the lens yellowing with age, thus literally colouring the image falling on the retina. However, this cannot be the full explanation, since some unfortunate elderly individuals who have had a lens surgically removed still perceive the world as having a yellow tinge. The reason is probably attributable to changes in the nervous system (Marsh 1980).

The elderly are also slower at processing visual stimuli, and need to see them for longer before they can be accurately identified. Also, their disadvantage grows disproportionately worse the dimmer the stimulus they are looking at. This slowing occurs in both the peripheral stages (i.e., the retina and nerves leading into the brain) and in the sections of the brain responsible for processing visual information (Moscovitch 1982, Walsh 1982).

The size of the visual field also diminishes. A relatively minor problem is that the elderly cannot move the eyeball as far up as younger adults, with the result that older people have to move their heads to see some objects above them which younger adults can see by eye movement alone. A more serious problem is a loss of peripheral vision (i.e., how 'wide' the field of view is). Onset of this decline occurs in middle age, but becomes far more pronounced in the over-75s (Jaffe *et al.* 1986).

The above problems can be serious and annoying for elderly people, but they are not necessarily crippling. In addition, many of the problems in vision arise prior to old age, in some instances as early as the mid-thirties (Corso 1987). However, it is pertinent to remember that about 7 per cent of 65–74-year-olds and 16 per cent of 75+-year-olds are either blind or severely visually handicapped (Crandall 1980). The three principal causes of this are **cataracts** (the lens becomes opaque); **glaucoma** (excess fluid accrues in the eyeball, and the resultant pressure permanently destroys nerve and receptor cells); and **macular degeneration** (the **macula** or 'yellow spot' on the retina, which has the greatest acuity of vision, degenerates).

These illnesses are not confined to old age, but they are certainly much commoner (Corso 1981).

HEARING

Hearing declines gradually throughout adult life, so that as young as 50, many people are impaired in at least some circumstances, such as listening to faint sounds (Bromley 1988). For some individuals the degree of hearing loss can be a severe handicap. Stephens (1982) estimates that 1.6 per cent of 20–30-year-olds have serious hearing difficulties, compared with about 32 per cent of 70–80-year-olds. This figure rises to over 50 per cent for those aged 80+ (Herbst 1982). Other commentators, using slightly looser criteria, posit even higher estimates for hearing difficulties, with figures of 75% for people age 70+ being not uncommon. The rate of hearing loss can be exacerbated by environmental conditions. Deafness among long-term workers in heavy industry is well documented (e.g. Sekuler & Blake 1985), and because men have tended to work in noisier workplaces then women, hearing loss is greater among the former than the latter. Generally, however, it is impossible to adduce how much of hearing loss is because of ageing *per se*, and how much is due to environmental damage, although undoubtedly both play a role.

Working from the outside of the ear inwards, the following changes may be noted. One of gerontology's more esoteric findings is that ageing ear lobes increase in size by several millimetres (Tsai, Chou & Cheng 1958). The functional significance of this change remains unclear, however. The elderly ear canal can get blocked with wax more easily, causing hearing loss, though this is easily treated. Changes in the middle ear are severer. The bones of the middle ear – the hammer, anvil and stirrup (or malleus, incus and stapes) – tend to stiffen with age, either through calcification or arthritis. This affects the transmission of sound, most particularly at high frequencies. The problem may be compounded by changes in the inner ear, where cell loss is usually concentrated in the receptors for high frequency sounds (Corso 1981, Crandall 1980, Kermis 1983, Marsh 1980). Leading from the inner ear to the brain is the auditory nerve. This bundle of nerve fibres diminishes in size with age. The atrophy is probably due to a combination of loss of blood supply, and bone growth restricting the channel for the fibres (Crandall 1980, Krmpotic-Nemanic 1969).

A frequent misconception about deafness is that all sounds are perceived as quieter and harder to hear. Some forms of deafness do take this form, but the commonest form of hearing loss in the elderly is a condition known as **presbycusis**. This condition can occur in several forms (Kermis 1983 – though see Corso 1981 for a critique of these divisions). However, the feature common to all of them is that there is a greater loss in perception of high than low frequency sounds. Sometimes the problem is exacerbated by a phenomenon known as **loudness recruitment**: higher pitched sounds are perceived as being of louder than normal intensity, often to the point of being painful and/or distorted. Presbycusis clearly handicaps a sufferer. At best the auditory world becomes muffled; at worst it is agonisingly painful. Crandall (1980) observes that, ironically, the best way to communicate with a presbycusis sufferer may be to whisper – this lowers the tone of the voice and reduces the painful effects of loudness recruitment. For many sufferers the biggest problem is that speech perception can become difficult if not impossible. Speech sounds are a composite of low and high frequencies, but it is usually the high frequency components which distinguish one speech sound from another (particularly consonants). The phenomenon is not confined to the severely deaf elderly. Old people with relatively robust hearing, and only the normal level of high frequency hearing loss, nonetheless are significantly impaired at identifying consonants (Kart 1981).

A further problem with the elderly's hearing appears to be another manifestation of the age x complexity effect. Generally, the more complex the speech signal, the more the elderly are disadvantaged relative to the young (Corso 1981). For example, when detecting signals played against a background of noise or of competing signals, compared to detecting signals played against a silent background (e.g. Bergman *et al.* 1976, Dubno *et al.* 1984). However, when the signals are familiar phrases or ones expressing familiar concepts, there is no or little age difference (Hutchinson 1989).

Within the normal elderly, other facets of hearing also decline. Not surprisingly, perhaps, there is a loss in pitch discrimination, and also in the ability to detect the direction of a sound source (Marsh 1980). In addition, up to 10 per cent of the elderly suffer from **tinnitus**, or what is commonly (if slightly inaccurately) known as 'ringing in the ears' (Kart *et al.* 1978). This can block out other auditory signals, as well as cause suffering. A complicating factor in studies of hearing loss is that the degree of handicap can only be partly explained by objective measures. Thus, the elderly's subjective ratings of their handicap are often at some variance with their actual decline in hearing thresholds, and Corso (1987) estimates that 'audiometric data explain less than 50 per cent of the variance in hearing handicap in the elderly' (p 45).

The effects of even mild hearing loss can be very damaging to an old person's social life. Herbst (1982) observes that society has held a grudge against the deaf from the start of recorded time. To the Ancient Greeks, the word 'deaf' was synonymous with 'stupid', and to the early Christians, deafness was a curse, because in pre-literate societies it blocked the person from holy teachings. In modern times this bias has continued. The deaf tend to receive less charitable support than, for example, the blind, because, Herbst argues, the latter are cut off from things while the former are cut off from people. This alienation of the deaf and hard of hearing is of course illogical, but it often leads to able hearers behaving like the archetypical 'Englishman abroad', complaining that his failure of communication is solely due to the natives having the temerity not to learn English. In other words, the speaker can never be at fault. The elderly person is well aware of this, and is often cowed into submission and silence rather than risk the anger or ridicule of normally hearing individuals. This removal from social intercourse can cause an old person to become depressed and still more withdrawn. This may be interpreted by the outsider as evidence of antisocial behaviour or even the onset of dementia, and the person is accordingly shunned even more. This can cause further withdrawal by the old person, and thus a vicious cycle is created. However, there is a danger that the social effects of hearing loss can be over-dramatised. For example, Norris & Cunningham (1981) and Weinstein & Ventry (1982) provide evidence that social isolation is only poorly correlated with degree of hearing loss. Such proof does not obviate the need for help, of course, and a variety of remedial measures is available (see Burnside 1976). However, as Herbst (1982) argues, one of the biggest problems is getting the elderly to seek help in the first instance – because of the perceived stigma, many do not seek medical attention at all until they are practically stone deaf.

OTHER SENSES

The declines in the other senses are of less interest to the psychologist because they do not impinge as directly on intellectual functioning as do the declines in hearing and vision.

> *Taste.* The tastes humans perceive can be divided into four primary types – bitter, sour, salty, and sweet. Commentators are divided on the extent to which ageing causes a decline in sensitivity to these. For example, Engen (1977) argues that whilst there is a general decline, sensitivity to bitter tastes increases with age. Weiffenbach *et al.* (1982) on the other hand, found a decline in sensitivity to bitter and salty tastes, but found no change in sweet and sour sensitivities. The data on detection of more complex tastes are far more clear-cut however, with the elderly being significantly worse than younger people at identifying blended foodstuffs (Murphy 1985, Schiffman 1977).

Smell: The associated sense of smell seems to fare better than taste, with virtually no decline in the healthy aged. However, in the case of elderly unwell people, there is a considerable decline (Corso 1981, Kermis 1983).

Touch: The touch sensors are housed in the skin. Accordingly, it would be very surprising if the obvious thinning and wrinkling of the elderly's skin did not herald changes in touch sensitivity, and indeed this is what is found: the elderly have higher touch thresholds (i.e. firmer stimulation of the skin is required before it is detected), and similarly, sensitivity to the temperature of objects decreases. However, the changes are not necessarily clear-cut. For example, the effects vary greatly in their magnitude across individuals. Again, sensitivity to vibration is different across the frequency range. At relatively high vibration speeds (250 Hz), the elderly are worse at estimating the strength of the vibration than are young people. However, at a lower frequency (25 Hz), there is no significant age difference (Verrillo 1982).

Pain: Some researchers have reported an increase in the pain threshold of the elderly – in other words, they can endure more extreme stimuli without perceiving them as being painful (e.g. Harkins *et al.* 1986). This may be due to a decline in the number of sensory receptors in old age. However, some studies have failed to find any change in pain perception, and this discrepancy in findings may be due to where on the body the experimenters inflict the pain (Bromley 1988). There are also serious methodological problems with pain studies. Apart from obvious ethical considerations which curtail the range and strength of pain inflicted, there is also the problem of creating a suitably objective measure for such a subjective feeling as pain.

OVERVIEW

The clear message from this brief survey of the ageing senses should be readily apparent – the information reaching the brain from the surrounding environment is constrained in its range, is less sensitive, and, given the general slowing of the nervous system, takes longer to arrive. This hardly bodes well for the aged intellect; nor indeed for the personality if an elderly person's self image is affected (it is known that illness is linked to level of depression in the elderly – Williamson & Schulz 1992). However, it should be noted that the ageing brain is in turn not making the best use of the incoming sensory information. A notable pattern of decline in the ageing perceptual processes is that the aged mind is less adept at integrating several strands of sensory information into a cohesive whole (e.g. complex versus simple tastes, complex versus simple auditory signals). As mentioned earlier in this chapter, the principal age deficits appear to happen when several simple processes must be operated simultaneously.

Basic anatomy of the nervous system

It is important that the reader has some knowledge of the nervous system in order to understand the psychological and neurological changes which occur in old age (particularly in the dementias). Accordingly, this section is devoted to a basic description of neuroanatomy. As far as is possible, this is presented in non-technical language. Those readers already familiar with neuroanatomy can safely skip this section.

The neuron

The basic building block of the nervous system is the **neuron** (or, less accurately, the 'nerve cell'). Neurons vary enormously in shape and size, but all have the basic function of receiving signals from other neurons or specialised sensory receptors (for touch, pain, heat, etc), and passing signals on to other neurons or sense organs. Neurons connect with each other at junctions called **synapses**, and signals are sent between these neurons via these synapses. When a neuron is activated, an electrical pulse passes down its length until it reaches a synapse. The synapse 'spits' a chemical onto the receiving neuron, causing it to do one of four things:

(1) It was dormant, and it is activated into sending a signal.

(2) It was already sending a signal, but the new input causes it to fire with greater vigour.

(3) It was already active, but the new stimulation makes it either to stop firing, or to fire with less vigour.

(4) It was dormant, and the new stimulation prevents other neurons exciting it into firing.

In cases 1 and 2, the effect is said to be **excitatory** and in cases 3 and 4 the effect is said to be **inhibitory**. Therefore, neurons can either spur each other on, or they can suppress activity. The chemical transmitters employed to do this are called **neurotransmitters**. On some occasions it is convenient to classify neurons according to the type of neurotransmitter they use. For example, there is the **cholinergic system**. This uses a transmitter called **acetylcholine**. About 90 per cent of the neurons in the brain are cholinergic. The other principal use of the cholinergic system is in the control of skeletal muscle. Conversely, the **noradrinergic system** (which uses **no-**

radrenaline) is primarily employed in the control of smooth muscle. Many neurons are covered with a layer of fatty substance called **myelin**, which acts rather like the insulation around electrical wires – it stops the signal from escaping where it is not supposed to, and also helps to increase the speed at which the signal is sent.

Anatomy of the nervous system

The simplest division of the nervous system is into the **central nervous system (CNS)** and the **peripheral nervous system (PNS)**. The CNS consists of the brain and the spinal cord, the PNS of the neurons connecting the CNS to the rest of the body. The nervous system consists of approximately 1010 neurons, most of which are in the brain. The fundamental difference between the neurons of the CNS and the PNS is that the former cannot be replaced if they die, while the latter can.

PNS anatomy

The PNS can be divided into sub-sections, according to function. **Afferent** neurons carry information into the CNS, and are said to be somatic if they carry information from joints, skin, or skeletal muscle, and visceral if they carry information from the **viscera** (intestines). **Efferent** neurons carry commands from the CNS to the body, and are said to be **motor** if they send signals to skeletal muscle, and **autonomic** if they send signals to glands, smooth muscle, cardiac muscle, and so forth (i.e. bodily functions over which there is little conscious control).

CNS anatomy

The **spinal cord**'s principal function is to channel information between the PNS and the brain. However, it is capable of some simple processing. By means of a mechanism called the **reflex arc** (a simple connection between afferent and efferent neurons), it can make the body respond to some forms of stimulation. Many reflexes (such as the well-known knee jerk reflex) are produced in this manner.

The spinal cord projects into the brain or, more accurately, the section of the brain called the **brain stem**. Many lay persons think of the brain as being a homogeneous mass of 'grey matter', but in fact the brain is a collection of distinct though interconnecting structures. For anatomical and functional reasons, the brain is often divided into four principal divisions. The first is the brain stem. Located behind this at the base of the skull is the **cerebellum**. Located above the brain stem is the **diencephalon**, or

interbrain. Seated above and overlapping the other three segments is the **cerebral cortex** (often simply called the 'cortex'), the wrinkled 'top' of the brain. Generally, the further a structure is away from the spinal cord, the more sophisticated its functions.

> *The brain stem* is chiefly concerned with the maintainance of 'life support' mechanisms, such as control of blood pressure, digestion, respiration, and so forth. It also receives the inputs from the senses, and channels them through to other systems in the brain.

> *The cerebellum* receives somatic input, and information from the semi-circular canals (the balance sensors located in the inner ear). Given this information, it is not surprising to learn that the cerebellum is responsible for coordinating movement.

> *The diencephalon* is a collection of several components. Among the more important of these are the following. The **thalamus** co-ordinates and channels sensory information and the execution of motor movements. Damage to this region gives rise to Parkinsonism (see Chapter 6). The **hypothalamus** might be loosely said to control bodily needs – hunger and satiety, sexual drive, anger, and so forth. The **hippocampus** is, in evolutionary terms, the oldest section of the brain. It is involved in emotional control, but of principal interest to psychologists is its role in memory. Some unfortunate individuals who have had this area of the brain destroyed (by disease or accident) cannot retain any new information in their memories for more than about two minutes. Therefore, the hippocampus is in some manner involved in retaining information in a long term memory store.

> *The cortex* is responsible for the execution of most higher intellectual functions. It is divided into two **hemispheres.** The divide runs vertically from front to back, along the centre of the head. The hemispheres are linked by several pathways which bridge this divide, of which the most important is the **corpus callosum**. For most individuals, the right hemisphere controls visuo-spatial skills, and the left hemisphere controls verbal skills.

The cortex can also be divided into lobes, based upon the psychological functions which each of them controls. The **frontal lobes** extend from the front of the skull back to the temples. They are mainly involved in the control and planning of actions, such as producing sequences of movements, getting words and letters in the right order in speech and spelling, and producing socially appropriate behaviour. The frontal lobes are also involved in memory – principally in identifying which events in memory occurred in the recent past and which in the distant past. The **temporal lobes** are situated in the positions of the right and left temples. One of their principal roles is in interpreting information, and in particular the left temporal lobe is vital in comprehending speech and print. The temporal lobes are also strongly involved in memory, particularly the long term retention of information. Because of the specialisation of the left and right hemispheres, the left temporal lobe tends to store verbal memories and the right temporal lobe tends to store spatial information. The **occipital lobes** are at the rear of the brain. They are involved in reading, but their principal function is in vision. Virtually all processing of visual information takes place in the occipital lobes. The **parietal lobes** are located on the top of the brain, surrounded by the other three lobes. In part they are responsible for maintaining awareness of the body's state and location. Their principal intellectual role might be said to be symbol interpretation, and they are involved in object recognition and reading.

Neuronal changes in old age

Researchers agree that the brain decreases in weight by 10–15 per cent in the course of normal ageing (Bromley 1988). This has potentially serious repercussions for psychological functioning: it is important to recall that cells in the central nervous system cannot replace themselves (i.e. when a cell dies, it is lost forever). The reasons why this loss occurs are far from clear. Most probably, several factors are responsible, and the relative contribution of each may vary from individual to individual. One possible cause is decreased cerebral blood flow, leading to neurons starving of oxygen and thus dying. However, Hunziker *et al.* (1978) demonstrated that changes in cerebral blood supply seem to be an adjustment to a decline in the number of neurons rather than vice versa. There are a number of important caveats to this. First, the same research group noted in a subsequent review that only individuals with very well-adjusted cerebral blood supply seemed to survive beyond early old age (<75) into late old age (>75). It is suggested that this results from genetic programming (Meier-Ruge, Hunziker *et al.* 1980). Second, many elderly suffer from miniature strokes or **infarcts**, where a minute portion of the brain atrophies because of the demise of the local blood supply. The old person is unaware of this happening, and it is worth stressing that usually the number of infarcts is small, and can be regarded as symptomatic of normal ageing. However, in some individuals they dramatically increase in numbers, giving rise to **multi infarct demen-**

tia (see Chapter 6). Third, it should be noted that if blood supply does not automatically affect neuronal numbers, it may nonetheless influence the efficiency and speed with which the CNS can operate, as was noted earlier. A fourth and final consideration is that the cerebral blood supply, when operating efficiently, filters out possible toxins in the blood before they reach the brain, by a mechanism called the **blood-brain barrier**. If ageing causes this to decline, then the brain might be exposed to potentially damaging toxins.

More important causes of cellular decline are the changes which occur in the neurons' own physiology. There is some debate over whether cells die, or if in fact they survive, but are simply reduced in size. It is documented that for many sections of the brain, neurons shrink in size in old age (partly because of a thinning in the myelin sheath) and decrease the number of connections with other cells. However, estimates of actual losses differ considerably between researchers because of the technical difficulties in taking measurements. Schaie & Willis (1991) from an overview of the literature, place an estimate of 5–10%. Perlmutter & Hall (1992) from their overview, observe that some of the claims for cell loss have come from studies of patients with diseased brains, and that studies of healthy elderly brains have tended to show no or little cell loss (though a reduction in cell size). The debate is far from resolved, but what is certain is that the neural networks in the brain are rendered less efficient. Again, Meier-Ruge, Hunziker *et al.* (1980), reviewing their own and others' work, argue there is a significant decline in the ageing brain's metabolic activity. This is especially serious because, as has been seen, the CNS is primarily a cholinergic system, and the cholinergic system is very energy demanding (see also Meier-Ruge, Gygax & Wiernsperger 1980). Again, the speed at which neurons can conduct signals declines (see section on 'Reaction times and ageing' in Chapter 2).

Elderly neurons may also absorb minute metallic fragments into their cell bodies. This phenomenon is observed in the brains of many older people, and is especially prevalent in the brains of demented patients. The effect of the absorption is either to kill the neuron, or severely to reduce its efficiency. Cells can also atrophy from other causes. Sometimes their manner of death leaves behind traces. **Neurofibrillary tangles**, caused by abnormal protein metabolism, are strands of protein looking (under a microscope) like knotted string. **Granulovacuolar degenerations** are a malformation of neuronal cell bodies containing a dense granule of malformed cell materials. **Senile plaques** are amorphous conglomerations of decayed neurons. **Hirano bodies** are abnormal crystal-like structures found in brain cells. These four types of decayed cell structures are found in most elderly people, though they are far more prevelant in demented patients (Adams 1980, Bromley 1988, Kermis 1983, 1986).

The deleterious changes at the neuronal level are reflected in the changes in the brain's anatomy and in mental performance, but some areas are more affected than others. For example, the hypothalamus is barely affected by ageing (Bromley 1988, Selkoe 1992). However, other areas are not so well preserved. A wide variety of studies has shown that cell loss or shrinkage and a decline in metabolic activity are concentrated in the cortex (particularly the frontal lobes) and the hippocampus: in other words, in the areas of the brain most strongly linked with intellectual functions and memory (Adams 1980, Kermis 1983, 1986, Meier-Ruge, Hunziker *et al.* 1980). Again, some sections of the brain stem are badly affected (Selkoe 1992) whilst others remain unscathed (Bromley 1988). However, this need not necessarily give cause for concern. The issue of how CNS neurons store information is hotly debated. Perhaps the most widely held current view is that the storage of a memory is spread across networks of thousands of neurons. The loss of individual neurons should not matter, because the remaining neurons in the network should retain enough of the encoded memory to be able to reconstruct it. Therefore, on a priori grounds, one cannot assume that cell loss will automatically lead to a decline in intellectual ability. In addition, recent evidence suggests that if neurons are lost, then the surviving neurons may produce new 'branches' to form new connections with other surviving neurons, to compensate for this loss (see Selkoe 1992).

In an attempt to resolve this issue, one must turn to studies where measures of anatomical and/or metabolic changes have been correlated with psychological performance. This has only been a practical proposition since the mid 1970s with the advent of body scanners. These are of two principal types – **computed tomography (CT)** and **positron emission tomography (PET)**. Essentially, the CT scan works by taking X-rays of the brain, with the difference that it can scan the brain in very fine slices. The PET scan measures how the brain metabolises a dose of (mildly) radioactive glucose injected into the cerebral blood supply: the more the metabolism, the more active is that area of the brain. Thus CT scans measure the structure of the brain and PET scans the brain's level of activity. Both methods have been used to study possible correlates between the elderly's physical and psychological states. Usually the subjects have been demented (see Chapter 6), but a limited number of studies has been run on the normal elderly. Conclusions from these studies are nearly unanimous in noting that age-related declines in brain mass and metabolism are correlated with decrements in intellectual and mnemonic performance (Albert & Stafford 1988, Metter 1988). However, a considerable fly in the ointment is that researchers have often disagreed on the physical location of the decline – some studies have found one area of the brain to be in decline, while later researchers have found it to be well preserved, and vice versa. This may reflect the fact that the technology of scanning is still in its infancy – the resolution of pictures from scans is improving yearly, but they are still rather fuzzy and hard to interpret. Thus, it would perhaps be fair-minded to suspend judgement for the present.

An older method of assessing the brain's physical activity relies on the fact that neurons transmit electrical pulses, and that, given sufficiently sensitive equipment, these pulses can be measured. This mechanism is called the **electroencephalograph (EEG)**. This measures the electrical activity on the scalp, and from this the activity of the brain within can be roughly surmised. The electrical pulses recorded by the EEG are transmitted across a range of frequencies, which can be grouped into frequency bands – **delta** (0–4 Hz), **theta** (4–8 Hz), **alpha** (8–12 Hz) and **beta** (>12 Hz). It used to be supposed that EEG frequencies slowed down in old age, but recent evidence shows that the situation is more complicated than was first supposed. Alpha activity is largely unaffected by ageing, whilst for other frequency bands there is 'a general desynchronization with age, characterised by decreased slowing and increased fast activity' (Duffy & McAnulty 1988, p 274). Several researchers have observed age differences in EEG recordings made while subjects perform a simple intellectual task, such as scanning a list of letters to see which has been presented in a previous exposure, or choosing the correct response in a reaction time task. Usually the age difference manifests itself as a less strong electrical pulse, and sometimes the pulse takes longer to be initiated (Marsh & Watson 1980). It is difficult to judge the weight which should be accorded to EEG findings. They have an obvious attraction because they provide a physiological correlate of psychological performance. However, they are also less accurate than CT and PET scans, and give only a general impression of neural activity. It is quite likely that EEG measures, although currently providing richer findings than other scanning methods, will rapidly be superseded.

Summary and overview

Ageing as a widespread phenomenon is confined to twentieth century westernised nations, resulting from lower infant mortality rates, and improvements in health care and lifestyle in earlier adulthood, rather than any intrinsic improvement in the way humans age. There is no single reliable measure of ageing – most gerontologists, as a rule of thumb, take an age of 60 or 65 years as indicating the onset of old age. About this age, declines in many physical and psychological processes become readily apparent, although the actual onset of this decay is usually in early adulthood. There are many suggested causes of physical decline, which may be grouped under the larger headings of **wear and tear theories** (parts of the body gradually 'wear out' with use) and the **cytologic theories** (that the body ages through exposure to toxins, including metabolic waste products). The disposable soma theory explains why ageing may be an evolutionally sound strategy for an individual's genes – certainly, ageing and death from 'old age' are not methods of population control, as many commentators have argued. Physiological ageing typically takes the form of cell loss coupled with loss of efficiency in the cells remaining. A consistent phenomenon is that age-related declines are greater for complex than for simple processes. The general effect of physical ageing is to provide the brain with poorer support. Perceptual changes in old age can be severe to the point of handicapping many elderly people. For those with less severe loss, the brain is nonetheless receiving a more limited and slower perception of the sensory world. The ageing nervous system also suffers. There is an some loss of central nervous system neurons, and a bad decline in the efficiency of those neurons remaining.

It must be stressed that the processes of social, biological and psychological ageing do not occur independently of each other. As has been seen, changes in the physical state of the body (and the brain in particular) can have profound effects upon psychological functioning. The point is at least tacitly acknowledged by many researchers, although not often spelt out. A useful model in this regard is that of Dannefer & Perlmutter (1990), which combines the concepts of biological, social and psychological ageing into a a single framework. The researchers argue that ageing can be seen in terms of 'physical ontogeny' (essentially, biological ageing); 'environmental habituation' (the process of coming to respond to items in the environment automatically, i.e., without conscious attention); and 'cognitive generativity' (at its most basic, conscious processing of information about the self and the environment). The ageing process is made up of a combination (and interaction) of these three factors. It is argued that some parts of ageing, such as physical ontogeny are largely beyond volitional control, but that others, and particularly cognitive generativity are what the individual makes of them. At a basic level, this is a restatement of the old adage that people must make the best of what they have been given, but the model is subtler than this, and interested readers are advised to consult the authors' work. An older and consequently further developed model by Baltes (e.g. Baltes & Reese 1984) argues that development is determined by three factors –

purely environmental, purely biological, and mixtures of biological and environmental. These influences express themselves through three strands of development. **Normative age-graded development** (a.k.a. age-normative development) is the basic developmental pattern one would expect to find in any normal individual (e.g. in terms of biological ageing, the onset of puberty, in term of social ageing, the effects of retirement on behaviour and attitudes). Within a particular society, the norms of 'correct' behaviour determine that everyone experiences these events. **Normative history-graded development** (a.k.a. history normative development) charts the effects of historical events which have been experienced by one age group but not others (e.g. experience of food rationing would be normal for most English people in their sixties, but would be unusual for people in their twenties). **Non-normative life development** measures the effects of major events unique to an individual's life (e.g. not everyone has experienced the effects of playing football, winning the Nobel Prize). The model neatly demonstrates how people's lives are made similar by the common experiences of normative development, how identification with one's own generation is shaped by history normative development, and how an individual's uniqueness is shaped by non-normative development.

In short, ageing is the result of a complex mixture of factors, and in the chapters which follow although, for the sake of convenience, isolated aspects of psychological functioning have been selected for scrutiny, it must not be forgotten that they form part of a wider pattern of development.

Suggested further reading

Schaie & Willis (1991) can be recommended as a general introductory text, as can Perlmutter & Hall (1992). Both are American in origin, and some examples may confuse or be inappropriate for British readers. However, overall they are very readable (Perlmutter & Hall is particularly strong on physical ageing). Two British texts may also be of interest. Bromley (1988) is another general textbook, is comparatively cheap, is well-written, and provides a solid (if now slightly dated) overview. The disadvantages are a paucity of references and an assumption that the reader is already familiar with basic medical and psychological jargon. Stokes (1992) is readable, and has a different format from many texts. It veers towards considerations of the impact of ageing rather more than other texts. This may be advantageous for some readers. Corso is the acknowledged authority on perceptual processes in the elderly, but much of his work is steeped in technical jargon. Slightly more readable is the collection of papers on visual perception (including one by Corso), edited by Sekuler *et al.* (see reference for Carter 1982). A good collection of papers on geriatric neuropsychology is edited by Albert & Moss (see reference for Albert & Stafford 1988). A useful overview is provided by Selkoe (1992) in a Scientific American article. A more advanced general text is the Handbook of the Psychology of Aging, edited by Birren & Schaie (1990). Chapters 1–3 are particularly relevant to this chapter. The book is a flagship of gerontological scholarship (however, it is also expensive). Economic, social and demographic aspects of ageing are well served by the literature. Binstock & George (1990), Jeffreys (1989), and Johnson & Falkingham (1992) may be of value to interested readers.

CHAPTER 2

Ageing and Intellectual Skills

Introduction

The chapter is a review of the relationship between ageing and intellectual skills. It begins by considering the effects of ageing on intelligence as measured by intelligence tests, in terms of general intelligence and the differential effects on fluid and crystallised skills. The issue of group versus individual differences in decline is assessed, as is the related topic of terminal drop. The relationship between intelligence and practice (the 'disuse theory') is considered and reaction times (the 'speed hypothesis') are then assessed. The chapter then turns to considerations of the effects of ageing on more specific intellectual skills. It closes with a review of the relationship between intellectual changes in old age and models of intellectual development in children, and attempts to build an integrated theory of development across the whole lifespan.

Intuitive beliefs about ageing and intelligence

Most commentators argue that people, if asked to describe the effects of ageing on intelligence, would say something along the lines that ageing brings an increase in general knowledge, but that this is at the expense of taking longer to think things through. In other words, it creates an increase in wisdom, but a decrease in wit. Berg & Sternberg (1992) found this to be a reasonably true representation. When asked to describe an 'exceptionally intelligent person' of 30, 50 or 70, subjects tended to emphasise 'ability to deal with novelty' in the 30-year-old person, and to stress 'competence' in the case of older adults. This reflects the finding that young and middle-aged adults have a greater tendency than older people to associate 'wisdom' with old age (Clayton & Birren 1980). Berg & Sternberg's study is interesting, but slightly misleading, because it is examining concepts of the very intelligent. Hence, it would not have been surprising to find the hypothetical 70-year-old was described as being very good at dealing with novelty, or the 30-year-old as being very competent, because that is what made them exceptional for their respective ages. Of more interest is the clear belief that many people have that intelligence can be modified (for better or worse) with age (only 3.8% of the sample believed that intelligence was fixed for life). Interestingly, and in comparison, people of all ages tend to provide the same phrases when asked to define 'wisdom' (Holliday & Chandler 1986, cited Perlmutter & Hall 1992).

A more revealing insight into everyday concepts of ageing and intelligence is perhaps to be gained from studies of the works of artists and writers. For example, painters and sculptors have conditioned one to accept that a depiction of a healthy old man looking pensive is automatically a representation of the epitome of wisdom, be it temporal or spiritual. It is very difficult for anyone brought up in a Western culture to think of a philosopher, saint, or even God, as anything other than an old man (long white beard optional). Paradoxically, the elderly are simultaneously portrayed as being slow thinking and dull witted. The old person, doddery of mind and body, has been the butt of jokes from Shakespeare to television situation comedy. Dogberry's famous adage in *Much Ado About Nothing* that 'when the age is in, the wit is out' expresses the guiding spirit for centuries of ageist humour. However, popular opinion is not necessarily synonymous with scientific fact. Is there any proof that ageing causes wit to decline, whilst wisdom is preserved? In order to answer this question, one must first decide if there are measurable intellectual traits which correspond to wit and wisdom.

Crystallised and fluid intelligence

When psychologists began to consider the issue in the early years of this century, it was generally felt that 'intelligence' was a unitary skill. In other words, no matter what type of intellectual task was set, be it verbal, numerical or visuo-spatial (i.e., shapes and figures), the same basic ability dictated a person's performance. This was christened **g** (for 'general intellectual capacity') by one of the founding fathers of intelligence testing, Charles Spearman. The term 'g', or 'Spearman's g', is still in use, although it is now employed more loosely, to describe overall ability or score on a battery of intellectual tests which have assessed a variety of intellectual skills (i.e., verbal, numerical and visuo-spatial). Most researchers now reject the more rigid definition of g, arguing that 'intelligence' is composed of several inter-related skills. What these are is still open to debate (Eysenck & Kamin 1981; Kail & Pelligrino 1985 and Rebok 1987). However, perhaps the most widely accepted theory has been the **hierarchical approach** (Cattell 1971). This argues that all intellectual skills make use of a general intellectual ability, but they also call upon more specialised skills, depending upon the needs of the task in hand. Cattell (1971) and Horn (1978) identified two of these specialised skills, and called them **crystallised intelligence** and **fluid intelligence**. These skills, it can be argued, correspond to the popular concepts of 'wisdom' and 'wit' respectively.

Crystallised intelligence measures the amount of knowledge a person has acquired during his or her lifetime. Usually it is measured by simple direct questions, such as asking the person to define obscure words (e.g. 'what is the meaning of *manumit?*'), or to answer 'general knowledge' type questions (e.g. 'what is or are the *Apocrypha?*'). These types of questions (to slip into jargon) find the limits of an individual's knowledge base. However, the questions can also be rather more abstract, asking the testee to provide solutions to problems. These can be practical (e.g. 'what do you do if you cut your finger?' – the correct answer is *not* 'bleed') or moral (e.g. 'why should we pay our taxes?'). Such questions can only be correctly answered if one already has the information in one's head: one cannot create concepts of antiseptics, sticking plasters, taxation systems and infrastructures from first principles. Fluid intelligence tests, on the other hand, draw on acquired knowledge as little as possible, and might be defined as the ability to solve problems for which there are no solutions derivable from formal education or cultural practices. In other words, it is the ability of the testee to solve novel problems. The most commonly used method is to ask the testee to identify a rule governing a grouping of items (verbal, numerical or visuo-spatial) and then provide either the next item in the series:

A C F J ?

or to spot the odd one out:

245   605   264   722

Typically, fluid intelligence tests have a time limit imposed on them so that, to be proficient, a testee must not only be accurate, but fast as well.

It would therefore seem that fluid intelligence and crystallised intelligence provide measurable psychological concepts which correspond to wit and wisdom. There is also the measure of overall intelligence, called g, which, according to Horn and Cattell's framework, is the aggregate of fluid and crystallised intelligence scores. In the next section it will be examined how these skills change (if at all) with age.

Age changes in general intelligence (g)

The earliest studies on the effects of ageing on intelligence were conducted in the 1920s and 1930s, and brought discouraging news for anyone aged 30 or above. In summary, the typical finding was that g increased until the mid-twenties, but thereafter there was a steady decline, although, as several researchers noted, verbal skills were relatively unaffected (Rebok 1987, pp.363–364). However, there is a potentially serious flaw with these studies, since they used **cross-sectional** samples of subjects. This simply means that a sample of people of different ages was tested at one time, and is in contrast to the alternative method of testing, called a **longitudinal study**. This latter method means that the same people are tested at one age, and then retested as they get older (usually they are retested at fixed intervals of time). The obvious advantage of the cross-sectional over the longitudinal method is the saving in time. For example, to compare differences between 20- and 60-year-olds will obviously take 40 years using a longitudinal method, compared with a matter of weeks or months (depending upon the sample size) for a cross-sectional study. The price to be paid for this convenience is that the researcher cannot be absolutely sure how much of an age group difference is due to ageing *per se*, and how much is due to the effects of different educational and socioeconomic backgrounds. The last hundred years have seen an enormous improvement in health care and standards of living. Young people may therefore outperform the elderly not just because they are less old, but also because they are healthier, have had more (and better?) education, and have been brought up in a culturally richer world. This difference is called the **cohort effect** (a cohort is a group of people born or raised in the same environment and/or period of history).

There are two ways of compensating for the cohort effect. The first is to try to match age groups for level of education, socioeconomic class, and so forth. This can be problematic because it is difficult to match large numbers of people in this way, and for certain forms of analysis, large numbers of experimental subjects are *de rigeur*. The second approach is to use the longitudinal technique: since the subjects all belong to the same cohort, the cohort effect should disappear. Indeed, the results of some early longitudinal studies seemed to confirm suspicions about the cross-sectional method, since such studies showed that g seemed to be preserved at least until middle age (e.g. Bayley 1968; Owens 1959) and in one subsequent follow-up study, preservation was found into the volunteers' sixties (Cunningham & Owens 1983).

However, interpretation of these findings must be cautious, since there are also potentially serious methodological flaws with longitudinal testing.

The first problem arises from the fact that many volunteers drop out of longitudinal studies. In some cases this is because they move to areas too geographically remote for the researchers' travel expenses. A more serious worry is that many volunteers quit for motivational reasons. No matter how hard researchers try to explain to the contrary, most experimental volunteers seem to regard psychological tests as a competition. Therefore, if a volunteer perceives him or herself to be worsening in intellectual performance, then he or she may be less willing to be retested. This means that as the longitudinal study progresses, the 'declining' subjects drop out, leaving a rump of 'well preserved' volunteers. For example, Riegel & Riegel (1972) showed that people who refused to be retested in a longitudinal study had significantly lower test scores than those volunteers who were willing to carry on taking part in the project. Another problem is that for those who remain in the study performance on tests can improve considerably (Salthouse 1992b). In other words, if the subject takes the same test over a period of several decades, performance will improve. To rebut the obvious criticism, it is *not* because the subject remembers the answers (parallel forms of the test with different questions are used). The phenomenon is probably due to a variety of factors. Subjects may become 'test wise' – they are increasingly at ease with the testing procedure (and hence perform better), they have increased general awareness of the ways in which psychological tests operate, and so forth. Again, the effect can be attributed to general environmental factors – improved cultural input, the greater availability of instructional materials and greater amounts of leisure time in which to study them, may all play a role in improving performance. However, for whatever reasons they occur, the result of these flaws is that the longitudinal method may underestimate the effects of ageing (whilst the cross-sectional method probably exaggerates them).

One method of side-stepping the problems of the two approaches is to combine them. In other words, compare several age groups on one occasion, and then retest them all on subsequent occasions. This was the approach adopted by Schaie in a justly celebrated study – the **Seattle Longitudinal Aging Study** (e.g. Schaie 1983). A group of volunteers, aged between 20 and 70 at the start of the project, was tested in 1956, and then retested in 1963, 1970, 1977 and 1984. The principal test measure was the **Primary Mental Abilities Test**, or **PMA** (Thurstone 1958). This is a **test battery** (i.e., a collection of tests with a common theme – in this case intelligence – although each test measures something slightly differ-ent). The authors of the PMA claim that it measures five distinct abilities: *number* (basic arithmetic and algebraic skills); *reasoning* (logical deduction); *space* (visuo-spatial skills); *verbal meaning* (knowledge of semantics) and *word* *fluency* (efficiency at producing words related to an example). On all four test sessions (i.e., in 1959, 1963, 1979 and 1977), the younger subjects were significantly better on all sections of the PMA than were their elders. However, Schaie was also able to show that part of this superiority was a cohort effect. Because of the study's design, it was possible to compare the scores of younger subjects reaching a particular age at the final test session with the scores of older subjects who had been the same age at an earlier test session. Any differences between these age matched groups could only be due to a cohort effect, and Schaie found such differences on three of the five sections of the PMA: namely, reasoning, space and verbal meaning. Having allowed for this cohort effect, however, there was still a decline with age, although this was not appreciable until the subjects had reached their mid-sixties. In other words, when the cohort effect is controlled for, the age decline in intelligence is still there, but its onset is 30 years or more further on than was reckoned by the early cross-sectional studies. This means that on average, the intellect is preserved at least through the period of a person's working life.

Age changes in fluid intelligence and crystallised intelligence

So far intelligence has been considered principally as a general measure. However, what of the changes in crystallised and fluid intelligence discussed earlier? Is it the case that fluid skills decline whilst crystallised intelligence is unaffected by the ravages of time? An often-cited study by Horn & Cattell (1967) would seem to support this notion, since they showed that there was an age-related decline in fluid intelligence, whilst crystallised intelligence remained stable. However, a note of caution needs to be sounded. The researchers used a cross-sectional method, raising problems of cohort effects. This fear seems to be justified, since if Schaie's longitudinal data are reanalysed in terms of ability on tests requiring fluid ability versus tests requiring crystallised ability, then some age-related decline in fluid skills is found, but it is of a lower magnitude than the decline reported by Horn & Cattell. Schaie, like Horn & Cattell, found no age decline in crystallised skills (Schaie 1979). Another caveat is that Horn & Cattells' subjects were mostly aged under 50, whereas Schaie did not find an appreciable decline in fluid intelligence until the mid-sixties.

Subsequent studies have almost universally acknowledged that fluid intelligence declines in old age, whilst crystallised intelligence remains largely unaffected. Cross-sectional studies usually place a higher estimate on the extent of this difference than the longitudinal studies. For example,

Cunningham, Clayton & Overton (1975) showed that young subjects had significantly higher scores on a common test of fluid intelligence – **Raven's Progressive Matrices** – than did older subjects. Furthermore, the magnitude of this difference was considerably greater than the age difference on a vocabulary test (a test of crystallised skills). Hayslip & Sterns (1979) found similar results using batteries of fluid and crystallised tests. An analogous point is made by Salthouse (1992a). He reviewed a number of studies and re-tabulated the scores of the elderly subjects on a variety of fluid intelligence tests in terms of the standard deviations (see Glossary for definition) of the scores of the younger subjects. On intelligence tests, he found that elderly groups were an average of 1.75 standard deviations (s.d.s) below the average for the young groups (figures extrapolated from Salthouse 1992a, Table 4.2, pp.175–176). In other words, the average elderly person was performing at the level which, amongst a group of young adults, would be *very* below average. Note, however, that many of the studies used in the calculations were cross-sectional, and accordingly there may be cohort effects. In addition, there is considerable variability in the size of the reported effects. For example, using the same test (PMA Reasoning) different researchers have found effects ranging from -1.62 s.d.s to -5.19 s.d.s Accordingly, these findings must be interpreted with caution.

It is important to note that the decline in fluid intelligence is not universal within an age group, and some individuals may be largely immune to age changes. For example, Rabbitt (1984) conducted a cross-sectional study in which 600 volunteers, aged 50–79, were tested on measures of crystallised and fluid intelligence. Rabbitt divided his subjects into age decades (i.e., of people in their fifties, sixties and seventies). He found that there was no significant difference between the age groups' mean scores on the crystallised intelligence test, nor was there a difference in the *distribution* of these scores. To all intents and purposes, they were identical. However, the fluid intelligence measures behaved differently. Here, not only was there a significant lowering of mean scores in the older groups, but the distribution of scores altered, so that there was an increased skew in the older groups' scores. Put in plainer English, this meant that, although the three age groups' scores fell within the same range (i.e., the lowest and highest scores for the three groups were identical), the proportion of low scorers increased in the older groups, with a corresponding lowering of the proportion of the elderly who were high scorers. None the less, 10–15 per cent of the 70-year-olds remained high scorers, at the same level of performance as the best of the younger subjects (note that Salthouse's (1992a) review of studies of age changes in intelligence found smaller proportions of 'well preserved' old people). It is possible that these gifted

70-year-olds possessed even higher scores in their youth, and had declined to this new level, but this seems unlikely, since Rabbitt found no individuals in the younger groups with the very high scores that would be necessary if this theory were correct. Therefore, on an individual basis, the decline in fluid skills does not seem to be an inevitable consequence of growing old.

Subsequent research by Rabbitt (e.g. Rabbitt 1993) has shown that variability in test scores is greater for the elderly than for the young on a variety of cognitive measures, such as reaction times (see below) and measures of mnemonic ability. A literature review by Morse (1993) also records similar findings on changes in variability in old age. This means that among themselves, older people differ more in their performance than do the young, and hence, in this context, it is harder to justify talking about a 'typical' old person than it is to talk about a 'typical' young person. Furthermore, it would seem that some fluid skills are better preserved than others, and the pattern of change can vary between individuals (e.g. one person may have skills A,B, and C well preserved, whilst for another person these may be the skills showing the greatest decline). Rabbitt observes that these changes might be linked to physical changes in the brain (e.g. they may reflect disproportionately heavy losses of neurons in particular cortical lobes, in the hippocampus, etc). This theory echoes that of 'critical loss' discussed in 'The terminal drop model' below.

A cynic might argue that the cause of the age decline in fluid intelligence test scores is not due to any change in intellectual processes *per se*, but rather is due to the fact that the elderly cannot write down the answers quickly enough. Earlier in this chapter, we noted that the fluid intelligence test usually has a time limit imposed on it. If the elderly take physically longer to respond, then they will obviously have less time to deal with the problems themselves. This issue has been investigated by Storandt (1976). She tested subjects on a test which is part of a widely-used intelligence test battery called the **Wechsler Adult Intelligence Scale**, or **WAIS**. The particular measure Storandt used was the **digit-symbol test**. This requires subjects to match up digits to printed symbols according to a preordained code (e.g. if one sees a square, write a 2 underneath it, and similarly a triangle equals 3, an oblong equals 4, etc.). To see how much time the elderly were losing in writing down their answers, Storandt measured how many symbols the subjects could copy within the time limit of the test (90 seconds). This was taken as a measure of the subjects' physical response speed. Storandt then compared this with the subjects' performance on the test itself. It transpired that the elderly were significantly worse at both tests, and Storandt was able to show, by statistical means, that about half of the difference between the young and the old groups was due to the older subjects' physical limitations.

However, the difference is by no means eliminated and, in a later study, Storandt was able to show that even if the subjects were given as long as they wanted to perform a fluid intelligence test, there was still a significant age difference (Storandt 1977). Therefore, it would appear that abolishing the time limit can only *lessen* the age difference – it cannot totally remove it. Increasing the size of the test items (to overcome eyesight problems) similarly does not remove age differences (Storandt & Futterman 1982).

Similarly, there is probably a response time difference in tests of crystallised skills. Core (unpublished, cited Rabbitt 1984) found that older subjects took significantly longer to reply to questions on a crystallised intelligence test (the **Mill Hill Vocabulary Test**). Had a time limit been imposed on the test, then the elderly would have scored significantly worse than the younger subjects. Hence, to a certain extent, whether an age difference is found or not depends upon whether the experimenter decides to apply a stopwatch to the test. Again, Botwinick & Storandt (1974) demonstrated that, although the elderly scored as well as the young on a vocabulary subtest of the WAIS, they nonetheless gave less 'perfect' answers than young subjects. The test criteria were sufficiently lax for this difference to go unmarked. There are other instances in this chapter (and in the rest of the book) where crystallised skills can be shown to decline with age. This is supported by Meacham (1990), who argues that 'the essence of wisdom is not in what is known but in how that knowledge is held and put to use' (p 188). This implies that once one moves beyond a straightforward recital of stored information to any form of *interpretation*, then a decline is at least possible.

The terminal drop model

So far, (with the exception of Rabbitt's work), changes in intelligence have only been considered with reference to the *average* performance of different age groups. How representative of the individual is this average group performance? It is known that if the average scores for age groups are taken, then the rate of decline appears to be fairly gentle – certainly there is not a sudden precipitous drop in performance after a particular age. If we plotted *individual* subjects' performances, then it is possible that they would similarly show gentle declines. However, an alternative hypothesis is that the change within individuals is much more sudden. The moribund name for this is the **terminal drop model** (Kleemeier 1962; Riegel & Riegel 1972). This argues that individuals maintain the same level of performance until a few months or years before death, and then their abilities plummet, as if their minds suddenly 'wind down' in preparation for death. But, it might be argued, if the decline is so sudden, why does the group decline appear so gentle? The answer is quite simple. The probability of dying rises from middle age onwards. Therefore, the older the age group, the greater the proportion of its members in the terminal drop stage, and hence the lower the *average* intelligence score for the age group as a whole. However, because the proportion of 'drop' subjects rises fairly gently across age groups, then the overall age group average declines only gradually. Thus, the terminal drop should only be apparent when individuals (rather than groups), are tested. Kleemeier (1962), working on longitudinal data, found that if on retesting, a subject showed a large drop in intellectual performance, then there was a high probability that the subject would die within a short space of time. Similar evidence was provided by Riegel & Riegel (1972). They tested a group of middle-aged and elderly volunteers, and then retested them 10 to 20 years later. Riegel & Riegel found that volunteers who had died before they could be retested had had significantly lower test scores at the initial test session than the 'survivor' volunteers who came for retesting. Every longitudinal study has similarly reported the terminal drop phenomenon (Jarvik 1983), although the magnitude of the effect varies from study to study and can to a certain extent be dependent upon the statistical analysis used (Palmore & Cleveland 1976).

Jarvik and colleagues developed the terminal drop model to include the concept of **critical loss** (e.g. Jarvik & Falek 1963; Jarvik ibid). This argues that if over a period of time (10 years in the original study) there are declines in abilities on intellectual tests which exceed certain boundaries, then the probability of dying within a short period of time is dramatically increased. The extent to which a skill can decline before it is considered critical very much depends on the skill in question. For example, Jarvik argued that the ability to detect verbal similarities can decline by up to 10 per cent without cause for concern. However, *any* decline in vocabulary size is counted as a critical loss. Blum, Clark & Jarvik (1973) conducted a longitudinal study on 62 elderly subjects, and found that 15 of them had suffered a critical loss. Within five years of retesting, 16 of the sample had died, and of these, 11 had been in the critical loss phase. Whilst accepting the concept of critical loss, other researchers have disagreed with Jarvik *et al.* as to precisely what constitutes a critical decline. For example, Botwinick, West & Storandt (1978) found that changes in verbal abilities did not predict terminal drop, whilst abilities on **paired associate learning** (i.e., remembering which items in a memory test have previously been seen together and which have not) and **psychomotor skills** (loosely, mental skills with a physical skill component) did. In complete contrast, Siegler, McCarty & Logue (1982) found that verbal skills were the best predictors of the probability of imminent death. To complicate matters further, Reimanis & Green (1971) found that *total* score on the WAIS test battery to be the best predictor. In other words, although researchers agree that something must be declining in the terminal drop phase, nobody seems quite sure what it is.

A further problem with the terminal drop model is that it only appears to apply to the young elderly (i.e., the elderly aged below about 75). For example, Jarvik (1983) and Riegel & Riegal (1972) reported that the deaths of subjects who had reached their mid eighties or more appeared to be almost random, and were not predicted by a battery of intellectual measures. Similarly, White & Cunningham (1988) showed that a drop in intellectual performance (in this case of vocabulary scores) only predicted death if: (a) the subject was aged under 70, and (b) he or she had been tested within two years of death. Why should this curious state of affairs occur? The reason is probably as follows. Death in younger old age is usually due either to a specific illness or to an accident (often in part caused by a physical decline, such as sensory impairment). Such a precipitous rate of decline presumably has a similarly deleterious effect on psychological functions. The old elderly (i.e., aged over about 75) have (obviously) survived these events, but have considerably frailer bodies, and death may occur not so much from disease, as from a steady decline, until one physiological system drops in performance past a critical point. This decline occurs slowly and almost randomly, and hence is unlikely to be reflected in a sudden drop in psychological skills.

Hence terminal drop does exist, but interpretations of it must be cautious, since researchers are undecided on which skills are involved and also, the phenomenon is probably restricted to the relatively young elderly. Having allowed for these criticisms, the terminal drop model allows for the exciting (though gruesome) possibility that in the future there may be a relatively cheap and straightforward method of detecting when a person is afflicted with a life-threatening condition, and hence be able to administer appropriate therapies.

Disuse theory

Several researchers have found that physical exercise can improve certain aspects of elderly intellectual performance. For example, Hawkins *et al.* (1992) demonstrated that a ten week exercise programme resulted in a significant improvement in attention tasks, and that in some instances, improvement was disproportionately greater for the elderly group relative to young controls. Again, Powell (1974) found cognitive improvements in elderly institutionalised patients given an exercise regime. There are many reasons why physical exercise might have a beneficial effect on the intellect. A healthy body is likely to function more efficiently (particularly the cardiovascular system) and, as was seen in Chapter 1, a healthy body can enhance neural and hence mental functioning. Again, an older person who feels fit and healthy is also likely to have greater confidence in what they are doing, and hence have a higher motivation to do well at mental tasks. However, what can mental exercise do?

A commonly-used expression is 'use it or lose it'. The equivalent psychological term is **disuse theory** – the belief that age-related declines are attributable to a failure to use skills, so that eventually they fall into a decline. The theory is not easy to prove or disprove. Finding that elderly individuals practise a skill less, and that the level of performance on that skill is lowered is ambiguous. The skill may be worse because of lack of practice but, equally, the skill could be practised less because the individual's abilities are worsening, and so he or she has a lower motivation (motivation has been shown to adversely affect older subjects on a variety of tasks (Perlmutter & Monty 1989)). However, in studies of very well practised individuals on tasks related to a skill they practise regularly, it has almost always been found that there is a decline in performance in older subjects. For example, studies of architects and airline pilots on spatial skills have shown age-related declines (Salthouse 1992a). It would seem, therefore, that practice cannot entirely stave off ageing effects.

However, it would be wrong to draw such a bleak conclusion, nor would it be correct to assume that an experienced older person is less able than a younger one. The experiments cited above used relatively abstract laboratory tests. If one considers more realistic situations, then the age difference is often rather less. Although the elderly may be slower and less accurate at some 'basic' skills, their experience may be able to compensate for this through greater knowledge of strategies, and so forth. For example, Charness (1981) demonstrated this to be the case for elderly chess players, and in an earlier study found the same phenomenon in habitues of bridge (Charness 1979). In this instance, level of experience outweighed any intellectual decline. Similarly, Salthouse (1984) showed that whilst there were significant differences in various reaction time and finger movement measures when older and younger typists were compared, there was no age difference in typing speed. This was attributed to the older typists being able to plan further ahead – they had larger 'eye–hand spans' – which enabled them to compensate for their slower movements. Bosman (1993) adds a caveat to this – if older experienced and less able typists are compared, then the latter display errors in key movements which the former do not, relative to younger typists (Bosman also replicated some of the original Salthouse (1984) study, and she links her findings to Salthouse's explanation).

Again, if the elderly actively fight decline, then many abilities can be preserved. For example, Baltes & Willis (1982) have shown that perform- ance on fluid intelligence tests (e.g. figural relations) can be improved by practice. Other researchers have also reported positive effects of training (Kermis 1983, Rebok 1987). Salthouse (1992a) criticises these studies because often there have been inadequate control groups, and/or the success of the training has been judged on too narrow a range of tests. Again, he (and other commentators) have suggested that training may not affect the root skill which is in decline, but instead may offer new strategies to cope with the situation. An analogous situation might be taking a painkiller for toothache – it does not cure it, but it enables one to cope with it. From a practical viewpoint, this argument may seem relatively unimportant (if the elderly can cope, why worry?) but the theoretical considerations are, of course, not trivial.

Reaction times

The **reaction time** or **RT**, is a measure of how long it takes a person to respond to the appearance of a stimulus: the *lower* the RT, the *faster* the person is responding (and vice versa). Obviously, having lower RTs is advantageous. Fast reactions will aid a sportsman and may mean the difference between life and death to a car driver. Other examples of RTs are less dramatic but more central to everyday life. For example, the speed at which one can think of the answer to a question is an example of a RT, as is the time taken to recognise a voice, a face or an object. Indeed, every single experience of the outside world must be processed by the CNS before it is perceived, and the time taken to do this is a RT. Thus, at the most basic level the RT is the measure of the time gap between reality and one's perception of it. Most research on RTs has confined itself to rather more mundane considerations, such as the time taken to make a simple response to a simple stimulus. Classical RT experiments adopt two basic formats. The first is the **simple reaction time (SRT)** study. This is a measure of how quickly a subject responds when there is only one stimulus and only one kind of response allowed. This is typically tested by requiring the subject to press a button every time a light flashes. The delay between the flash and the button press is the RT. The second measure is the **choice reaction time**

(CRT). In this instance, the subject is presented with an array of stimuli and a choice of responses. For example, there might be three stimuli and three possible choices, and the subject is told to press button *A* if a red light flashes, *B* if a green light flashes, and *C* if a blue light flashes. Subjects have to give more consideration to what they see in a CRT experiment, and thus responses tend to be slower in a CRT than in a SRT study. Similarly, within a CRT study, the more stimuli and responses a subject has to choose between, the slower he or she is.

It is well established that reaction times get slower as people get older (e.g. Lindenberger *et al*. 1993). A belief shared by many gerontologists is that the elderly are disproportionately slower on a CRT than on a SRT task. A corollary of this is that, within a CRT task, the bigger the number of choices, the more disadvantaged old people become. This decline can be seen in stylised form in Figure 2.1 (a). There are many published studies supporting this finding (e.g. Botwinick 1973, Kermis 1983, Salthouse 1985). A slowing of nerve impulses (see Chapter 1) explains why the elderly have generally slower RTs. However, why should they be especially disadvantaged when the range of choices to be decided between is increased? A very basic explanation can be constructed as follows. The greater the range of choices, the more mental processing has to be done before a decision can be reached (hence SRTs are less than CRTs). Presumably, the greater the processing required, the more nerves have to be employed for the task. However, if, as in ageing, nerves become slower to conduct signals, then the greater the number of nerves, the greater the decline in processing speed. Hence the findings of RT studies where the range of choices (and hence processing demands) has been increased.

To quote Rabbitt (1980, p.427), 'This would be a simple and satisfying story and it is a pity that there is no reason to believe that is true'. Probably the most serious criticism of the evidence is that this age x complexity interaction only occurs when the experimental subjects have little practice at the tasks. If young and old subjects are allowed to practise the tasks over several days, then the elderly no longer display a disproportionate disadvantage. They are still slower than the young, but this now takes the form of a constant lag across all conditions (Rabbitt 1980). This is represented in stylised form in Figure 2.1 (b). Thus, the traditional explanation for ageing RTs can only at best hold true for tasks which are relatively novel – for practised individuals, another explanation has to be found. Probably the simplest explanation is that subjects' responses become automatic.

Most skills, if practised for long enough, become automatic. The definition of an automatic process is that it is done without conscious control. There are many examples of this in everyday life. At one point one

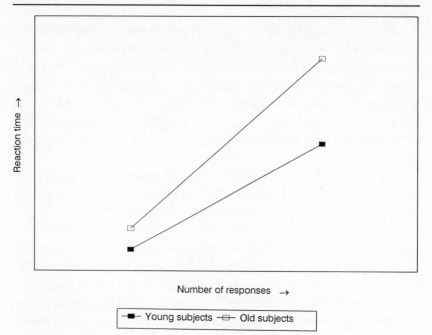

Figure 2.1 The traditional view of the relative effects on young and old subjects of increasing choices of response in a reaction time task

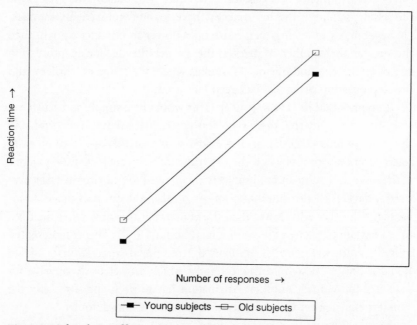

Figure 2.2 The relative effects on young and old subjects of increasing choices of response in a reaction time task, after serveral thousand practice trials

had to learn how to do such things as tying shoelaces, walking downstairs, reading, and so forth, but now they are second nature. To take the example of reading. In learning the skill, one had to think constantly about what each word meant. Now, however, words are instantly understandable, without one having to deliberate over their meaning. A similar procedure probably occurs in CRT tasks. As the responses to particular stimuli become familiar, subjects simply give the right response to the right stimulus, and no longer have to think about it first. This considerably cuts down the time taken to react to the stimulus. Botwinick (1973) demonstrated that the principal difference between unpractised old and young people's RTs was attributable to a slowing of neural transmission in the CNS. Practice removes this difference in central processing (presumably automatic processes take much the same length of time for young and old alike), and the constant age lag which remains is an expression of a slowing in peripheral factors, such as lower efficiency of muscular control, and so forth. Hasher & Zacks (1979) argue that automatic processes are relatively unaffected by ageing, although more recent commentators (e.g. Burke *et al.* 1987, Myerson *et al.* 1992) have found some instances where this is not the case.

Traditional considerations of age differences have considered mean RTs. Rabbitt (1980, 1988a, b) has observed that this is misleading, because it presents the impression that the elderly are no longer capable of the fast responses of their youth. In fact, if the distribution of response speeds is considered, than a different explanation emerges. The old can give response speeds just as fast as the young, but they make fewer of them. The elderly tend to produce a wider variety of response speeds compared to the young, who are fairly consistent in their rate of response. This is particularly the case when reactions to errors are examined (an error occurs when, in a CRT task, the subject presses the wrong button). Subjects are usually aware when they have made a mistake, and young adults respond by slowing down their RT on the trial after an error, before picking up speed again. Elderly subjects, however, will slow down for several trials after they have made an error, and will pick up speed comparatively slowly. This means that relatively speaking, young subjects can 'shrug off' their mistakes, whilst the elderly become overcautious. It thus seems that the young find an optimal speed of response (i.e., as fast as they can go without making too many mistakes) and stick to it, whilst the elderly seem to lack this degree of control and thus oscillate in their RTs. When the average performances of the two groups are considered, this difference expresses itself as a difference in mean response speeds.

Rabbitt & Goward (1986) found that if groups of elderly and young adults are matched for intelligence test scores, then there is no age difference in their CRT performance. Hertzog (1991), Salthouse (1991a) and Schaie (1989) similarly report that when the effect of speed of processing is statistically controlled for, differences between age groups are significantly lowered, or disappear altogether. This is at first sight discouraging, because it implies that the decline in RTs is nothing more than part and parcel of the decline in g. In a sense it is, but a more interesting explanation, argued by many researchers, is that declining RTs are not the effect but the *cause* of declining intelligence (e.g. Eysenck 1985, Salthouse 1985), an argument known as the **speed hypothesis** (or **general slowing hypothesis**) of cognitive ageing. If two items are correlated, there is no mathematical method of showing which is the prime mover. However, it can be logically argued that RTs are measuring a more fundamental process (and hence an earlier stage in the chain of causation) than are intelligence tests. RTs provide a parsimonious method of assessing how quickly nerves can send messages. This in turn indicates how quickly the CNS processes information. Botwinick (1973) demonstrated that the majority of CRT processing time is spent in the CNS. If the elderly have slower RTs, then they have slower CNS processing speeds, and this alone might explain much of the age-related deficit in performance on timed intelligence tests. This does not just apply to the elderly. Within any age group, there is a correlation between RTs and intelligence test scores – the faster the subject is, the better his or her scores (Eysenck 1985). However, as was noted in the studies of Storandt (1976, 1977) cited above, a decline in response speed only explains about half of the young–old age difference. Therefore, a further argument is needed, and this is provided by the fact that the ageing decline which causes a slowing of neural conductivity also causes a decrease in the number of synaptic contacts neurons make with each other, and generally signals are transmitted less accurately (see Chapter 1). The slowing RTs are a strong indication of this general loss of efficiency and accuracy of neural processing, which may greatly contribute to the loss in problem solving abilities. The decline in neural transmission cannot be the sole cause of intellectual decline, however. Factors such as experience and learning must play an important contributory role (as in the elderly chess players considered above). Again, as noted in Chapter 1, a decline in the bodily functions, particularly the senses, also has an important part. Nonetheless, on *a priori* grounds, it would seem logical that changing RTs (or rather, what they represent) are a key determinant of intellectual decline in the elderly.

The speed hypothesis also makes another important contribution to the understanding of ageing and intellectual skills. This is best explained by an example. Suppose that a particular specialised intellectual skill is chosen – for example, speed to complete a crossword. The researcher collects the findings of all the studies ever done on age differences in crossword solving. Each study obligingly provides the following pieces of data – the average time taken for a group of young adults to complete the crossword, and the average time taken by a group of older adults (for the sake of example, assume that the young are always faster than the old). The researcher draws a graph, with the old group time on one axis, and the young group time on the other. He or she then takes the first study to hand, and plots the point made by these two average times. He or she then repeats the exercise, plotting the average young versus old times for each study on the graph. When the researcher comes to join up the points on the graph, it is found that they form a straight line. This indicates that there is something remarkably consistent about age changes in crossword performance. The researcher then repeats the whole exercise using studies of another intellectual skill, and finds the same phenomenon – namely the plot of old and young average speeds is a straight line. This now begins to appear to be more than just a phenomenon of crossword solving, so several more sets of studies of other skills are assessed, in which performance is measured by speed of processing, and there is an age group difference. In all cases a straight line relationship is found. This indicates that the difference between old and young groups is subject to a consistent trend, and the most parsimonious explanation for this is that the old groups' responses are subject to a general slowing. Within a particular skill (or 'domain') older people will be consistently slower than the young.

The above is a simplified example, but the real life research on general slowing has followed the same basic principles. Across a wide variety of tasks, where average old and young speed of response measures can be compared, linear relationships have been found (e.g. Cerella 1990, Lindenberger *et al.* 1993). There are several caveats to this. The first is that the relationship is not determined by drawing a graph, as in the example. Instead, statistical analyses (regression equations) are used, which mathematically describe the shape of the line. Also, in some instances, the line is not absolutely straight, but may be slightly curved. Again, Myerson *et al.* (1992, p.266) make the important point that, within a particular domain, 'the term *general slowing* would appear to capture the fact that the degree of slowing does not appear to depend on the nature of the task or the specific cognitive processing components involved'. In other words, slowing must involve something more basic, such as changes at a neural level (Cerella 1990). However, this does not stop the old–young speed relationship being influenced by other factors, such as compensatory strategies used by the elderly:

'Because of the compensatory effects of life-long knowledge accumulation, for instance, some domains of cognitive functioning may be less affected by slowing than others. Recent evidence showing that slowing is less pronounced in tasks requiring lexical decisions as compared with analogous tasks requiring nonlexical decisions is consistent with this assumption.' (Lindenberger *et al.* 1993, p.207)

This indicates that some caution must be taken in reading too much from the shape of the line – it would be unwise to assume too much about the relationship between young and old subjects on a single type of task. In addition, although the phenomenon would appear to be robust, recent evidence by Perfect (in press) suggests that similar straight lines can be generated from sets of unrelated data. In other words, the straight lines maybe a statistical artifact, rather than evidence for a genuine psychological phenomenon.

Given the above arguments, it is perhaps surprising to note that RTs seem at first sight to be remarkably poor predictors of ageing performance. Salthouse (1985), reviewing a wide variety of studies, found an average correlation of .28 between age and SRT and .43 between age and CRT. For those unfamiliar with statistics, this means that ageing can only account for about 8 per cent of the variability in SRTs and about 19 per cent of CRTs. This at first sight indicates that the magnitude of the change in RTs does not merit much attention. However, Salthouse himself has provided a rejoinder to this. His argument is mathematically complex, but the essence of it is that changes in intellectual skills are *mediated* by the decline in processing speeds (Salthouse 1985, 1991b, 1992b). The full argument is too detailed and technical for an introductory text such as this, but interested readers are urged to consult it (Salthouse 1992b is probably the most approachable).

So far discussion has centred on RTs as measured by classical SRT and CRT experiments. However, as was noted above, RTs are involved in a much wider range of skills than these, and attention will now be focussed on the effects of ageing on the speed of processing of more complex intellectual tasks. Salthouse (1985) provides an admirable critical review of studies investigating this issue, and the overwhelming conclusion is that the elderly are indeed slower at performing virtually all intellectual tasks. These range from card sorting (Botwinick *et al.* 1960) to generating as many words as possible beginning with *s* within a time limit of two minutes (Bilash & Zubek 1960). There are some exceptions to this rule (e.g. the evidence regarding the speed of spoken replies is inconclusive), but overall it would appear to be a remarkably robust phenomenon. Furthermore, the age difference gets disproportionately larger the greater the intellectual demands of the task. This is known as the **age x complexity effect**. For example, in Botwinick *et al.'s* (1960) card sorting task, the age difference increased the more sets the cards had to be sorted into. It is possible that the age x complexity effect is echoing the findings of the early stages of a classical RT experiment – that is, if the subjects were given enough practice, the effect would disappear. However, as yet no subjects have been rehearsed long enough on a complex task for this to have been found.

Salthouse (1985) raises several cautionary points regarding the age x complexity effect. Two of the more important caveats are that, first, it is difficult to objectively measure how complex a task is. For example, because task A takes twice as long to do as task B does not automatically make it twice as difficult. Different processes which take longer to operate might be used in task A, but they are not necessarily subjectively experienced as being more difficult. Second, researchers have tended to stress results which fit the age x complexity phenomenon, and to ignore findings where the elderly are not as disadvantaged as the theory would predict. Thus, although a useful generalisation, the age x complexity effect must be treated with caution when more detailed conclusions are sought.

Thus, RTs, an expression of speed of neural processing, slow in old age, and this has an influence on the decline in *g*. The magnitude of this difference can be influenced by amount of practice and by the complexity of the task involved. However, to place this issue into perspective, it will be recalled that earlier it was noted that about 10–15 per cent of the elderly retain a youthful level of intelligence, and hence, by corollary, their RTs are also preserved.[*]

Intelligence level and its relationship with specific intellectual skills

A great many intellectual skills (particularly those heavily reliant on fluid intelligence) decline in old age (Horn 1982) by becoming slower and/or less accurate. Skills as diverse as memory for word lists, identifying briefly presented visual targets (Walsh *et al.* 1979), or pattern recognition (Walsh 1982), all show an age-related decline. Furthermore, the cause of these changes is usually easy to find. In a review of the literature, one author concluded that:

---

[*] The related issue of semantic facilitation, which uses the RT technique, is dealt with in the section on 'Word Recognition' in Chapter 4.

'such changes in intellectual competence as may occur with ageing are much better picked up by a simple, brief, timed test of general intelligence than by any single specific cognitive measure we have yet explored.' (Rabbitt 1984, p.113)

Rabbitt is probably deliberately overstating the case, but certainly most intellectual changes in old age are strongly tied to, if not uniquely explained by, the decline in general intelligence. This raises a serious problem for some researchers. Suppose that an experiment discovers that elderly people are significantly worse than the young at mental arithmetic, and suppose also that this is explained by the general fall in intelligence. If one is interested in discovering what makes old and young people different from each other, then this finding is dull, because it tells one nothing *new* about ageing – the drop in arithmetical skills has been shown to be part and parcel of a general declining process already well documented. It is about as earth shattering as the finding that elephants have big toenails. This is not to say that the experiment is of no value at all. For example, the researchers may be able, from their results, to construct a detailed model of how ageing affects mental arithmetic (i.e., *why* the changes take place). If a model is not constructed from the results, then the study might still be of value from a practical viewpoint. Thus, the study above might lead one to exhort old people to use a calculator when they go shopping.

Throughout this book there are examples of tests of intellectual ability, many of which demonstrate that the decline in a skill is attributable to the general intellectual decline, and their value must be weighed against the above considerations. It is the instances where the decline in a skill is *not* in tandem with the general pattern of changes which are often more interesting. There are a variety of ways in which the effect of general intelligence on performance can be assessed. The two simplest are **matching** and **partial correlation**. The former involves comparing groups of people who are known to have the same level of ability at a certain skill. Thus, any difference between the groups cannot be due to that skill. For example, suppose young and old people with the same level of intelligence are compared on a task, and an age difference is found. It can be validly concluded that differences in performance on this task are not due to general level of intelligence. Partial correlation is a statistical technique which is quite complex to perform, but relatively easy to explain. It assesses whether the relationship between two variables is due to the common influence of a third variable. To take a standard example. Suppose some strange passion drove a researcher to measure schoolchildren's feet sizes and to compare these with their scores on a maths test. It is highly probable that there would be a good **positive correlation** between the two measures – that is, on average, the bigger the foot size, the bigger the test score. There is obviously not a causal connection between the two measures, so why the correlation? The answer lies in a third factor – age. Older children have bigger feet and also will perform better on maths tests. Therefore the feet–maths correlation is a coincidental effect of the influence of a third variable (i.e., age). This can be demonstrated mathematically using the partial correlation technique. The children's feet sizes, test scores, and ages are fed into the equation, and the coincidental influence of age is removed mathematically – that is, age is said to be **partialled out**. If, after this has been done, there is no longer a significant correlation between feet size and test scores, then it is valid to assume that the effect was attributable to the coincidental effect of age. The partial correlational technique is an important one in gerontology, because it enables researchers, amongst other things, to test if an ageing decline on an intellectual skill is solely due to the coincidental effect of a general fall in g. Further information about the mathematical rationale behind the method can be found in any general statistical textbook.

Another important caveat concerns the cohort effect, which can manifest itself in several forms, and can skew results either to exaggerate or diminish ageing effects. For example, there is evidence that some cognitive skills are well preserved in old age because, although some aspects of performance (such as memory) decline, the elderly person's greater experience can compensate for this, as was seen in Charness's studies of bridge and chess players and the training studies in intellectual skills cited above.

Attentional deficits in ageing

Attention is the ability to concentrate on and/or remember items, despite distracting stimuli (which may have to be simultaneously mentally processed). Attention manifests itself in several forms. The ability to simply concentrate on the task at hand without being distracted is known as **sustained attention**. A typical test of this might be to require a subject to respond every time a particular letter appears in a continuous stream of letters presented on a computer screen. Ability on sustained attention tasks is known to be quite well preserved in old age: there is some decline, but it is not appreciable (Salthouse 1982).

Selective attention refers to the ability to concentrate on the task at hand whilst there are other distracting stimuli present. A popular method of testing this is the **visual search task**. Subjects are shown a display of (for example) letters, and are told to find a particular letter. Rabbitt (1979) showed that the elderly are much slower than the young at this task. Furthermore, the elderly did not take advantage of a feature of the experiment: namely, that the target appeared more often in some positions than others. Older people's responses were the same speed whether the target was in an often- or a rarely-used position. Younger subjects, on the other hand, were faster for the frequently used positions. This was not because the elderly were unaware of the phenomenon: after the test session was over they could accurately identify where the target was most likely to appear. Hence they could accrue information, but they could not act on it. Furthermore, repeated practice did not seem to improve their performance (Rabbitt 1982). Other researchers, however, have failed to replicate Rabbitt's findings. For example, Gilmore *et al.* (1985) found that the elderly can use information conveyed by the visual array, and Nissen & Corkin (1985) showed that, in their experiment, elderly subjects responded faster to a target repeatedly appearing in the same position. Other studies have shown that the presence or absence of an effect depends upon relatively peripheral features of the experimental design, such as the size, shape and brightness of the stimuli involved (Albert 1988). Where age differences are found in visual search tasks, Walsh (1982) has demonstrated statistically that the slowing and loss of accuracy in the elderly cannot be solely due to a general slowing in the rate of neural transmission.

In another test of selective attention, McDowd & Filion (1992) gave subjects the task of listening to a tape of a radio play, whilst a number of tones were played. In the key experimental condition, subjects were told to ignore the tones and concentrate on the play. The degree to which subjects succeeded in this task was measured by testing skin conductance and heart rate – if the tones were being ignored, then neither measure should show a change when they were played. After the first few tones were played, young subjects successfully ignored them, but older subjects could not, and their responses remained at the same high level throughout the experiment. Again, Friedman *et al.* (1993) found that brain potentials (electrical activity produced by the brain) were far more pronounced in older than in younger subjects when presented with a repeated stimulus. These findings reflect the studies of Bergman *et al.* (1976) and Dubno *et al.* (1984) cited in Chapter 1, which found that the elderly are disproportionately disadvantaged when trying to follow auditory messages played against noisy backgrounds. This is evidence of a more serious attentional problem than has been found in many visual attention tasks. Whether this is because the visual attention tasks are intrinsically easier, or because the elderly display a greater decline in aural than visual skills, has yet to be resolved.

Divided attention refers to the ability to attend simultaneously to and process more than one source of information. Many **working memory** tasks (see Chapter 3) thus fall into this category. The best-known method of assessing divided attention is probably the **dichotic listening** task. Using stereo headphones, the subject is presented with a different message in either ear. The subject then has to report what he or she heard in either ear separately. Many researchers have shown that the elderly are bad at this task (e.g. Horn 1982, Salthouse 1985), and various theories have been advanced to explain this. Salthouse (1985) argues that the effect is yet another manifestation of the age x complexity phenomenon. This is for two main reasons. First, because on simpler attention tasks (e.g. sustained attention) the age effect is less. Second, if the information load is lessened, then the age difference is also diminished (Albert 1988). *Why* the age x complexity effect should manifest itself is harder to explain. Wichens *et al.* (1987) demonstrated statistically that the effect is not completely explained by the general decline in processing speed. Salthouse (1985) showed that the elderly are as able as the young at shifting and allocating attention in a divided attention task, and thus it can be concluded that the old and the young are using the same working methods. The most parsimonious explanation is that the elderly suffer from a loss of processing resources: in other words, through the wastage and/or drop in efficiency of nerve cells, the elderly no longer have the mental capacity to attend to as much at one time as they could in their youth. This explanation seems to fit the available evidence. Salthouse (1985; especially Chapter 7) provides more detail and fleshes out the theory convincingly, but the technical details of his arguments go beyond the scope of this book.

Conceptual organisation

As reaction times measure the mind's immediate reactions to stimuli, so **conceptual organisation** describes the ability to treat items at an abstract level, in order to uncover basic rules and principles. For example, a man, a gerbil and an elephant are visually dissimilar, but at an abstract level they are all examples of mammals. Again, a proverb such as 'people in glass houses shouldn't throw stones' is of value only to greenhouse owners unless it is treated at a symbolic level. Researchers have shown that, in many instances, the elderly have difficulty in moving from the concrete to the abstract. Perhaps most surprising is the finding of Albert *et al.* (1987) that older subjects were worse at interpreting the meaning of proverbs. This applied whether subjects were left to provide their own answers unaided, or were given a multiple choice test. This is at first sight a contradictory finding, because one would suppose that proverb comprehension is part and parcel of crystallised intelligence, which is supposedly age-invariant. It is possible that Albert *et al.'s* results are attributable to a cohort effect. However, as has been remarked above, it is also possible that crystallised intelligence is less 'ageing proof' than most commentators believe.

Another test of conceptual abilities is the 'twenty questions' type of task. This is a version of the parlour game in which the subject is told that the experimenter is thinking of an object, and by a series of questions, to which the experimenter can only answer 'yes' or 'no', the subject tries to elicit the name of the object. Clearly, the optimal method is to narrow down the field by asking questions which progressively narrow down the choice of alternatives (e.g. 'is it an animal?', 'is it a mammal?', 'is it a household pet?'). This is called a **constraint seeking strategy**, because the choice of possibilities is increasingly constrained by each question. Eventually, when the list is down to a small number, it is best to switch to a **hypothesis scanning** question, where a specific item is named (e.g. 'is it a dog?'). If a hypothesis scanning question is asked when the list is still large, then this is a foolish strategy, because the chances of hitting on the right name are too remote (e.g. asking 'is it a dog?' having only established that the animal is a mammal). Denney & Denney (1974) found that the elderly are far less efficient than the young at a twenty questions task. They had to ask more questions than the young before they got the right answer, largely because they asked fewer constraint seeking questions. The elderly are disadvantaged in an analogous fashion when they are given a range of items, and asked to divide them into groups. Clearly a good strategy would involve the grouping of items into superordinate categories (e.g. 'animals', 'items of furniture'). The elderly perform less well than the young on such a task, producing more grouping in which the linkage between items is illogical to the observer (e.g. Denney & Denney 1973). It might be argued that the decline in categorisation skills is due to an artifact of declining memory (i.e., the elderly cannot simultaneously keep in mind everything they need to sort through). However, varying the memory load by varying the number of items to be categorised has no appreciable effect on age differences in performance (see Rebok 1987). Differences in education level cannot provide a total explanation (Cicirelli 1976, Laurence & Arrowood 1982). Neither can a cohort difference in knowledge of how to deal with this sort of task, since even after being shown the best strategy, old subjects failed to use it as extensively as younger controls (Hybertson *et al.* 1982).

Another explanation (and perhaps also the most parsimonious) is that declines in classification skills are tied to the general decline in *g*. Laurence & Arrowood (1982) compared the performance of (Toronto) university students, elderly alumni from the same university, and hospitalised elderly, on a classification ask. No significant difference was found between the alumni and the students, but both groups were significantly superior to the hospitalised elderly. Although no IQ test data are provided, it would be reasonable to assume that the alumni's intelligence levels are well preserved (this would accord with other studies of similar groups). Hence, classification skills probably only decline when intelligence begins to fall, as in the case of the hospitalised elderly. Laurence & Arrowood also noted that the error made most often (43%) by the hospitalised subjects was to make a **sentential grouping** – items were linked together because they fitted into a sentence (e.g. 'the *bunny* ate the *carrot*'). This was rarely if ever done by the other two subject groups, who made some errors, but these tended to be due to relatively minor slips of logic. Thus, deleterious ageing can result in quantitative and qualitative changes in classification skills. Furthermore, Arenberg (1982), in a longitudinal study, showed that young subjects' performance on a conceptual formation task improved on subsequent test sessions, whilst the elderly subjects' got worse.

It may be observed that when people make 'errors' in a classification task, they are only 'wrong' because their classifications do not conform with what the experimenter wanted. Grouping a carrot with a rabbit is perfectly sensible; although, in the wider scheme of things, it is not the most elegant solution, it is perhaps more fun (that subjects might seek amusing solutions does not seem to occur to many experimenters). Denney (1974) argues that the elderly make grouping mistakes, not because of any 'decline' but because they forget the accepted 'correct' way of grouping things as defined by educational practice, and instead adopt an arguably more 'natural' method of grouping. This may be coincidentally related to education level and intelligence because brighter, better educated individuals may stay in touch with formal methods of thought in 'white collar' jobs and activities for longer than others.

If a 'failure' of grouping does occur, then the fall in skill need not be as bad as it may first appear. The decline observed by Arenberg was not appreciable until the subjects were in their seventies. More encouragingly, Labouvie-Vief & Gonda (1976) found that the elderly can in some circumstances improve their classification skills with practice. Also, old people perform better if the tasks have an obvious practical slant rather than being purely abstract. For example, Arenberg found that the elderly were better at working on problems where items of food were grouped to produce 'safe' and 'poisonous' combinations than when given structurally identical problems of set formation using abstract shapes.

Creativity in old age

Running in tandem with general intelligence is **creativity**. Researchers are divided on how best to describe the skill, but most would agree that for an act to be creative, it must be novel, and it must be appropriate to the situation. The best way to demonstrate what is meant by this is to consider a typical creativity test. The subject is presented with a house brick and is asked to think of as many uses for it as possible. There are two types of response which are classified as being 'uncreative'. The first is appropriate but conventional (e.g. 'use it in building a house'). The second is novel but inappropriate (e.g. 'use it to cure insomnia by knocking oneself out with it'). A creative answer would be something like 'scrape the surface of the brick to make rouge': i.e. something which is both novel and feasible. People who produce a lot of creative answers are said to be good at divergent thinking (i.e. given a simple situation they can produce answers which diverge from mainstream thought). Studies have found that the elderly are poorer at divergent thinking tasks than the young. It might be argued that this is because the elderly are on average duller witted, and hence have not the necessary mental agility to perform divergent thinking tasks. However, the age difference persists even when the older and younger experimental subjects have been matched for intelligence and education level (Alpaugh & Birren 1977, McCrae *et al.* 1987). Among individuals who have always been very creative, this difference may be lessened or even not be present (e.g. Crosson & Robertson-Tchabo 1983). An important caveat to the findings of the above studies is raised by Simonton (1990), which is simply that the applicability of divergent thinking tests is debatable, and that they may not be reliable indicators of 'real life' creative abilities in all cases.

Another way to consider creativity is the biographical approach. By this method, the lives of acknowledged leaders in fields of activity where originality of thought is highly prized are examined, to see what made or makes them 'better' than others. Some generalisations can be gleaned from such studies. Artists and musicians tend to display their talents early in life (e.g. Mozart), whilst scientists are usually in their twenties before they show signs of outstanding ability. In addition, scientists are often competent, but not outstanding, students, until the area of specialisation in which they will become preeminent grips their imagination (Hudson 1987). Charles Darwin was a classic example of this. Thereafter, most eminent persons make their major contributions to their field before the onset of old age. Most have a peak of creative output before the age of 40. This applies to disciplines as diverse as mathematics, chemistry and musical composition. It is important to note that 'great' and 'routine' pieces of work tend to be produced in tandem. In other words, in a prolific period, a creative person will produce the same ratio of good to indifferent work as he or she will during relatively unproductive periods – the **quality ratio** stays fairly constant (Simonton 1990). Creativity has for *most* people died away by their sixties (Rebok 1987). However, this is not *universally* true, and Butler (1967) has made a spirited counter-attack to this view, citing numerous masterpieces produced late in their creators' lives. Titian, for example, continued to paint into his nineties, and most critics agree that his later work far surpasses his earlier output. However, Butler cites notable *exceptions*. For the majority of creative people, ageing means an inevitable decline.

It can be argued that the sensory and physical declines of ageing will affect creative people especially hard because above all others they need a precise, accurate and untiring view of the world (Rebok 1987). Undoubtedly in some creative fields, where physical fitness is *de rigeur*, this is true. Opera singers and ballet dancers are never at their peak in old age (but equally, there are very few ballet dancers over 35 who still perform on the stage). However, for the majority of creative persons, another explanation must be sought, since there is a long list of innovative people who have succeeded in spite of, or even because of, physical incapacity. For example, it is well known that Beethoven was deaf in his later years, and this fact may account for some of the innovations in his later works, when he had to rely upon an imagined world of sound. Degas was practically blind in his later life. Mahler suffered from a crippling heart condition, which probably contributed to the especially *angst*-ridden nature of his later work (indeed, the irregular rhythm of his heart beat is incorporated into the opening of his ninth symphony). Stephen Hawkins, perhaps the most eminent of contemporary theoretical physicists, is nearly completely paralysed by motor neuron disease, a condition, which by his own admission, has encouraged him to think about his work. In short, there is plenty of evidence that creativity need not be affected by physical declines even more severe than those experienced in normal ageing. Similarly, attribution for the effects of ageing cannot be laid upon a general intellectual decline, for two main reasons. First, because as was seen from Alpaugh & Birren (1977) cited above, the old are less creative than the young, even when intelligence levels are matched; and second, because intelligence is in any case a poor predictor of creativity (Hudson 1987). Therefore, another explanation must be sought.

One possibility is that creative people are victims of their own success. Scientists who achieve preeminence in their field are likely to find themselves quickly elevated to headships of departments or research groups. Once in this position, much of the running of experiments and 'hands on' experience is passed on to research assistants, whilst the head of department finds himself or herself embroiled in an increasing quantity of administrative duties. Thus, the eminent scientist's reward for success at a particular endeavour may be to have future activities in that field restricted, thus causing a decline in creative output. A different set of values probably applies to people preeminent in the arts. First, far more than scientists, artists (of any type) rely for their success on critical and public opinion. Accordingly, the worth of an artist depends upon what is fashionable at the time, and to be considered creative, the artist must be seen as a leading interpreter of the fashion and/or to have been a creator of that fashion. A second consideration is that few artists are able to support themselves if their craft in itself does not pay. Accordingly, if they do not achieve success in early life, they are likely to withdraw from full-time creative activity, and seek alternative employment. It follows from these two premises that the creative person usually becomes noticed by being a skilled exponent of a current fashion at an early stage in his or her career. Obviously, the artist seeks to capitalise on this, and accordingly becomes increasingly identifiable with that fashion. However, opinions change, and almost inevitably the artist becomes a representative of a movement which is now unfashionable. The more successful he or she was, the more strongly he or she is now identified as being unfashionable. In short, the artist is hoist by his or her own petard. The only solution for most artists is for them to move with the fashion. Since this probably involves a radical change of style, their output is likely to suffer since they are unfamiliar with new techniques, and thus their creative output declines. The speed at which these changes occur vary from discipline to discipline. Anyone keen on pop music will know that a cycle such as the one described occurs every three or four years. However, in any field, there are very few artists who produce 'timeless' works which rise above the mercurial changes of fashionable opinion. For example, a quick perusal around a secondhand book shop or through Grove's musical dictionary will readily reveal how many 'geniuses' of literature and music from previous generations are now completely forgotten.

Thus, the reasons behind the changes in creative output across the lifespan may be due far more to the lifestyles and job demands of the gifted than to ageing *per se.* The elderly may have 'lost' their creativity because they were too good at their job earlier in life.

Piagetian conservation

Papalia (1972) demonstrated that the elderly are bad at some of the **Piagetian conservation tasks** (named after their inventor, Piaget). This is a surprising finding, because most normal seven-year-olds can successfully perform them. The tasks in question test subjects' knowledge that two items of equal volume remain of equal volume, even when one of them changes shape. The subject is shown two balls of modelling clay of equal size and shape, and agrees that each is composed of the same amount of clay as the other. The experimenter then rolls one of the balls into a sausage shape, and asks the subject if the two pieces have the same amount of clay in them, to which of course the answer is 'yes' (pedants note that one ignores the minuscule quantities lost on the hands and table surface during rolling). It is surprising that ageing should cause people to fail such a simple task (and indeed, Piaget thought it impossible). Several other researchers have recorded the phenomenon (Blackburn & Papalia 1992), but the explanation for it is unclear. Some studies have shown that when the subjects' education levels are controlled for, then the age difference disappears (Rebok 1987). Blackburn & Papalia cite the work of Denney (see section on conceptual organisation above) which argues that age-related changes in concepts may reflect the rejection or forgetting of methods of formal analysis taught in schools, and the adoption of other, perhaps simpler methods used in childhood. This is not due to neural decline, but to lifestyle (many people do not need a lot of what they learnt at school, and so over the years it is forgotten). Coincidentally, adults with higher levels of education may retain the 'correct' method of interpretation, because their activities are more likely to keep them involved in formal methods of thinking. That the elderly have not lost the ability to conserve is proved by the fact that with training, they can once again succeed at Piagetian tasks (Blackburn & Papalia 1992).

This is an interesting argument, but there is still much which needs to be answered. It is possible that some older people are either deliberately or accidentally adopting a different way of thinking. However, it is a rather uncomfortable coincidence that this change occurs at a time when IQ is in decline. That the elderly can be trained to recover their skills is also not surprising, since unless their intelligence has fallen below that of an average seven-year-old, then this should be perfectly feasible. In addition, at least one other skill shows a 'reversion' in older people. Stuart-Hamilton (in press) found that approximately 10 per cent of elderly people make an appreciable drawing 'error' called **intellectual realism**. This occurs when the subject draws what he or she knows to be there, rather than what can be seen. In this instance subjects were shown an apple with a knitting needle pushed through it. The 'intellectually realistic' subjects drew the apple with the whole of the pin visible (i.e., as if the apple was transparent). This drawing error is not usually seen in children aged over eight years. It also should be noted that work on conservation has concentrated on the simpler conservation tasks. Other, more complex tasks, such as judging if two objects of equal volume but different shape displace the same amount of water have not been assessed. Nor does the relationship between intelligence level and conservation skills appear to have been systematically examined.

This relative neglect of studies of how performance on Piagetian tasks can change across the lifespan is surprising, because it would provide a conceptual link by which to view the whole of human psychological development. As a quick survey of current textbooks on developmental psychology will reveal, the lifespan is compartmentalised. There is a considerable literature on all aspects of development up to and including the early teenage years. Thereafter, research has tended to concentrate on social changes until after the midlife crisis, whereupon interest resumes in a wider variety of psychological matters in old age.

This is not true of all researchers, however, and a number of them have devised models to account for adult development. An interesting example of this is provided by Labouvie-Vief (1992), who proposes the concept of **postformal thought**. This is a stage of intellectual development, which, it is argued, occurs in adulthood, after the stage of **formal operations**. 'Formal operations' is the final phase in Piaget's theory of cognitive development, in which subjects begin to think in genuinely abstract terms. The stage commences at about 11 years and is completed by the late teens for those who attain it (some individuals never attain full formal operations). This method of thought is very systematic and relies on formal logic. However, it can reasonably be argued that people do not spend their lives being logical, and that many important decisions are made by not only relying on cold logic, but also consideration of emotions and other subjective feelings. Accordingly, postformal thought refers to this ability to weigh up and balance arguments created by logic and emotion. It is not necessarily better, but it is appreciably different. Whilst this is a useful operational distinction, it is debatable whether formal and postformal thought are intrinsically different, since arguments created from an emotional source and arguments created from a logical source can be combined logically, without the need for a 'new' kind of thinking. A cynic might argue that a further danger is that the theory might be used to excuse some age-related declines in intellectual performance by relabelling failures to perform tasks as examples of alternative strategies. However, this area of study is still developing, and promises much.

Another view is provided by Schaie (1977) who argues that intellectual development is characterised by four phases. In childhood, the individual acquires knowledge and skills which he or she then applies in the teens/early adulthood to solving problems, taking exams, and so forth, which will define his or her status in terms of academic achievement, job, or societal status. In later adulthood, he or she attains responsibilities (e.g. to a partner and children), which in come cases may involve having to make managerial or executive decisions. In old age comes a period of reintegration, in which the person reviews their knowledge and skills, and hones in on those which are still of value, sweeping away unwanted mental clutter. The concept is a useful description, but again, needs a greater empirical justification before it can be examined in detail.

Summary

The elderly have traditionally been seen as retaining their wisdom (crystallised intelligence) whilst losing their wits (fluid intelligence). Research has backed this conclusion, although it should be noted that: (a) some of the elderly have preserved fluid intelligence and (b) the size of the age difference is in part an experimental artifact. For many, however, the change in intellect is considerable, being on average nearly two standard deviations lower than the mean scores of younger adults (though note that this is before cohort effects are considered). There is some evidence that in the young elderly, a sudden sharp decline in intellectual abilities is a warning of imminent death (the terminal drop theory). However, note that commentators are divided on what measures predict morbidity, and the model is in any case inapplicable to the old elderly. Various models to explain the age-related changes have been proposed, including the disuse theory (that skills decline because they are insufficiently practised) and the speed hypothesis (that the changes are sué to a slowing in neural conduction). The former may have some validity, but cannot explain certain phenomena (e.g. why well-practised older individuals display considerable worsening of skills). The latter theory is backed with some intriguing evidence, including the phenomenon that young and old mean reaction times for the same type of task, when plotted against each other, show a linear relationship. However, it is acknowledged that previous experience and training may ameliorate changes caused by declining processing speed. Declines in more specific intellectual skills, such as attention, conceptual organisation, creativity, and Piagetian conservation tasks have all been well documented. In all instances, however, cohort effects may have exaggerated the size of the change. Indeed, in general, it would appear difficult if not impossible firmly to decide how much of a change is attributable to cohort effects. The chapter concluded with a consideration of how studies of ageing intelligence are related to theories concerned with development in general. It would appear that often commentators have compartmentalised human development into separate and often unconnected stages. Some models of change in adulthood are available, but they are general and as yet lack sufficient empirical examination for more detailed conclusions to be drawn.

Suggested further reading

There are innumerable textbooks on intelligence and intelligence testing. However, the issues are technically very complex, and the writing sometimes reflects this. Some knowledge of psychology and basic maths is often required. This should not deter the interested reader, but he or she has been warned! Perhaps the best (and most readable) summaries of the issues pertaining to old age are provided by Rebok (1987) and Perlmutter & Hall (1992). Salthouse (1991a,b, 1992a,b) provides a superbly exhaustive (and exhausting!) critical review of the ageing and intelligence literature. For a discussion of the fluid–crystallised dichotomy, Kausler (1982, pp.584–598) is recommended, as is Rabbitt (1984, 1993). Regarding the declines in more specific intellectual skills, Craik & Trehub's edited collection (see Horn 1982 reference) is a collection of thoughtful, well written papers, as is Poon et al. (1989 – see reference for Perlmutter & Monty 1989). Butler (1967) gives a detailed consideration of creative acts in old age, whilst Simonton (1990) provides an intelligent and interesting summary of the recent literature on the subject.

CHAPTER 3

Ageing and Memory

Introduction

The study of the psychology of memory has generated a large number of concepts and technical terms, and a brief survey of at least some of these is necessary before an examination of the effects of ageing on mnemonic skills can begin. A belief held by many lay people is that memory is a homogeneous skill: that is, everything is memorised in the same way. This is erroneous, simply because physiological research has shown that different types of memories (e.g. for words, pictures, physical skills) are stored in anatomically different sections of the brain (see Chapter 1). Furthermore, psychologists have found that these memory systems also behave in different ways. Accordingly, when researchers talk, for example, of 'verbal' or 'visual' memories, they can be confident that they are discussing anatomically and functionally distinct systems.

One of the simplest ways of categorising memories is by the length of time over which they are retained, and this usually means a division into **short term memory (STM)** and **long term memory (LTM)**. These are also known as primary and secondary memory, respectively. STM is the temporary storage of events and items perceived in the very immediate past: that is, no more than a few minutes ago, and usually a much shorter period (i.e., the last few seconds). The classical test of STM requires the experimenter to read out or show a list of letters, numbers or words, and get the subject immediately to repeat it back. The longest list of these **to-be-re-membered (TBR)** items which the subject can reliably repeat back is called his or her **span**. Spans vary according to the nature of the TBR items and, thus, there is usually a prefix denoting the materials used in the test. Thus, **digit span** denotes memory for numbers, **word span** memory for word lists, and so forth.

One of the problems with the classical span experiment is that it is not very realistic: people simply do not spend their time learning arbitrary lists. Another point is that STM is impermanent: unless an especial effort is made, the memory fades within a brief time. A popular explanation of why there is a short term store, and how it might function is provided by Baddeley & Hitch's (1974) **working memory model**. Working memory is defined as:

'the temporary storage of information that is necessary for such activities as learning, reasoning, and comprehension.' (Baddeley 1986)

Thus, typical tasks involving working memory:

'are those in which the person must hold a small amount of material in mind for a short time while simultaneously carrying out further cognitive operations, either on the material held or on other incoming materials.' (Morris *et al.* 1990, p.67)

This is a form of STM which most people can intuitively appreciate that there is a need for. For example, in listening to speech, it is necessary to keep in mind what a person has just said in order to make sense of what is currently being said. Another example of working memory in action is mental arithmetic. All the figures of the sum have to be retained (in the right order) while the arithmetical transformation is performed on them. Note that in both these instances something has to be remembered while another mental operation takes place.

Full details of how the working memory model is presumed to operate are complex and far from finalised (Baddeley 1986, 1990). However, in its basic form the system is said to be controlled by the **central executive**. This is in part a memory store (though with a limited capacity) and in part a controller of several **slave systems** (the imagery is taken from computing terminology rather than any more unsavoury source). The slave systems have larger memory capacities than the central executive, and each specialises in only one type of memory. Thus, there are separate systems for verbal material, pictures, and spatial position. The verbal material system is termed the **phonological loop** (in some older texts it is called the **articulatory loop**). The phonological loop deals with words in the broadest possible sense, and thus not only memorises letters and words, but also numbers. The central executive controls the depositing and retrieval of memories to and from the slave systems. When **concurrent processing** is required (i.e., maintaining a memory and doing another attention-demanding task at the same time) the central executive helps co-ordinate these. It is important to note that if there are too many TBR items to fit in the slave systems (i.e., the slave systems by themselves cannot remember everything sent to them), then some or all of the items can be transferred to LTM, which thus acts as a backup.

Memory traces quickly fade from STM for the simple reason that the vast majority of information taken in is only of value at the time, and afterwards is highly redundant. To return to the example given above, one wants to remember the numbers in a mental arithmetic problem at the time, but to keep remembering them afterwards would be both an irritation and a waste of memory space. However, there is obviously some information which *does* need to be remembered more permanently, and this is the role of LTM.

LTM seeks to be a permanent store of information. Whether it has a maximum capacity, and how much information is lost from it are unanswerable questions. However, it is certainly the case that for normal people, 'essential' and 'everyday' information is never lost. For example, people do not forget their native language, their names, the name of the capital of France, or toilet training. In all probability this is because such information is either very important to them and/or it is so frequently **rehearsed** (i.e., the memory is recalled and thus 'practised') that they form strong, unshakeable **memory traces**. Some information *is* lost from LTM, however (e.g. old addresses, telephone numbers, etc., tend to be forgotten when friends move). These lost memories tend to be either information which is now irrelevant and has been superseded, or is unimportant, so that it is infrequently rehearsed. The classical test of LTM is the same as the STM 'span' procedure, except that the subject is required to hold the TBR items in memory for a longer time (typically anything from 30 minutes up to several days). If the reader is wondering why subjects do not forget the TBR items as with the STM experiment, the simple answer is that the subjects are encouraged to rehearse them.

Another method of dividing memory is into **episodic** and **semantic memories** (Tulving 1972). Episodic memories are of events relating to a person's own life: a kind of mental autobiography. Semantic memory is for items independent of personal experiences and is a store of facts, such as general knowledge, or academic learning. A further system divides memory into **explicit** and **implicit memories** (Graf & Schachter 1985). This refers to the distinction between a memory which is consciously sought (e.g. trying to recall the date of the Battle of Waterloo) and one which appears unbidden (or perhaps even exerts its influence without the subject being consciously aware of it). A common method of testing implicit memory is to expose a subject to a list of words in the guise of a psychological task (e.g. grading words for imageability). At a later time, the subject is given a **word completion task**, in which the subject, given the first letter or letters of a word, must complete it (e.g. 'complete FOR- - -'). The subject is more likely to provide a word which he or she has encountered in the previous list (e.g. 'FOREST' rather than 'FORGET'), even though he or she is unaware that these memories are being drawn upon.

Tangential to the above domains of memory are the skills of planning and overseeing. One of the commonest uses of memory is to remember to do something in the future, or **prospective memory**. Closely related to this is **metamemory**, which is knowledge about one's own memory – what its capacity is, how best to remember things and so forth.

Memory systems can also be considered in terms of how they work: for example, how memories are created for storage (**encoding**) and how they are retrieved. There is a considerable debate within psychology as to whether memories are lost through inefficient encoding or inefficient retrieval. The inefficient encoding hypothesis can be likened to a library, where an incompetent librarian shelves books in the wrong places, so that when a search is made for a book, it cannot be found in its logical place. Similarly, memories that are inefficiently encoded will be lost because they cannot be retrieved. The inefficient retrieval argument is that memories are lost because, although they are stored properly, the search for them is inefficient. To return to the library analogy, it is as though a person with severe dyslexia was sent to find a book. This issue is of especial importance in discussing the memories of demented patients (see Chapter 6).

Memory can be tested in a variety of ways. The commonest distinction is between **recall** and **recognition**. The former requires a subject to report as much as possible of a list he or she has been set to remember. In an **ordered recall** task, the subject is only marked correct if all TBR items are repeated in their exact order of presentation (e.g. TBR items are *17654*; subject must repeat *17654: 71654*, for example, is not sufficient). In a **free recall** task, the order of recall does not matter (thus, *71654* or any other permutation is acceptable). A recognition task is considered to be easier than a recall task. Both begin with a presentation of the TBR items. However, in a recognition task, the subject's memory is tested by having to select the items he or she has just seen (the **targets**) from a list which also includes items which were not in the original list (the **distracters**). Subjects tend to remember more items in a recognition than in a recall task, because the memory load is lighter (see the section on STM below for a more detailed explanation). It is also worth noting that the recognition and recall processes are almost certainly controlled by different mental mechanisms. In a **cued recall task**, the subject is in effect given a hint about the answer (e.g. he or she might be given the first letter or letters of a TBR word).

Having thus briefly considered some of the technical terms, theories and techniques employed in memory research, attention will now shift to how ageing affects mnemonic processes.

Ageing and short term memory (STM)

If a basic STM span test is administered (where the subject simply repeats back what the experimenter has just said or shown) several studies have shown a small but significant decline in old age (Craik & Jennings 1992). There is some evidence that younger subjects can remember slightly more of the items presented at the end of a list (see Salthouse 1991b, Chapter 6), but the effect is probably due to the effects of long term memory rather than any short term deficit (see Craik & Jennings 1992 for a full explanation). When any extra demands are placed on subjects, then age effects generally become very apparent.

One method of complicating a STM task is the **backward span** procedure, where the subject is required to repeat the items back in the reverse order of their presentation (e.g. TBR items are *75123*; subject must reply *32157*). This is clearly harder than straightforward recall, since subjects must keep in store the items in their correct order while constructing their reverse. Bromley (1958), among others, has shown that the elderly are significantly worse at this task. Several causes have been suggested. One is that because the items in the forward and reversed lists are identical, it is easy to confuse the two, and thus form a garbled amalgam. Again, the older subjects might lack the mental processing capacity of younger people, and simply not have the 'processing space' necessary to manipulate the TBR items. A refinement of this is to argue that the items are transferred to LTM for rearrangement, because the slave systems' memory capacity is too inadequate (see Introduction). Either items are lost during the transfer process, or the LTM in some manner fails to store the items efficiently.

This suggestion is supported by the findings of Morris *et al.* (1990). They gave young and elderly subjects a conventional working memory task, in which subjects had to remember a short list of words while simultaneously deciding if a simple sentence was true or false (e.g. 'a sparrow can build a nest'). The older subjects' subsequent recall of the words was significantly worse than the young, and the magnitude of this difference increased the more words had to be remembered at one time. Morris *et al.* argue that this age difference occurs because the younger subjects not only encode information in their working memory, but also send a copy of the memory trace to a LTM store. If the memory trace is lost from working memory, the younger subjects can retrieve the spare copy from LTM. Older subjects, however, are less able to make a copy, either because they lack the 'mental capacity' to do it, or because their LTM is in some manner inefficient (see next section). Thus, if the memory cannot be retained in a working memory store, it either cannot be retained at all, or at best it is retained inaccurately. Note that the logical consequence of this argument is that it is possible that the old and the young may have equally efficient STM stores – the difference lies in the fact that the elderly have poorer encoding and/or retrieval strategies.

Baddeley (1986) cites the central executive as the prime cause of this age-related decline. As evidence for this, one can consider the experiments on backward span and concurrent processing which were discussed above. Other studies have shown that increasing the complexity of the distracting task in a working memory test disproportionately affects the elderly's recall (e.g. Morris *et al.* 1988). According to the working memory model, these processes are overseen by the central executive, which in the elderly is failing to combine memory and concurrent processing. Thus, the root of the problem lies in the control of mnemonic processes rather than in memory *per se*. When a 'basic' span task is used, no, or a very small, age difference is found; it is only when the elderly have to divide their attention and/or manipulate the TBR information that a decline becomes apparent.

However, the above is not the only problem besetting the elderly. A study by Belmont *et al.* (1988) suggests that the elderly may encode information in STM less efficiently than the young. This concerns a mnemonic process called **chunking**. Given a long string (>4) of TBR items, a better strategy than trying to remember them as one long string is to think of them as a series of groups of 3 or 4 items. For example, instead of trying to remember *345172986142* as *345172986142*, a better strategy would be to think of it in chunks of three as *345 172 986 142*. Precisely this principle is used in the presentation of credit card and telephone numbers. Belmont *et al.* demonstrated that the elderly are less likely than the young to chunk long digit lists when trying to encode them. However, it is worth noting that some elderly subjects *did* chunk, and their spans were as good as the best of the younger subjects. Other researchers have also noted that the elderly do not arrange TBR items, and that without prompting they do not pay as close attention to them (i.e., they do not process the items 'deeply' enough) as younger subject do (e.g. Craik & Rabinowitz 1984; though note that Salthouse 1991b argues that evidence of depth of processing changes in the elderly is equivocal because of methodological flaws in the studies concerned).

Perlmutter & Mitchell (1982) concur that the elderly have an especial problem in encoding material, but also note that ageing affects the retrieval and/or storage processes. In support of this argument, they note that on some STM tasks, the elderly subjects were disproportionately better on the recognition than the recall tasks. As was noted in the Introduction, recognition is easier than recall because the subject does not have to possess as clear a memory of the TBR item in order to get the right answer. This can be explained conceptually as follows (though no claims that this is actually what takes place in the brain are intended!). Suppose that young and old subjects are given the following list of TBR items:

duck clock table glass phone pack

Suppose also that the young and old encode equally well, and that any problems that arise occur after this stage, in either storage or retrieval (experimentally, it is difficult to distinguish between the two processes). Finally, suppose that any errors that occur consist of forgetting letters in the words (indicated by xs below). If the storage/retrieval of the older subjects is worse, then the memories they retrieve may be something like this:

Young: dxck clock table gxass xhone pack

Old: dxck clxck table gxass xhone pack

In a recall task, only those items completely clearly retrieved can be recalled. Thus, the recall scores for the old and young would be 2 and 3 respectively. However, in a recognition task, the subjects can compare their 'fuzzy' memories (e.g. dxck) against the items in front of them. If there is a strong correspondence between the fuzzy memory and a possible answer (e.g. dxck and duck), then either the subjects' memories may clear (thereby recognising the x as a u) or they may make an educated guess. Either way, the elderly's performance should match the young's, because a crystal clear memory is no longer de rigeur. Following this argument a step further, it should be apparent that the elderly's memory for items is not so much less, as slightly but critically more inaccurate. Recognition would not aid the subjects if they had no memory trace of a TBR item, or at best a very poor one (e.g. the memory trace of duck being xxcx). This is supported by a study by Parkin & Walter (1992), in which subjects were asked to state if a word they claimed to recognise was one which they could distinctly remember, or if they 'knew' it was on the list but had no clear recollection. The researchers found that the proportion of 'definitely know' to 'just know' answers shifted towards the latter with increasing age of the subjects. Furthermore, this shift was related to evidence of a decline in the functioning of the frontal lobes (see Chapter 1) which are in part responsible for monitoring memories.

Belmont et al. and Perlmutter & Mitchell provide evidence that the elderly can encode and retrieve as well as the young, but they do not do so spontaneously. If not deliberately prodded or aided into such strategies, then they choose less efficient methods of encoding and retrieval. Waugh

& Barr (1982) also note that elderly subjects are less good at encoding if TBR items are presented quickly in succession (rather than slowly). This indicates that the encoding processes of the elderly are slower and less efficient. However, by Perlmutter & Mitchells' own admission, the 'younger subjects' used in their (and indeed most other researchers') memory studies are college/university students, who are likely to be better versed in mnemonic tasks (and hence using mental *aides memoires*) than the community resident elderly. This places a question mark over these studies – are the elderly worse because of their age *per se*, or because of a cohort effect? The debate surrounding this issue has yet to be fully resolved, but from the combined longitudinal and cross-sectional studies of Schaie and others (see Chapter 2), which have included memory measures, it appears there are genuine age differences, but that these are *in part* the result of a cohort effect.

However, there is evidence that, with training, at least some age deficits can be overcome. One method is to train the elderly in the **method of loci** technique. This involves memorising a series of mental pictures of rooms (e.g. the rooms in one's house) or other familiar scenes. Each TBR item is mentally placed in a scene, and then the list is recalled by making an imaginary journey, recalling what was stored in each picture. Suppose that one was given the list *15794* to recall. One might imagine entering one's house. A *1* is sticking through the letter box, a *5* is in the umbrella stand. Entering the living room, *7* is sitting on the sofa, whilst next door *9* is helping himself to a large scotch. Going into the kitchen, *4* is peeling potatoes. The purpose of the technique is to make each image as vivid as possible, and accordingly more memorable. Smith *et al.* (1984, cited Rebok 1987) using native Berliners as subjects, found that they could increase their digit span by using familiar Berlin street scenes as loci. Herrmann *et al.* (1988) have also reported improvements in the memory of elderly subjects after training, but noted that training only aided the particular mnemonic task involved – the advantages did not transfer to other forms of memory. Improving digit span, for example, does not automatically aid recall of pictures. This effect has been noted in all age groups (i.e., it is not just a phenomenon of ageing). It must also be borne in mind that the method of loci technique is also used more efficiently by younger than older adults. Lindenberger *et al.* (1992) found that elderly subjects performed less well than younger subjects on a method of loci task, even in comparisons of elderly experienced graphic designers (with good spatial skills) and younger subjects with no especial spatial skills.

Ageing and long term memory (LTM)

As mentioned in the Introduction, the 'basic' LTM and STM tasks are identical, save that the time gap between presentation of the TBR items and the request for their recall is a few seconds or minutes in STM, and approximately half an hour to several days in LTM studies. Whereas there is no appreciable ageing effect in basic STM tasks, there is a pronounced effect in LTM, with encoding being the prime area of decline (Albert 1988). This may not be very surprising, since much of the information passing into LTM must first be processed by STM, and any defects in the latter will be reflected in the poorer performance of the former. Much of the recent work on ageing, however, has moved beyond the rather arid 'laboratory studies' of long term retention of arbitrary lists of words and digits, to more realistic everyday memory tasks, and the chapter will concentrate on these.

Remote memory

Remote memory is for non-autobiographical events which have occurred within a person's lifetime. It is usually tested by giving subjects a list of names and/or descriptions of events which have been 'in the news' over the past 50 or so years, and asking them to indicate which they can remember. Several obvious precautions are taken by test designers. First, to prevent people getting full marks simply by saying 'yes' to everything, a few fictitious names and/or events are included in the list ('Prince Babylon', 'The assassination of King Marvo of Ruritania', etc). A more pressing problem is ensuring that the subjects are genuinely recognising a remote memory, and not a more recently stored piece of information. To take an example. Most English people aged over 35 can remember England winning soccer's World Cup in 1966 (they beat West Germany in the final by four goals to two). The event drew a record television audience in the UK for the time. Therefore, asking a question such as 'Did England beat Germany 4–2 in the 1966 World Cup final?' might seem to be a sensible question to include in a remote memory test. Most older people would be able to correctly answer this question. However, it is very improbable that they do this by consulting a memory laid down in 1966 and not consulted since. This is simply because highlights of the said soccer match have been repeated very frequently on the television ever since. Hence a subject could be answering 'yes' having consulted a memory of a television broadcast from the week before. It is also very probable that subjects aged under 25, who could not possibly remember the match as a live event, would also be able to answer such a question correctly. This is because they too have memories of the event, drawn from the same media repeats. It might well be argued that memories of such well-known events of 'historical importance' (others might include VE Day, the assassination of President Kennedy) are more rightly treated as semantic memories, rather than reminiscences.

To escape this 'too famous' problem, more obscure names and events have to be chosen. If too obscure items are chosen, then one has the reverse problem that nobody has heard of them. Luckily, the media has an agreeable habit (as far as experimenters are concerned) of making some people very famous for a brief time, after which they sink back into obscurity once more. This is in no way to belittle their achievements – often they are considerable – but the inevitable hunger for news or the arrival of new champions in their field of endeavour causes a shifting of attention. The **Famous Names Test**, or **FNT** (Stevens 1979) is a test which uses these 'briefly famous' names. The FNT comprises a list of names of people such as John Conteh, Sid Vicious, Issy Bonn and Reggie Whitcombe. Any reader aged over 30 may recognise the first two names, but unless he or she is over 70, then it is improbable that the final two will be known.* The argument is made that since their period of fame, the above names have not been frequently mentioned in the media. Thus, if subjects recognise a name, it is because they are recalling a genuinely remote memory, and not just remembering the name being mentioned in a recent media presentation. To assess the depth of a person's remote memory, the names on the FNT can be divided into categories: namely those briefly famous in the 1970s and 1960s; the 1950s; the 1940s; and the 1930s. (Several extremely famous names, such as Winston Churchill, Margaret Thatcher, etc, are also included, but these are intended for severely demented patients – see Chapter 6.) A number of fictitious names are included to prevent cheating.

Stuart-Hamilton *et al.* (1988) tested subjects aged 50–80 on the FNT, and the pattern of results obtained can be seen in Figure 3.1. As can be seen, for all ages, memories for recent names are better than for distant ones. This phenomenon has been observed by many other researchers (e.g. Craik 1977, Perlmutter, 1978, and Poon *et al.* 1979), and contradicts the once popular **Ribot's hypothesis** (Ribot 1882). This argues that in the elderly, memory for recent events should be worse than for remote ones. A useful analogy to explain this argument is to think of the brain as a long deep

---

*   For those readers still wondering, Mr Conteh was a boxer, Mr Vicious a now dead
      exponent of punk rock (now also mercifully defunct), Mr Bonn was a music hall
      comedian, and Mr Whitcombe was a champion golfer.

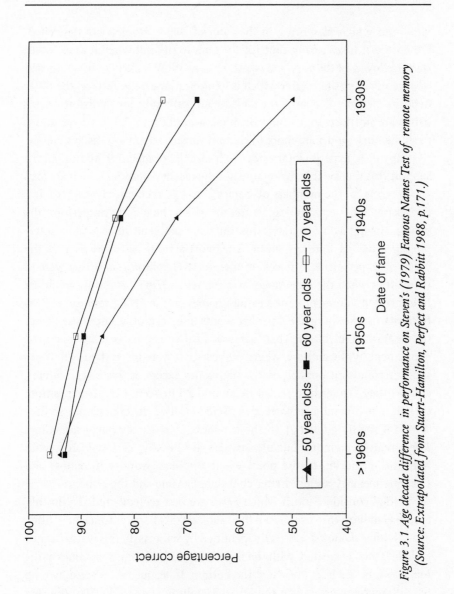

Figure 3.1 Age decade difference in performance on Steven's (1979) Famous Names Test of remote memory (Source: Extrapolated from Stuart-Hamilton, Perfect and Rabbit 1988, p.171.)

tank, into which memories, in the form of water droplets are deposited. Obviously, it takes a long time for the tank to fill, but when it does, water starts to flow over the edge and is lost. This overflow is likely to be composed of recently deposited water which is lying near or on the surface: the older deposits of water deeper in the tank are unlikely to be much disturbed and hence are not lost. In a similar manner, according to Ribot's hypothesis, fresh memory inputs are more likely to displace recent than distant memories. However, experimental evidence from remote memory studies fails to support this theory: it is the remote not the recent memories which are lost.

In terms of the numbers of names correctly recognised, the FNT is a rare example of a psychological test on which the elderly outperform the young. Having acknowledged this, there are problems in accurately interpreting what its findings mean. The most serious difficulty is that the youngest experimental subjects in the Stuart-Hamilton *et al.* study were in their fifties when the experiment was run (circa 1987), and thus would be hard-pressed to remember the earliest names on the FNT (from the 1930s) from firsthand experience. In other words, they can only know the names from semantic memory. This fact was further emphasised by a second experiment by the authors, where 20-year-olds were given the FNT. These subjects could not possibly know the names except as 'historical' figures, and yet they managed to recognise around 25 per cent of the names from each decade (the subjects correctly rejected most of the false names, so they were not simply guessing). In short, remote memory tests may sometimes assess remote memory, but the answers are heavily 'contaminated' with semantic memories, to the point where one may wonder if remote and semantic memory are not better considered as one and the same.

A final consideration is which *names* are best remembered. To do this, Stuart-Hamilton *et al.* reanalysed their subjects' FNT scores to see how often an individual name was correctly identified by subjects. In this way, a 'league table of fame' is created, with the most commonly recognised names at the top, down to the least known at the bottom. If league tables are drawn up for different age groups (in the Stuart-Hamilton *et al.* study, 50-, 60- and 70-year-olds) then a remarkable similarity in the ordering of names is found (and this is borne out by statistical analysis). Thus, the same names have the same relative level of fame for different age groups. This in turn suggests that the same processes control remote memory across a wide age range of people. The nature of these processes is more properly the preserve of a sociologist, but it is not unreasonable to suggest that supposedly 'forgotten' names from the past get a revival in the media occasionally, and the similar league tables reflect just how uniform the effect of such media coverage on different age groups can be. The higher overall scores of the elderly merely reflect that they have endured more media input, and thus have had more opportunities to rehearse the names.

Thus, while remote memory may exist, testing it remains fraught with difficulties, and measuring 'pure' remote memory, free from the 'bias' of semantic memory and 'post-fame' media coverage, is probably impossible.

Eyewitness memory

As the title suggests, eyewitness memory refers to the ability to recall information from an incident (usually dramatic) which has been seen once. In 'real life', eyewitness memory forms the basis of many legal cases, and experimental measures of eyewitness testimony have tended to present subjects with an enacted incident (either 'in the flesh' or on video tape). Generally, the elderly are found to be as good as younger subjects at remembering the main points of an incident, but to show some worsening of recall for visual details, such as the appearance of the participants (e.g. Adams-Price 1992).

One of the key features of eyewitness testimony is remembering the source of a particular event or utterance (e.g. who said what). Ferguson *et al.* (1992) demonstrated that the elderly have greater difficulty in remembering the source of an item than younger subjects. The subjects listened to sets of spoken words played over a stereo system, and had to remember which speaker produced particular words. The elderly subjects found this harder to do when both speakers played voices of the same sex, and although advantaged by having different sex voices in either speaker, other permutations worsened recall (although they improved the recall of younger subjects). This implies that the older subjects cannot make use of the same range of information as the younger subjects. Although not an eyewitness memory experiment, the findings have an obvious link to issues of recall of detail from different locations and persons.

Again, in a review of the literature, Cohen & Faulkner (1989) note that the elderly are more prone to believing that an interpretation of an event is an actual memory of the event. This means that there may be a greater danger of the memory of an event being distorted to fit a subsequent interpretation, thereby removing the objectivity of an eyewitness account.

Text recall

Because recall of text is strongly linked with linguistic skills, this topic is dealt with in detail in Chapter 4. A summary of the findings is that, essentially, there are no or relatively few age differences in the recall of the main·points of a story (the 'gist' of the text) but that memory for details may worsen, especially in older people of relatively low levels of intelligence. However, there are a number of occasions when this rule breaks down, and interested readers should consult the appropriate section in the next chapter.

Semantic memory

Semantic memory might be expected to survive ageing in a fairly robust state, because memory for facts and information is part of the definition of crystallised intelligence, which is known to be relatively age-invariant (see Chapter 2). Indeed this appears to be the case – in general, the elderly are as good as, if not better than, the young at recalling facts and information held in semantic memory (e.g. Camp 1988, Fozard 1980). A contradictory note is sounded by Hultsch *et al.* (1992) who, in a three-year longitudinal study, found a significant decline in general knowledge for world events in their sample of elderly subjects (along with declines in other mnemonic and intellectual measures). However, this may in part have been a cohort effect.

Perhaps of greater interest to researchers is how the elderly gauge the accuracy of their responses, a process known as **metaknowledge**, or **feeling of knowing (FOK)**. A typical FOK experiment might require subjects to look at a question and then declare how confident they are that their answer is correct. For example, the subject might be confronted with the following:

> QUESTION: What is a *pangolin*?
>
> HOW CONFIDENT ARE YOU ABOUT GIVING THE CORRECT ANSWER TO THIS QUESTION?
>
> 1. Complete guess
>
> 2. Educated guess
>
> 3. Fairly confident
>
> 4. Completely confident
>
> PLEASE GIVE YOUR ANSWER..

Several researchers have shown that subjects are quite accurate in their judgements. Namely, the more confident they are that they are right, the greater the probability that they *are* right. There appears to be no age difference in FOK accuracy (e.g. Fozard 1980, Perlmutter 1978). However, although this may be the case, old people do not necessarily believe it. For example, Camp (1988) reported that the elderly thought that their semantic memory had declined. Other researchers have similarly reported low self-confidence in the elderly (e.g. Botwinick 1967). How justified these feelings are will be further examined in the section on metamemory below.

Implicit memory

Evidence on implicit memory points to there being no significant age difference or, at worst, only a very slight decline (Craik & Jennings 1992, Salthouse 1991b). Park & Shaw (1992) argue that in studies which have found an age difference, it has not been established if the younger subjects had realised that they were taking part in a memory test, and so deliberately concentrated harder on the items. Park & Shaw cite the work of Light & Albertson (1989) which found that, if aware subjects were excluded from the analysis, an age difference in implicit memory performance disappeared. Park & Shaw's own study found no evidence for an age difference in implicit memory on a word completion task 'regardless of whether [subjects] aware of the memory test were included or excluded' (Park & Shaw 1992, p.632). Jennings & Jacoby (1993) demonstrated that implicit memory was preserved, even when a distractor task was employed (though explicit memory worsened).

Salthouse (1991b) suggests that with further research, age differences may be found in implicit memories for some materials but not for others. At the time of writing, there are as yet insufficient experimental data to productively pursue this argument in depth, although some recent studies raise interesting caveats. For example, Harrington & Haaland (1992) gave subjects the task of performing various hand movements. The movements were either performed in a set sequence which was repeated over and over again, or they were done in random sequences. It was anticipated that, in the first condition, the regular repetition should aid implicit memory for the movements far more than the random sequence. For young subjects, the first condition improved movement time more than the second condition. However, for older subjects, there was no difference between the two conditions. This implies that the elderly subjects were less able to make use of the implicit information (explicit recall of the movements was also worse in the elderly group), although note that another study showed that placing an explicit order on a physical act through list organisation *improved* the elderly's explicit memory for the act (Norris & West 1993). Again, as was seen in Chapter 2, although subject to experimental artifacts, it has been found that the elderly are less capable of implicitly learning that a target will appear with greater frequency in some locations than in others in a visual search task. However, countering this is the finding that the elderly are disadvantaged to the same extent as the young when a regular predictable sequence of stimuli in a reaction time task is replaced with a random sequence (Howard & Howard 1992).

Another warning is raised by McEvoy *et al.* (1992), who found an apparent worsening ability to *use* implicit information. In one of their experiments, they gave subjects a set of words to remember, and then tested recall using cues (in this case, words related in meaning – for example if the TBR word was 'butter' then the cue might be 'bread'). For the younger subjects, recall was worse if the TBR word had a lot of potential associates than if it had very few (e.g. the word 'car' could have lots of potential associates, whilst a word like 'basilisk' has very few). The same pattern of response was true for the older subjects, but the size of the effect was significantly diminished. This, it is argued, indicates that the elderly are less able to make use of implicit associations. It is probable, however, that the elderly subjects took longer to respond (no response latencies are recorded by McEvoy *et al.*). Therefore, the effect of the implicit associations may be diluted by the extra time spent in processing.

Although implicit memory may in many instances be unaffected by ageing, there would appear to be other occasions where it is not (although this is not true for every instance of the same general experimental paradigm). This may be support for Salthouse's assertion that implicit memory may be better preserved for some skills than others. However, it may also be the case that implicit memory is better preserved where the subjects simply have to receive it passively, and that a decline occurs only when some additional processing has to be done to make use of the implicit information. Until more evidence is gathered, these remain moot points.

Autobiographical memory and ageing

Several major problems beset autobiographical memory research. The most often cited of these is the issue of reliability. For example, an elderly subject may reminisce about a picnic in 1926, held with her now dead parents. How can one possibly verify the accuracy of this recollection? This is not to say that the subject is deliberately lying but, usually, reminiscences have been recalled many times before over a person's lifespan, and with each retelling, details alter to improve the flow of the narrative (Bartlett 1932). Thus, the recounting of a story five years after the event in question may have the same plot as a retelling 50 years on, but the details of the two narratives are likely to be different. This argument is supported by the findings of a longitudinal study by Field (1981). Comparing reminiscences of the same events 30 and 70 years on, there was a reasonably high correlation for points in the basic plot (r=0.88), but only a 16 per cent concordance for recall of more peripheral details (r=0.43).

Another serious methodological flaw concerns how the memories are elicited. Asking subjects for their most *vivid* memories produces a glut of reminiscences from the early part of their lives. So does giving subjects a cue word, and asking them to produce a reminiscence associated with it (e.g. JAM – 'Oh, yes, I remember helping my mother make jam when I was a child'), provided the subject has to put a date on each memory after producing it. However, if the subject is allowed to produce a whole list before any dating of memories is done, then the bias shifts in favour of a preponderance of memories from the recent past being produced (Cohen 1989). Thus, how the subject is asked determines the age of memories produced, and there is certainly no evidence to support the cliché that the elderly live in the past. Indeed, many studies have shown that the young and the old produce equal numbers of reminiscences from childhood (e.g. Cohen & Faulkner 1988). This is not necessarily due to subjects of all ages wallowing in nostalgia. Rabbitt & Winthorpe (1988) found that, when memories are divided into 'pleasant' and 'unpleasant', reminiscences from early life fall predominantly into the latter category. Another problem is that subjects may censor their memories. It is a reasonable assumption that, human nature being what it is, people's most vivid memories include a largish proportion of sexual experiences. However, strangely, these seem to be rarely mentioned by the elderly.

An issue related to what is remembered is the vividness of the recall. Introspection shows that some memories are clearer than others, and generally, earlier memories are perceived as 'dimmer' than later ones (Cohen & Faulkner 1988). This was also demonstrated by Nigro & Neisser (1983), who found that distant memories are usually perceived as if watching the events taking place as a bystander (i.e., as though watching oneself), while more recent events are remembered from one's viewpoint at the time. Furthermore, the reasons why an event is perceived as vivid change across the lifespan. Cohen & Faulkner (1988) found that young and middle-aged adults were affected by how emotionally charged the event was – the greater the feelings, the greater the vividness. For the elderly, however, the biggest cause of vividness was how often they had thought about the event subsequently. Cohen & Faulkner suggest that, because age blunts the vividness of memories, it is only by rehearsing them that their details can be retained (rather like taking pieces of silverware out of the cupboard to polish them, to prevent tarnishing). Why memories lose their perceived vividness is still open to debate. However, given that 'vividness' is a subjective measure, it is possible that as people become more world-weary with advancing age, so they become more jaded in their reminiscing. Another possibility is that a decline in the LTM causes people to forget details of a memory, and it becomes less clearly focussed as a result. In turn, this is interpreted subjectively as a loss of vividness.

Rabbitt & Winthorpe (1988) note that the elderly are generally slower to produce reminiscences. Indeed, in general, older people give poorer quality responses in autobiographical memory tests. For example, they produce vague rather than specific answers (e.g. 'I remember going on a picnic when I was a child' versus 'I remember going on a picnic on Salisbury Plain for my seventh birthday'). However, Winthorpe & Rabbitt (1988) demonstrated that this was not due to ageing *per se*, but to the coincidental decline in fluid intelligence and working memory (which is used to keep track of what has been said and what needs to come next in the narrative). In a subsequent study by the researchers, it was found that detail in the reminiscences was determined by age, fluid intelligence and crystallised intelligence (Holland (*nee* Winthorpe) & Rabbitt 1990). This was interpreted as meaning that although the ageing process and the fall in fluid intelligence cause a decline in reminiscence skills, the age-invariant crystallised intelligence may to some extent compensate for this.

Moving away from considerations of qualities of autobiographical memories, it is worth noting that reminiscence can have a therapeutic effect. Some commentators believe that 'reminiscence therapy' for the elderly should be encouraged, since it enables them to come to terms with their lives before they die (Kermis 1983). For many old people, reminiscence may be a response to boredom:

'Older people may experience an increasing contrast between an unmemorable present and an eventful past. Remote events may be more often researched and rehearsed in memory as the theatre of the mind becomes the only show in town.' (Rabbitt & Winthorpe 1988, p.302)

Prospective memory

As many recent textbooks have noted, one of the principal functions of memory is not to remember the past but to plan for the future. In part this means learning from one's experiences and mistakes in order to cope better with situations when they next arise. This can be considered as part of wisdom/crystallised intelligence. Another, more literal aspect is prospective memory, or the ability to remember to do something in the future. It might be supposed that prospective memory is simply another form of LTM, since it involves retaining a piece of information over a lengthy time period. However, there is ample evidence to disprove this notion. First, on theoretical grounds the two memory types are distinct. In retrospective memory, it is sufficient to recall an item or event for the action to be considered a success. In prospective memory, however, the item can be recalled any number of times, but it is only successful if the person remembers to do it at the right time and acts upon it (West 1988). A second consideration is that the memory types are empirically distinct, with little correlation either in accuracy or in types of mnemonic strategies used (Jackson *et al.* 1988, Kvaviloshvili 1987, Wilkins & Baddeley 1978).

Methods of recall in prospective memory vary greatly between individuals but, broadly speaking, they can be divided into two classes – **internal** and **external strategies/cues**. External cues are such familiar things as entries in a diary or the knot in the handkerchief. In other words, prompts which the person places in the external environment. Internal cues, on the other had, are purely mental strategies, where the subject hopes to prompt him- or herself at the appropriate time. This division is not as clear cut as some commentators seem to suppose, however. For example, a common strategy is to remember to do something in conjunction with a familiar daily routine, such as after the habitual breakfast coffee (Maylor 1990a, Appendix A). Is this an internal strategy (simply remembering to add another action onto the end of a familiar sequence) or an external strategy (the sight of the coffee cup acts as an *aide memoire*)? Similarly, an external cue such as a diary entry requires an internal strategy to remember to look in the diary. Therefore, the functional distinctions between these mnemonic methods are blurred, and certainly are too ambiguous to bear deep analysis. Therefore, for the rest of this section, internal and external methods will be treated purely as practical strategies, avoiding the question of how they work.

Prospective memory appears to be an area of mnemonic performance where the elderly generally can outperform the young, at least under experimental conditions (see the self-report questionnaire studies cited in the metamemory section below). A typical prospective memory task requires subjects to remember to phone the experimenter at prearranged times. Poon & Schaffer (1982, cited West 1988) and Moscovitch (1982) found that the elderly remembered to phone more often and they were more punctual. However, this could in part be a cohort effect. Old people may lead more sedate lives and thus have less to distract them from making calls. Again, they might have been brought up to place a higher value on punctuality and keeping appointments than the young, and were thus more *motivated* to make the calls. This latter supposition is supported by Poon & Schaffers' finding that increasing the monetary reward for making a call improved the elderly's performance, but not the young's. One method of minimising the cohort effect is to take subjects in their fities as the 'young' group, who perform (psychologically speaking) practically on a par with younger adults, but who are more similar to the elderly in their upbringing. Maylor (1990a) did this, and furthermore selected subjects who had similar lifestyles. The participants had to phone once a day for five days, either at a specific time (the 'exact' condition), or between two specified times (the 'between' condition). Maylor found no significant difference between age groups in punctuality nor in number of calls remembered. She also found there was no age difference in the types of cues used to remember to phone. This contradicts earlier findings that old people tend to use more external cues (e.g. Jackson *et al.* 1988, Moscovitch 1982). Possibly this reflects a cohort effect. Studies other than Maylor's have often used students as younger subjects, who may be forced to take part in the test as part of their degree programme. (Much psychological research takes place under the guise of practical classes.) Given the typical undergraduate enthusiasm for practicals, the younger subjects may be apathetic, and they may use internal cues because it is less effort than creating external reminders. In Maylor's study, the younger subjects were all active volunteers in an ongoing large scale research programme into the effects of ageing, and thus they were probably more motivated.

Maylor did find an age effect, however, in the efficiency with which subjects used external and internal cues. Namely, internal cue users who made errors were significantly older, and external cue users who made errors were significantly younger. Thus, those subjects who continue to rely solely on their memories worsen, whilst those who turn to external aids improve (probably because they become more practised). However, to some extent subjects use strategies according to the task at hand. Maylor found that the 'between' condition generated greater use of external cues than did the 'exact' condition. She suggests that this was because of the perceived difficulties of the two tasks (i.e., the condition thought to be harder demands a more positive response in the shape of preparing an external cue). West (1988) has reported similar links between use of cues and task demands.

In the main, older people's prospective memory is well preserved or even better than younger people's when tested under laboratory conditions. However, it is important to bear in mind the caveat about cohort differences, and to note that some studies have found an ageing decline. For example, Cockburn & Smith (1988) found that elderly subjects were worse on tests of remembering an appointment and remembering to deliver a message. Again, West (1988) noted that old subjects were significantly worse at remembering to deliver a message during a test session. In Cockburn & Smiths' study, intelligence test measures were taken, and these could not account for the decline. Maylor also noted that general intelligence did not affect performances in her study. Why the elderly should be better at some prospective memory tasks than others remains an open issue. It is possible that remembering to phone someone (or by extension, when someone is going to call) has become so well practised over the lifespan that it has become a crystallised skill. However, running errands and delivering messages is not something which the elderly do very often, and so by dint of disuse these abilities have declined. That the level of intelligence does not influence performance indicates that prospective memory is not particularly difficult to do. Given that the subjects are free to use *aides memoires* if they so wish, this is not surprising. Probably the answer lies in an amalgam of practice, prompts and motivation.

Metamemory and ageing

To what extent can the elderly gauge their mnemonic abilities? The answer to this question seems to depend very much on the type of memory being considered. It appears that for semantic memory and FOK, ageing has little effect (see *semantic memory* section above and Perlmutter 1978). In a FOK study, the subject is required to judge the suitability of an item he or she has already retrieved from memory: in other words, passing judgement on a mnemonic act already completed. The elderly and the young are also matched in ability to decide in general terms what types of TBR items are easiest to remember, and the best mnemonic strategies to use (Perlmutter 1978). However, other aspects of metamemory do show an age-related decline. Principally, age differences occur when: (a) judgements are asked on a mnemonic act which is incomplete or (b) global judgements on past and future performance are required. Furthermore, as will be seen below, methodological problems with the testing of the latter make much of the research literature uninterpretable in any case.

A prime example of an incomplete mnemonic act is the **tip of the tongue (TOT)** state. This is a familiar experience to most people. The word one is searching for cannot quite be recalled, yet one can remember some features of it, such as its first letter, the number of syllables, words which sound like it, and so forth. Brown & McNeill (1966) were the first to investigate this phenomenon intensively, by giving subjects definitions of obscure words, and asking them to provide the words. Often, subjects either knew the word or simply had no idea, but on some occasions a TOT state was generated. Often, subjects could indeed provide details of the word (e.g. 57% of the time they could identify the word's first letter). The TOT state is nothing more than an annoyance when confined to defining rare words. However, if it creeps into everyday speech, then it is a potential handicap. Burke *et al.* (1988) decided to study the TOT state in the elderly, partly because older volunteers in a gerontological study they were running had complained about it being a problem. Indeed, in general old people are bad at remembering names (Crook & West 1990). The researchers asked their subjects to keep a diary record of all the TOT experiences they had over a four-week period. Subjects were asked to record all the details of the word they could remember whilst in the TOT state, and whether they eventually discovered what the word they were looking for was (i.e., if the TOT state resolved itself). Burke *et al.* found that the old subjects reported significantly more TOTs than the young. However, there was no age difference in the percentage of resolved TOTs (over 90% of the time both young and old eventually found the word they were looking for). However, whilst in the TOT state, the young subjects could report significantly more details of the word (a finding echoed by Maylor 1990b). There was also an age difference in the types of words which generated TOTs. Both young and old generated TOTs most often for proper nouns, but for the remainder, elderly subjects had the greatest difficulty with the names of everyday objects, and the adults with abstract nouns. A final difference the researchers noted was that the young tended actively to mentally search for the desired word, or even ask someone else for help, whilst the old subjects usually simply hoped that the word would 'pop up' (although some did try the same strategies as the young).

In a similar study, Cohen & Faulkner (1986) had subjects complete a two-week diary of TOTs for proper nouns (i.e., names). Surprisingly, the majority of these (68%) turned out to be for names of friends and acquaintances. Perhaps, as Cohen (1989, p.104) notes, 'there are more opportunities to forget names that are in frequent use'. Again, the elderly seemed to rely on a strategy of waiting for the name to 'pop up'. Given these findings, one can surmise that the elderly have a problem with retrieving faint mnemonic traces. This can be seen in the facts they have more TOT states and that when in a TOT state, they have fewer details of the word. Because they lack many details of the word, it is probably not worth their while to search for it on the basis of the little information they have available (the product of another metamnemonic strategy?). Conversely, younger subjects, who can identify more about the word in a TOT state, and thus have more information to act on, will probably find it worthwhile to indulge in a search of their memories.

A further aspect of metamemory is what a person knows about the general state of his or her memory. Typically, this is assessed by requesting subjects to complete a self-report questionnaire. This includes assessments of everyday mnemonic competence (e.g. from 1 for 'poor' to 5 for 'excellent'), and asks subjects to estimate how often they forget things from the important (e.g. forgetting an appointment) to the trivial (e.g. going into a room to fetch something and forgetting what one went in for). To gauge the accuracy of subjects' metamemories, scores on the questionnaire are usually correlated with a battery of tests of memory spans and often other psychological measures as well. Results from such studies have been conflicting. Some studies have found the elderly reporting a decline in their abilities and a concomitant rise in acts of absent mindedness, and so forth (e.g. Perlmutter 1978). Other researchers have found the reverse – namely it is the *younger* subjects who report a greater number of memory lapses (e.g. Baddeley 1983, Rabbitt & Abson 1990). The relationship between questionnaire scores and memory spans is similarly muddled. Many researchers report a poor correlation between self-predicted performance and actual mnemonic skills (e.g. Herrmann 1984, Rabbitt & Abson 1990, Zelinski *et al.* 1993). However, others have found a correlation (e.g. Maylor 1990a). Taylor *et al.* (1993), in a longitudinal study, found a correlation at a group level between some memory scores and self-report (but not with a measure of fluid intelligence). However, when individuals were considered, then no significant relationship was found.

Why is there this confusion? The answer lies in the methodology used. First, people are notoriously bad at quantifying their abilities (hence the need for professional psychologists!). Rabbitt (1984) observes that a person can only judge how his or her memory is by comparing it with that of other people. But whom? Younger people (or him- or herself when younger)? Contemporaries? An idealised hyperintelligent being? Subjects may differ markedly in their value judgements, and hence ratings of mnemonic abilities are most probably not being set against a common scale.

A related problem concerns self image. Old people expect to be forgetful; the young do not. Accordingly, older subjects may be more sensitive to memory lapses, and so unrealistically downgrade their mnemonic abilities. It is not surprising to find there is a correlation between the elderly's self ratings of forgetfulness and depression (Rabbitt & Abson 1990, Thompson et al. 1987). Another frequent criticism is that, perversely, questionnaires may still overestimate the mnemonic skills of the worst subjects. Information about subjects' memories comes only from them – there is usually no corroborating evidence. However, with the self-confessed forgetful, how can they remember all that they have forgotten? This is an ingenious and untestable argument. However, there are some indications that it is overly pessimistic, since several studies involving the spouses of subjects have found a good correlation between self-reported mnemonic skills and spouses' estimates of the same (Cohen 1989). However, even the most fervent supporter of the questionnaire method would admit there will inevitably be inaccuracies in self-ratings.

The generally poor correlations between self ratings and actual mnemonic spans probably arise because usually questionnaires ask subjects how their memories are in real life, whereas spans are taken from tests run under laboratory conditions. For example, most 'standard' memory tests assess a single type of memory in quiet unstressful conditions. In real life, such opportunities rarely arise (Cohen 1989, Rabbitt & Abson 1990).

It is also worth noting that, under realistic conditions, many memory lapses may not be due to memory at all. For example, Tenney (1984) found that a frequent cause of misplacing items by the elderly was that they had literally overlooked the said items in a systematic search for them. In other words, the problem is often one of misperception rather than memory per se (though note that memory for spatial location is worse for older than younger subjects – Uttl & Graf 1993). Rabbitt & Abson also note that in general the correlations between memory tasks are poor anyway. For example, training subjects to be good in one type of memory in no manner improves their performance on another, as was noted earlier. Therefore, expecting to find a general all-embracing metamemory measure which will simultaneously predict all types of memory is a misplaced ideal: there is no mnemonic equivalent of intelligence's g. In studies such as Maylor (1990a), which have reported a correlation between self-report and degree of failure, the effect is usually due to specific items on the questionnaire rather than overall score.

Summary and overview – how *does* ageing affect memory?

The familiar complaint of many old people that their memories 'aren't what they used to be' seems in the main to be justified. Memory *does* decline in old age, and despite a few areas of preservation (e.g. 'basic' STM span and some aspects of metamemory), the outlook is downwards. However, although there is a general trend, a general mnemonic principle does not seem to underlie it, because there is a poor correlation between the spans of different types of memory. Many factors have been suggested as key determinants of age-related decline. For example, emotional state, socioeconomic background, and educational background have been suggested as possible determinants of intellectual performance (see Chapter 2). West *et al.* (1992), in an impressively large study of nearly two and a half thousand subjects, assessed performance on a wide variety of 'realistic' mnemonic tasks (remembering people's names, face recognition, etc). The researchers also took measures of chronological age, 'vocabulary, education, depression, gender, marital status, and employment status' (West *et al.* 1992, p.72). Perhaps not surprisingly, vocabulary level (also indicative of general intelligence, and crystallised intelligence in particular) accounted for performance on a measure of prose recall, and also generally could account for some of the variability in some of the other memory scores. Gender proved a significant predictor of mnemonic tasks in which subjects had to memorise a grocery list. The female subjects were better – given the traditional gender roles, this is not a surprising finding (note that Larrabee & Crook 1993 found that memory for such stereotypically 'female' tasks showed a gender bias across the lifespan, and was not disproportionately altered in old age). However, with these exceptions, chronological age was the best predictor of mnemonic performance, and overall was unquestionably the best.

In another three-year longitudinal study, Zelinski *et al.* (1993) took a rather smaller sample (508 men and women, of whom 227 were available for retesting) and assessed the relationship between mnemonic skills, vocabulary, and tests of 'higher reasoning' (essentially, measures of fluid intelligence). Measures of length of schooling and other biographical data were also taken. The researchers found a less clear-cut picture than West *et al.* Although age was a good predictor of performance on some memory tasks (especially for those subjects who had displayed very marked decline), 'higher reasoning' also had a significant effect independent of any influence of age. This should not be surprising, if one recalls Rabbitt's caveat, cited in Chapter 2, that practically any intellectual decline can be tied to a fall in fluid intelligence (as the authors in fact acknowledge). However, Zelinski *et al.* found that age had a strong relationship with mnemonic decline which could not be attributed to the coincidental effect of changes in fluid intelligence. Probably the most parsimonious explanation of the results is that there is no parsimonious explanation of the results. It would, however, be surprising if ageing and fluid intellectual decline were *not* at least in part responsible for mnemonic decline. However, this begs the question – what is the nature of the link?

It has been suggested that mnemonic decline may in part be due to the selective physiological changes in the brains of ageing people, and that the decline in neural functioning is reflected in a concomitant decline in fluid and mnemonic skills. It is well documented that the hippocampus suffers disproportionate degradation. The hippocampus has a pivotal role in memory, relaying information from short- to long-term memory stores, and in attention (Winocur 1982). Damage to this area alone can neatly explain many of the mnemonic deficits suffered by the elderly. The reason why there is a poor correlation between different memory types is that they are reliant to different degrees upon the hippocampus. Those processes which use the hippocampus as a central part of processing will be affected more seriously than those which use it solely as a 'relay station'. Unfortunately, knowledge of hippocampal functioning in the elderly is relatively limited, and accordingly, the above theory is as yet untestable.

A psychological explanation, not incompatible with the hippocampal hypothesis, may also be advanced. It can be observed that the memories which do *not* decline are very much part of crystallised intelligence – knowledge of facts, of strategies, and so forth. Problems occur when subjects have to process novel information and concurrently deal with other problems and distractions (this can be seen most clearly in the working memory studies). It might be supposed that the fall in fluid intelligence underlies the decline in these mnemonic functions. Fluid intelligence is very much involved in processing novel information and is probably an expression of the general efficiency of the CNS (central nervous system), as are measures of reaction times (see Chapter 2). Rabbitt (1988b) found empirical support for this argument. He tested a group of subjects aged 50 to 79, and gave them a test of fluid intelligence, a CRT (choice reaction time) task, and several measures of STM and LTM. Correlations between the memory measures were not significant when the coincidental effects of intelligence scores had been controlled for. Some mnemonic measures were also influenced by the subjects' CRT speeds. Thus, many age-related declines in memory may be attributable to changes in the efficiency with which information is processed in the CNS. It is also worth noting that many aspects of 'crystallised' memory, supposedly age-invariant, are probably determined by fluid skills. This is because someone with a high level of fluid skills is likely to learn more and thus accrue a greater amount of knowledge. For example, Stuart-Hamilton *et al.* (1988) found that subjects with a high fluid intelligence score also scored more highly on the FNT of remote memory. However, Rabbitt is at pains to point out that not all of the decline can be attributed to changes in fluid intelligence or CRT. For example, the rate of memory loss from STM when rehearsal of TBR items is blocked is not predicted by intelligence test score. Changes in fluid intelligence cannot explain all aspects of ageing memory, but they certainly form a key part of the process.

Suggested reading

Baddeley (1983) provides an immensely readable introduction to the general psychology of memory, and the book is warmly recommended. Baddeley (1990) is a more advanced text, but it is still reasonably accessible. Good general introductions to studies of ageing and memory are provided by Chapter 11 of Schaie & Willis (1991) and Chapter 8 of Perlmutter & Hall (1992). There is an interesting collection of writings on ageing memory in a two volume work edited by Gruneberg *et al.*, entitled *Practical Aspects of Memory* (see reference for Winthorpe & Rabbitt 1988). Another useful selection is contained in Poon *et al.'s* edited collection, *Everyday Cognition in Adulthood and Late Life* (see reference for Cohen & Faulkner 1989). There are also two useful chapters, by Craik & Jennings (1992) and Light (1992), contained in a generally very good textbook on ageing and cognition edited by Craik & Salthouse, two of the leading lights of modern gerontology. Salthouse (1991b, 1992b) provides an interesting analysis of ageing mnemonic changes, linking them to general intellectual changes. These works, although excellent, are, however, intended for a readership already well versed in psychological terms and techniques.

CHAPTER 4

Ageing and Language

Introduction

The effect of ageing on linguistic skills is rarely given much consideration
in general gerontological texts, beyond a cursory glance at changes in the
physical characteristics of the voice and the decline in the ability to recall
stories. This is a pity, because there is a considerable research literature on
the subject – not as vast as that on ageing and memory or on dementia,
perhaps, but nonetheless sufficient to merit more than a passing nod.
'Language' comprises not just speech production and comprehension, but
also, of course, writing and reading. This chapter will concentrate on the
last of these skills, because it is the one for which perhaps the best developed
theories are available, and upon which most research has concentrated.

Introspectively, reading is perceived as being a fairly automatic and
instantaneous process but, in fact, it involves the coordination of a variety
of different skills, from the very basic to the complex. On *a priori* grounds,
normal reading must involve at the very least the following processes. First,
there must be a process for identifying individual letters, to distinguish them
from, say, random splodges of ink, or items from a foreign alphabet.
Furthermore, there must be a method of identifying whether sequences of
letters form real words or whether they are merely nonsense strings (e.g.
xyllfrg), and also of judging how to pronounce the word (i.e., of converting
the printed into the spoken representation). Following from these stages
must be a skill of judging if sequences of words form meaningful phrases.
Phrases have to be judged for both their **syntactic** and **semantic** accept-
ability. For example, the phrase:

    goldfish make suitable pets

is sensible, if banal. The phrase:

    hypotheses make suitable pets

is more interesting, but is obviously nonsense, and is said to be semantically
unacceptable (loosely, semantics is the expression of meaning). However,

the phrase's syntax (loosely, its grammar) is acceptable. Conversely, a phrase such as:

goldfish makes suitable pets

is syntactically unacceptable (because it is grammatically incorrect), but it could be argued that it still conveys a meaning, and thus is semantically acceptable. A final stage in the reading process must involve extracting meaning from the phrases. Introspection shows that one does not remember every word of what has been read – instead one recalls the gist of the story. Thus, readers must possess a method of extracting the key features of a piece of text. It must not be supposed that all the processing is in one direction from the fairly basic skill of letter recognition to the relatively complex one of meaning extraction, since the latter operations can send information back down the processing chain to speed up the reading process. For example, suppose one is reading a passage of text written in an appallingly untidy hand, and suppose that some letters are completely unrecognisable, represented below by *x*s:

Ix is xoubtful if anx moxe axxixtance is rexxired. Remxmbxr the xroverb: txo maxy coxks xpoil the xxxxh.

Most readers should have little difficulty in decoding this. There are several reasons for this. First, some words like *xoubtful* and *xroverb* can *only* be *doubtful* and *proverb*. Thus, the reader makes use of knowledge of which letter combinations make real words to work out what the indecipherable letters stand for. In other instances, semantic knowledge is used. For example, *Ix* alone could be *If, It, In,* or *Is*. However, *Ix is* only makes sense if *Ix* is *It*. The final word in the passage – *xxxxh* – is unrecognisable by itself, but is easily recognised as *broth* because it is the last word of a well-known saying. This is an example of **semantic facilitation**, where the semantic content of a passage enables one to predict the words coming up. This does not just apply to reading sloppy handwriting. For normal print, one uses one's expectations to facilitate word recognition, and it has been demonstrated that words which are logically linked to what has just been read are read faster than less predictable words. Thus, if one has just been reading about animals, then one would read *tiger* faster than *armchair*. In formal experimental situations, the phenomenon is tested by presenting subjects with a word or sentence (the 'prime') and then presenting them with a word which may or may not be semantically related to the prime. Subjects are usually asked to decide if the word is a word or not, or to say the word out loud. In both instances, responses are faster if the prime is semantically related. How facilitation occurs is still hotly contested but, generally, it appears that the mind places semantically related words on 'standby' in a kind of mental dictionary, so that if they appear in print, their meaning is accessed faster.

A final consideration is the role of memory. Obviously, without LTM (long term memory), it would be impossible to read a story and understand it, simply because one would keep forgetting the plot. Less obvious is the need for working memory (see Glossary), but one must be able to keep in mind what has just been read, otherwise by the time one reaches the end of the sentence, one would have forgotten the point of it, and this would be especially true of long convoluted sentences such as this.

Thus, reading involves the active integration of a number of perceptual, cognitive, linguistic and mnemonic skills. It will not have escaped some readers' attention that the processes involved in the comprehension of spoken language are similar. There must be the capacity for recognising individual letters and words; for identifying whether they are correctly pronounced; for identifying meaning, and whether phrases are syntactically acceptable; and finally, for extracting the gist of a spoken message. Obviously, there are differences – reading is accessed visually, speech acoustically, so readers can look back at something they have not understood, while listeners usually have fewer opportunities to do the analogous thing, and ask a speaker to repeat a point they have difficulty with. Speech and writing also have different conventions. Writing, for example, tends to be more formal and grammatically correct. Indeed, there is a considerable debate whether speech and writing share *any* processes in common (Olson *et al.* 1985). In this chapter the debate will not be addressed, but given that reading and listening have functionally analogous processes, examination of the effects of ageing on the two skills will be conducted in tandem, with reading examined first and then listening skills (where research evidence on them is available). It is not necessarily implied, however, that a change in a reading sub-skill is automatically linked to a change in the analogous listening sub-skill. It should also be noted that the effects of ageing on the skills of speech production and writing have received relatively little attention, but such experimental findings as there are will be placed at appropriate points in the commentary.

The role of reading in old people's lifestyles

Because reading is a sedentary activity, it is often assumed that the elderly spend more time engaged in it than younger people. In fact, some evidence points in the opposite direction (e.g. National Council on Aging 1975). Despite worthy intentions, people do not read more once retirement presents the opportunity to do so through increased leisure time. Old people who read a lot were almost invariably voracious readers when they were younger. If solely those older adults who are active readers are considered, then there are some intriguing differences between them and their younger counterparts. The elderly active readers spend more time reading (e.g. Rice 1986a), but significantly more of this time is spent on newspapers and magazines (e.g. Ribovich & Erikson 1980, Rice 1986a). This means that the reading 'practice' the elderly obtain may be of a poorer quality, because the content of newspapers may be facile compared with the demands of, for example, a 'heavyweight' novel. In the same manner that failure to train strenuously reduces an athlete's performance, so a failure to read sufficiently demanding texts may cause a decline in reading skills. Why this change in reading habits should occur is open to debate. Reduced mental resources may mean that some old people no longer have the intellectual rigour to plough through Dostoevsky et al. Alternatively, when old age is reached, many people may feel that they have read most of the fiction they wanted to read, and have no desire to reread works of which they already know the plot. A more cynical view is that the elderly feel there is too little time left to waste it on wading through tedious 'classics'. Young adults may read 'heavy' works to 'improve' themselves. The elderly may no longer have this competitive urge. For whatever reason, old people select 'easy' reading over 90 per cent of the time, be it periodicals, newspapers, or 'light' fiction. Furthermore, they seem to get the same level of enjoyment out of reading as do younger adults (Bell 1980, Rice 1986a).

Physiological constraints

As was noted in Chapter 1, the eyesight of most old people worsens, and visual acuity ('focusing power') is reduced. This will clearly have a deleterious effect on the elderly's hearing and reading abilities. One study (Bell 1980) estimates that about 23 per cent of community resident old people are incapable of reading normal print. A solution to this problem is to print books in a larger typeface (for the technically minded, 18–20 point). Perhaps the best known example of this is the *Ulverscroft* series. The larger print makes easier reading for the those with poor sight, but a study has shown that in the UK at least, there are disadvantages. The first arises from the fact that large print books have a relatively small market. Young visually handicapped adults tend to use magnifying equipment, enabling them to cope with normally sized print. Therefore, the principal market is the elderly. This is further restricted by the fact that few readers buy large print books – most borrow from the local library. These considerations mean that publishers tend to stick to fairly 'safe' lightweight fiction, which will appeal to the largest numbers of old people, such as that by James Herriot, Agatha Christie, Catherine Cookson and so forth Whilst there is nothing wrong with these authors *per se*, this policy means that an elderly person with eyesight problems is restricted in his/her choice to texts which are unlikely to stretch his/her reading abilities. An additional consideration is that many elderly people are limited in the amount they can read. Large print books are heavy, and old people may take fewer books home from the library than when they were younger, simply because they cannot carry more (Bell 1980). Furthermore, there is some evidence that while large print size may increase the rate at which words can be read aloud, it may decrease the speed with which they are read silently (Bouma *et al.* 1982). The font face used can also affect reading speed (Vanderplas & Vanderplas 1980), although note that Cerella & Fozard (1984) found that making print harder to read did not differentially affect older people relative to younger people.

It should be noted that many elderly are unaware that they have problems with their vision. Holland & Rabbitt (1989) noted that all subjects from the age of 50 onwards gave near-identical subjective ratings of their vision, although in reality there was a marked deterioration as the subjects got older. A decline in perceptual abilities does not just mean that the elderly need large print and/or hearing aids, however. A sensory loss can directly affect the efficiency with which information is processed. For example, Rabbitt (1989) noted that elderly people with mild hearing loss (35–50 db) had great difficulty remembering lists of spoken words, even though they were earlier able to repeat them all perfectly as they were spoken to them. It appears that the hearing impaired elderly can perceive words, but it takes greater effort to do this, leaving fewer mental resources to encode and remember them. That there is nothing especially wrong with their memories can be shown by the fact that if the subjects were shown *printed* lists of words, then there was no difference between their and normal hearing controls' performance (i.e., the effect was confined to when hearing was part of the processing chain).

The voice also undergoes changes. The obvious superficial alterations, in a raising of pitch and a weakness of projection, arise from a variety of factors, including muscle wastage and a reduction in lung capacity. Other changes may result from relatively modern phenomena, such as (ill fitting) dentures and smoking (Thompson 1988). This loss of vocal efficiency also shows itself in a slowing of articulation rate, both for normal impromptu speech, reading a passage of prose, and reaction times to pronouncing words (e.g. Laver & Burke 1993, Oyer & Deal 1989, Ryan 1972).

Word recognition

There are a variety of ways to test the ability to read single words, but two of the commonest are the **lexical decision** and the **naming latency** tasks. The former requires subjects simply to decide if a group of letters forms a word (note that the subject does not have to identify what the word 'says'). A naming latency task measures how quickly a subject can read a word aloud. Generally, old people are no worse at these tasks than younger subjects (e.g. Cerella & Fozard 1984). However, if the tasks are made harder, then often an age decrement may appear. For example, Bowles & Poon (1981) found this when subjects were given a modified lexical decision task. Subjects had to judge pairs of letter groupings, both of which had to form real words for a 'yes' response to be given.

In semantic facilitation experiments, the elderly are generally slower than younger subjects (as with many reaction time experiments – see Chapter 2). However, elderly subjects gain a disproportionately greater advantage than do young people from the priming when compared with the recognition of words seen in isolation (Laver & Burke 1993, Myerson *et al.* 1992; although note that earlier commentators, such as Craik & Rabinowitz (1984) found no age difference). At one level the explanation for this phenomenon is simple – 'a slow horse will save more time than a fast horse when the distance is reduced by a constant amount' (Laver &Burke 1993, p.35). If one horse runs at 40 kilometres per hour, and another at 20 kph, then cutting the race distance from 40 to 20 kilometres will save 30 minutes for the faster horse but an hour for the slower one. In a similar manner, if the elderly are reacting less quickly than the young, then facilitation (which in effect cuts the computational 'distance') will be of greater benefit to the older subjects. However, the issue is complicated by the debate over what causes the slowing. The substance of this goes beyond the range of an introductory text, but essentially is concerned with whether the age difference is due to a general slowing of processes, or whether slowing is specific to particular processes. Evidence for either viewpoint is reliant on relatively complex statistical techniques, but since even minor changes in the data sets used can result in radically different final results (e.g. see Laver & Burke's reinterpretation of Lima *et al.*'s (1991) data), perhaps the issue is in any case too mercurial for a firm interpretation to be made as yet (for those readers interested in pursuing this matter, Laver & Burke (1993) is a useful introduction).

Knowledge of pronunciation of words might also be expected to be preserved in old age, and indeed early studies seemed to support this idea (note that the *speed* with which words can be pronounced may slow – see above). Typically, pronunciation knowledge is tested by presenting subjects with a list of irregularly spelt words (e.g. *yacht, dessert*), and asking them to say them aloud. Because the words do not obey conventional spelling rules, their pronunciation cannot be calculated from first principles. For example, pronouncing *dessert* by conventional spelling principles would yield the spoken representation of *desert* (and vice versa). Those readers who have already read Chapter 2 will appreciate that pronunciation abilities are therefore part and parcel of crystallised intelligence (general knowledge), which is largely age-invariant. It therefore follows that pronunciation ability should remain stable in old age, and indeed there is empirical support for this argument. Nelson & O'Connell (1978) examined the pronunciation abilities of 120 adults aged 20–70 years, and found no significant correlation between test score and chronological age (Nelson & McKenna 1973). The word list used in this experiment is now widely employed in the UK, and is known as the National Adult Reading Test or **NART**. A subsequent study by Crawford *et al.* (1988) found a slight negative correlation between age and NART score, but this disappeared when either length of education or social class was partialled out of the equation. Hence, concluded Crawford *et al.*, 'age has little or no effect on NART performance' (p 182). Because of such arguments, the NART has become widely used as a quick assessor of crystallised intelligence, where elderly patients with some kinds of brain damage have retained the ability to read while being incapable of some other intellectual tasks (e.g. Brayne & Beardsall 1990, Nelson & O'Connell 1978, O'Carroll *et al.* 1987, O'Carroll & Gilleard 1986).

However, there is a problem with the manner in which the age invariance of NART scores was proven. Both Nelson & O'Connell's and Crawford *et al.*'s studies correlated NART scores with subjects' ages. However, as the age range used was 20 to 70, the majority of subjects were not even old. As has been noted before, appreciable decline does not even commence until the mid sixties. Therefore, in the studies in question, only the very oldest subjects were likely to be showing a decline, and this would be masked in statistical calculations by the relative stability of the under-65s, who formed the majority of the groups. To avoid the potential masking effect, Stuart-Hamilton & Rabbitt (research note 1) gave the NART to a narrower age band of subjects, aged 50 to 79, and found that NART performance declined in old age (by about 10%). However, it would be rash to assume that old age *per se* 'caused' this decline. So what did? Subjects were matched for level of crystallised intelligence, so this (the most obvious factor) could not be the explanation. However, the researchers were able to show that the decline was due to three other factors. The first of these was amount of schooling – the older subjects had received less full-time education, so it would not be surprising to find that they had a smaller pronunciation vocabulary. Thus, part of the age difference was a cohort effect. This conclusion is supported by the findings of Rodgers (1984), who argues from what little demographic evidence is available that reading standards of schoolchildren improved with each generation up to the 1970s. Thus, not only the quantity but also the quality of the teaching has increased. A second factor was a measure of knowledge of authors and their works. It was argued that the more a person knows about literature, the 'better read' he or she is likely to be. The elderly subjects were less well informed about literature (despite having the same level of crystallised intelligence as the younger subjects) and this echoes the findings of Rice and others on the quality of reading practice mentioned above. The final factor to affect NART performance was the subjects' level of fluid intelligence. This is surprising, because irregular word pronunciation should be a crystallised skill *par excellence*. A possible explanation is that the level of fluid intelligence determines how well the pronunciation of a word is learnt in the first place, and thus, whether knowledge of it is retained when memory begins to fail. Other research findings by Stuart-Hamilton & Rabbitt (unpublished) note that the elderly's spelling abilities show a similar decline, chiefly explicable by a fall in fluid intelligence.*

Syntactic processing

Relatively little research has been conducted on semantic or syntactic processing independent of concurrent considerations of text recall. However, one notable exception is a series of excellent papers and articles by Susan Kemper on changes in syntactic processing in the elderly. Kemper (1986) requested young and old adults to imitate sentences by creating new ones with the same syntactic structure. She found that the old subjects could only reliably imitate short sentences: long sentences, particularly those containing embedded clauses, were the hardest to imitate (although note that Stine *et al.* (1986) did not find this effect). This syntactic decline is reflected in spontaneous everyday language. Kynette & Kemper (1986) noted that the diversity of syntactic structures declines with age, whilst there is an increase in errors such as the omission of articles and the use of incorrect tenses. Kemper & Rash (1988) reported other examples of this decline. For example, the average number of syntactic clauses per sentence fell from 2.8 for 50–59 year olds to 1.7 for 80–89 year olds. The researchers

---

* Readers may also be interested in consulting the section on 'tip of the tongue' states in the section on 'Metamemory and Ageing' in Chapter 3.

also assessed the **Yngve depth** of the syntax. This is a fairly complex technique which gives a syntactic complexity 'score' to a phrase or sentence (the higher the score, the more sophisticated the construction). Yngve scores declined with age, but more intriguingly, Yngve scores correlated well (r=.76) with digit spans (see Glossary). Thus, the better the memory, the better the syntax. There is an attractively simple explanation for this finding. Syntactically complex sentences are almost invariably longer than simple ones, and to construct or comprehend them, greater demands are placed on memory (simply, more words have to be remembered at one time). This is a plausible explanation of why the elderly simplify their syntax – they know that their working memory no longer has its youthful capacity, so sentences are simplified and shortened to cope with this. However, as Kemper herself has acknowledged, this is an overly simplistic explanation. More probable is that declines in spans and syntax are both manifestations of a general decline in fluid intelligence.

Comparable results are reported by Gould & Dixon (1993). They asked young and older married couples to describe a vacation they had taken together, and analysed the descriptions for linguistic content. The general finding was that the younger couples produced a greater amount of detail (e.g. more details of schedules and location of events in time). The researchers attribute the elderly couples' 'failure' to do this to a decline in working memory. However, they also acknowledge it is possible that the age-related change is due to a change in attitude – 'the younger couples... may have given less consideration to being entertaining than did the older couples' (Gould & Dixon 1993, p.15). Again, Adams (1991) notes that, compared with a group of young controls, elderly subjects' written summations of stories tended to interpret the text at a more abstract level, and placed less emphasis on a *précis* of the story's structure. This qualitative difference may arise through compensation for loss of processing capacity (e.g. if the elderly cannot remember as much of the story, then talking about it in more abstract terms may be a wise strategy). An alternative response is that the elderly are deliberately using a different mode of thought, and Adams cites the emerging work on developmental models of change (see Chapter 2) as a possible theoretical framework by which to judge these changes.

Kemper (1987a and b) examined six diaries kept by people for most of their adult lifespans. Drawn from museum archives, the diaries commenced between 1856 and 1876, and finished between 1943 and 1957. Kemper found that the language used became simpler over the writers' lifespans. Sentence length decreased, as did complexity of syntax. For example, the number of embedded clauses declined. and there was an increase in the failure of **anaphoric reference** (e.g. referring to 'he' without specifying which of two previously cited males is meant). At the same time, the sophistication of the narrative declined, and increasingly events were described as a catalogue of facts, rather than as a 'story' with a plot and a conclusion. This decline cannot automatically be attributed to an intellectual failing. As anyone who has kept a diary for some time will know, writing it can be a chore. Thus, the older they got, the less motivated the subjects might have felt to write a 'story'. Again, rereading their attempts at creative writing might have so embarrassed the subjects that they decided to resort to a less florid style. It may also be the case that as the subjects grew older, writing styles relaxed, and thus the subjects deliberately adopted a simpler style. Indeed, Kemper (1987b) could identify a cohort difference even with her small sample. The writers born earliest in her group used significantly more infinitives ('to go', 'to do', etc) than did the younger ones.

Bromley (1991) gave subjects aged 20–86 years the task of writing a description of themselves. Analysing the results, he found that the syntactic complexity and breadth of vocabulary exhibited in the writing was related to the subject's age, but that other factors, such as word length and readability, were affected by the subject's educational level and level of vocabulary (as measured by the Mill Hill vocabulary test, a common measure of crystallised intelligence – see Chapter 2). Interestingly, fluid intelligence (as measured by Raven's Progressive Matrices) did not play a significant role. However, Bromley's findings can be criticised in the same manner as Kemper's – namely, it is possible that the changes represent a cohort difference or a deliberate change in writing style, especially since the changes do not appear to be heavily reliant on processing skills.

A related argument concerns how the changes in elderly people's language can be linked to linguistic usage in childhood. In other words, do the elderly regress to a childlike language state? This is known as the **regression hypothesis**. The argument does not seem plausible, because the grammatical usage of elderly people is still far more sophisticated and varied than that of young children (see Kemper 1992). This should not be surprising. It was seen in Chapter 2 that vocabulary is largely a facet of crystallised intelligence, and it has been seen that certain other linguistic skills are also related to it. It might be argued that since the level of crystallised intelligence does not alter during normal ageing, many facets of language are likely to be preserved, even if a lack of processing capacity means that there is less frequently the chance to employ them.

Therefore, although there are changes in the elderly's spoken and written language, and these are reflected in the simplification of linguistic structures, a firm interpretation of these shifts cannot be made. The results may reflect a decline attributable to the worsening of working memory and fluid intelligence. However, there is also evidence that the changes are confounded by crystallised skills, cohort effects, and possibly a deliberate change in linguistic style (though whether this in turn is a response to a lowered processing capacity is a moot point).

Story comprehension

Story comprehension has attracted more research interest than any other linguistic topic in gerontology. This is not surprising, because ultimately the efficacy of listening and reading must be judged by how much information can be absorbed and comprehended. Because of the large number of studies, it is perhaps most convenient to itemise this field of research.

General aspects

The basic story comprehension paradigm is simple – a subject listens to or reads a short passage of text (usually 3–400 words long) and then either repeats back as much of it as possible, or is given a multiple-choice recognition test. Most studies have found that the elderly remember less than the young (e.g. Byrd 1985, Light & Anderson 1985, Petros *et al.* 1983). However, this is not a universal finding, and varying the types of experimental subjects and/or test materials can have a crucial effect, as will be seen below.

Choice of subjects

Some experimenters, using groups of 'old' subjects with an average age in the sixties, have failed to find an old–young group difference (e.g. Mandel & Johnson 1984). Age differences are only reliably found and are at their greatest when the 'old' subjects are in their mid seventies or older (Meyer 1987). Another important consideration is the education level of the subjects. Studies have sometimes found no age difference when elderly subjects with a high verbal ability (and hence high IQ/education level) have been used (e.g. Taub 1979). Thus, as has been noted in previous chapters, those with a well preserved intellect can maintain a youthful level of performance. The findings of Rice & Meyer (1986) criticise this assumption, however. They found that the quantity of reading practice declined in old age, and tended to concentrate on simpler reading materials. This suggests that the decline might be due to a change in reading experience rather than intelligence. However, Rice *et al.* (1988) showed that, although quantity and quality of reading practice were important in determining level of text recall, chronological age *per se* and level of intelligence were still the best predictors. Holland & Rabbitt (1990) found that among a battery of measures, the best predictors were age, and fluid and crystallised intelligence test scores. Cavanagh & Murphy (1986) noted that personality type and level of anxiety also significantly influenced level of text recall.

Choice of presentation of materials

The findings within this field have been mixed. Cohen (1981) found that the elderly were significantly worse at recalling spoken than written materials, whilst for the young there was no difference (Zacks *et al.* 1987). This is what would be predicted from Rabbitt's (1990) findings on auditory versus visual recall of word lists reported above. Presumably the decline in hearing is in this instance more disadvantageous to the elderly than is the decline in their sight. Attempts to manipulate the presentation of the story itself have met with variable results. Some alterations have no effect. For example, requiring subjects to read aloud versus reading silently does not affect the quantity of information recalled (Taub & Kline 1978), nor does giving subjects a choice of subject matter for the to-be-read text (Taub *et al.* 1982).

Varying the speed of presentation of the story has yielded mixed results. Where subjects are free to read at their own speed, usually no age difference is reported, but there have been exceptions (Meyer 1987). Subjects can be forced to read faster by setting time limits on how long they have to read a piece of text. Auditory presentation rate can be increased simply by the narrator speaking faster. Obviously, the faster the presentation rate the faster one has to process information to comprehend it, and one would logically expect old subjects to be disadvantaged. Indeed, there are several studies supporting this argument, but a sizable minority have failed to find an age difference. Furthermore, Petros *et al.* (1983) found that when both presentation and semantic difficulty were varied, there was no appreciable disadvantage to the elderly beyond that also experienced by the younger subjects. Conversely, Tun *et al.* (1992) found that elderly subjects were differentially disadvantaged when recalling quickly-spoken passages. However, this age difference was not affected by having to perform a concurrent task of picture recognition (i.e., the magnitude of the difference remained the same).

Stine *et al.* (1989) demonstrated a significant age difference in recall of spoken words when the they were 'jumbled up' so they made no sense, and this difference increased the faster the rate at which the words were presented. However, this difference diminished when the words made syntactic sense (e.g. 'bright deep gorillas fructate omnivorously'), and became non-existent for all but the very fastest presentation rate when the words formed conventional phrases (i.e., that made both syntactic and semantic sense). This implies that the elderly may be limited in processing the spoken input (e.g. through poorer hearing, a lower capacity working memory), but that they can compensate for this by making greater use of the semantic facilitation provided by normal phrases. However, this implies that processing the jumbled prose is the normal way in which speech comprehension takes place, and that subjects make use of semantic and syntactic information only as extra help when it is needed. In other words, the elderly cannot process speech by the simplest method of simply joining together the words as they are heard, and so must rely on contextual aids. However, as was seen in the introduction to this chapter, listening to speech relies on a *simultaneous* combining of all levels of information. Therefore, the unusual conditions are the syntactic and jumbled sentences. If the elderly do less well on these, it may be because they normally make greater use of semantic and syntactic information, but it could also be because they cannot attune to a different (and artificial) manner of speech comprehension as well as the younger subjects can.

Because of these issues, probably the safest conclusion is that the issue of age and presentation rates is as yet unresolved, and is very much an artifact of the experimental method used.

Some other manipulations of text have an effect. For example, Connelly *et al.* (1991) gave subjects short passages of prose to read. Interspersed in the to-be-read prose were segments of distracting prose, printed in a different font, which the subjects were told to ignore. It was found that the distractors had a disproportionately deleterious effect on older readers compared with younger controls (they both read the passage more slowly and correctly answered fewer comprehension questions). This was especially noticeable when the insertions were related to the to-be-read text.

Generally, the more complex the recall task, the worse the old person's performance. This shows itself in several forms. For example, Byrd (1985) found elderly subjects to be impaired on the simple recall of a passage, but to be disproportionately disadvantaged when they had to *summarise* it. In other words, when the passage had to be simultaneously remembered *and* processed, then the elderly were at a severe disadvantage. This seems to be another case of the age x complexity effect and/or working memory decline marring processing, and several types of study support this thesis. Hamm & Hasher (1992) found that the elderly had greater difficulty than young subjects in drawing inferences from ambiguous stories in which the text began by implying one thing before finally resolving itself in a different direction from the one initially anticipated. They attributed the age-related decline to a lessening ability to process information in working memory (i.e., to keep the initial story 'in mind' whilst resolving the contradiction introduced at the end of the story). Light & Albertson (1988) found that ability to draw inferences from sentences was only marred when the sentences were complex and/or concurrent processing of another task was required. Again, Cohen & Faulkner (1984) demonstrated that old subjects were especially disadvantaged at a recognition task when they had to integrate separate facts gleaned from the story to answer correctly. Smith *et al.* (1989) tested memory for prose of three types; 'standard' (self explanatory); 'scrambled' (sentences with no coherent links); and 'interleaved' (two or more stories alternating with each other sentence by sentence). The old and young subjects performed qualitatively the same for the standard and the scrambled texts. However, for the interleaved condition, the old subjects performed qualitatively as they had done for the scrambled prose, whilst the young performed qualitatively as they had done for the standard prose. In other words, the young had sufficient processing capacity to untangle the interleaved prose and treat it as a standard text, whilst the older subjects could not.

It is tempting to ascribe the above changes to a decline in the mnemonic skills of the elderly. However, it should be noted that some researchers have found a poor correlation between text recall and other mnemonic measures, such as digit span (e.g. Light & Anderson 1985). Other, more linguistic factors may also contribute. For example, Kemper & Rash (1988), reviewing their own and others' studies, found that the quantity of information recalled varied directly with the syntactic complexity of the to-be-remembered passage. Given the evidence on syntactic changes presented in the previous section, this is not a surprising finding. More remarkable perhaps is the contrast in the recall of details versus main points of a text. An often reported finding is that older subjects remember as many main points of a story as the younger subjects, but that they are significantly worse at remembering details (Cohen 1989). For example, in remembering a story, an old person might remember that it involved a girl entering a shop and buying a dress, but he or she might not recall the colour of the purchase. A failure of memory for details is not surprising if one argues that they require more processing to be remembered, and thus are less likely to be memorised than main points, which are more modest in their processing requirements (Cohen 1988, Holland & Rabbitt 1990). However, as the next section will demonstrate, this phenomenon is not universally true.

Interaction between subject type and reading materials

It might be supposed that if the prior experience of the subjects was relevant to the reading matter, then this might have an effect, but Morrow *et al.* (1992) did not find this to be the case. They tested groups of old and young adult subjects who were a mixture of airline pilots and non-pilots, on stories, some of which had a flying theme and some of which did not. There was a significant age difference in ability to recall items (specifically, subjects were asked which character was being referred to as 'he' or 'she' in a sentence they had just read). However, level of flying expertise had no effect on the age differences.

In an excellent review of the literature, Meyer (1987), drawing principally on work by Dixon *et al.* (1984), observes that age differences in recall of main points and details is not as clear cut as some commentators have supposed. Instead, the main points-details balance seems to depend upon the (verbal) intelligence of the subjects and the type of text being used. Normally, well-structured text with a clear, logical plot is used. When young and old high verbal ability subjects are tested on this type of text, then there are bigger age differences for details than there are for main points (if indeed there is any difference for main points at all). However, low ability subjects tested on the same type of material show the opposite pattern (i.e., the age difference is principally in recall of main points). This pattern is reversed when subjects are required to read unstructured text (i.e., where there is an incoherent narrative thread to the story). In this instance, high ability

Table 4.1 Relative differences in recall of main points and details
(adapted from meyer 1987)

		Prose Type	
		Well Structured	*Ill Structured*
Level of Subjects	*High Verbal Ability*	Difference bigger for details	Difference bigger for main points
	Low Verbal Ability	Difference bigger for main points	Difference bigger for detail

subjects show a principal age difference for main points, and low ability subjects for details. This argument is summarised in Table 4.1.

Two major explanations have been proposed to account for age declines in story recall. The first, introduced above, is that it is simply due to a decline in processing capacity. This can comfortably explain why in some instances main points are better remembered, because they are less demanding of mental resources. However, the theory cannot, without modification, explain the qualitative difference in performance across types of text. The second explanation is that differences between high and low verbal ability subjects are due to differing reading strategies. Thus, the low ability subjects have chosen a strategy which is diametrically opposed to that of the high ability subjects. However, this theory in its 'strong' form is difficult to defend, because it implies that low ability subjects go out of their way to choose the wrong strategy (Cohen 1988). By combining elements of the capacity and strategy theories, however, it is possible to gain an insight into why age changes affect story recall in such an intriguing fashion.

The high verbal ability subjects will be considered first. Meyer (1987) plausibly argues that they are more likely than low ability subjects to be responsive to an author's intentions. If someone writes a passage of prose with a relatively obscure plot, then it is probably the case that the author expects readers to pay more attention to details. An extreme example of this is a telephone directory but, more commonly, authors of many textbooks employ this strategy when wishing to impress the reader with the range of the topic being covered. Murder 'whodunits' provide another example where, to resolve the issue, the details must be attended to, and the plot, such as it is, is merely a device for accruing clues. Conversely, where there is a strong narrative thread to the story, the author clearly intends the reader to attend to this, with details intended to add a little local colour, and little else. It therefore follows that in well structured prose, high verbal ability subjects attend primarily to the main points, and details are only processed for storage if there is any spare processing capacity left over after the main points have been gathered. Given that the processing capacity of high verbal elderly people is likely to be less than that of the young high verbal subjects, it follows that for the elderly there is less room for the gathering of details. Conversely, in ill structured prose, the details hog the attention, and it is the main points which are processed only if there is sufficient capacity left over. Hence, for high ability subjects, the main points–details balance shifts according to what they think the author is stressing as being the more important. For low ability subjects, a different explanation is required, which hinges on the likelihood that they have relatively inefficient reading strategies. There is some evidence from child and adolescent readers that poor verbal abilities are reflected in poor or ill-coordinated general reading strategies (e.g. Fredericksen 1978, Stuart-Hamilton 1986), and Hartley (1988) has provided some tentative evidence that this also applies to elderly subjects. Note that it is not being argued that poor readers have chosen a strategy which is the reverse of good readers' – only that they are *less efficient*. Low verbal readers, like high verbal readers, know that they must concentrate on the main points in a well structured text, and on details in an ill structured one. However, they are less efficient at searching out and encoding the information, and thus do not take in their fill. However, because structured text places greater emphasis on main points, subjects tend to notice more of them. The difference in the processing capacity of young and old subjects means that the former encode more of them than the latter. For ill structured text, the emphasis falls on details, and the reverse pattern applies. An objection to this argument is that in terms of numbers, there may be an equal number of details and main points in well and ill structured texts. However, this ignores the concept of **pragmatics** (understanding of intent as opposed to explicit meaning). Thus, simply counting the numbers of details and main points ignores their relative subjective importance.

The above arguments are perhaps made clearer by an analogy. Suppose that the low and high verbal subjects are like riflemen on a shooting range. Targets appear, and the riflemen have a limited time in which to shoot down as many targets as possible. In the same manner, readers have only a limited time in which to take in as much information as possible. Suppose that some targets are worth twice the points of others (in the same manner that main points and details can be more important than each other in different types of text). High verbal readers are like good marksmen, who pick off the high value targets first, and then in the time remaining go for as many lesser valued targets as possible. The older marksmen will be slower at shooting, and although they may get as many or nearly as many high value targets as their younger counterparts, they have less time left over to go for the lesser targets. The high ability old and young readers behave in a similar manner – each gets roughly the same number of 'important' pieces of information – the main difference appears in secondary factors. The low ability readers are like poor shooters – they will aim at anything, and hit much less than the marksmen. However, assume that the targets are so arrayed that shooting randomly, some targets will be hit more often than others. In a similar manner, some types of text will cause some types of information to be more memorable than others. The younger poor shots will hit more targets than the old, not because they are better at aiming, but simply because they can fire more shots in the time available.

Ecological validity

The above findings have to be weighed against the argument that the experiments reported above lack ecological validity (i.e., they are not very realistic). The standard story recall test – of reading a passage of 3–400 words then attempting to regurgitate it whole – is hardly an everyday activity. Rice (1986b) observes that the only activity where anything approaching this skill is required is studying for exams, an activity which few of the elderly indulge in. The experience is probably more central to the younger subjects, thus creating a bias against the older subjects. However, even in hardened exam takers, attempts at verbatim recall do not consist of attempting to learn 3–400 words on one reading. A far saner strategy would be to learn such a length of prose sentence by sentence (and evidence for an age difference in this activity is more equivocal). In short, the text recall paradigm is unrealistic, and much of the age difference may be a cohort effect. Another consideration is the length of the prose passage used. Experimenters have usually chosen items of about the same length as magazine or newspaper articles – the commonest items read by the elderly (Rice 1986b). However, they do not accord with other reading experiences. Meyer (1987) observes that a 'very long text' used in only a minority of studies is about 1600 words. Given that a moderately sized novel is circa 60,000 words, even the longest texts currently being used in standard experiments fall well short of a realistically long piece of prose. The reason for this observation is that, as librarians know to their cost, old people are often appallingly bad not only at remembering the plots of books, but also *which* books they have read before. Clive James, the writer and television presenter, once worked as a librarian, and describes the phenomenon thus:

> 'I ran out of answers for the little old ladies who wanted to know if they had already read the books they were thinking about taking out. The smart ones used personalised coding systems... There were hundreds of them at it all the time. If you picked up a book by Dorothy L Sayers or Margery Allingham and flicked through it, you would see a kaleidoscope of dots, crosses, blobs, circles, swastikas, etc.' (James (1983), Ch 8)

The phenomenon seems to be widespread. The author has spoken to a number of librarians who practically gave a paraphrase of Mr. James's observations. However, this shining failure of recall for lengthy passages of prose seems to have escaped researchers' attentions.

Summary and overview

The study of language changes in the elderly is currently fragmented. Some areas have been covered in depth, while others have barely been touched upon (e.g. there is a woeful lack of studies on the elderly's writing skills). Furthermore, there have been few attempts to see how linguistic sub-processes integrate together – usually specific skills have been studied in isolation. This is a great pity because, as outlined in the Introduction, it is known that the different processes interact, and it would be of considerable theoretical interest to see whether some skills are being 'propped up' by others which have been less severely hit by the ageing process. Because the picture is incomplete, interpretations must be guarded.

It should first be noted that declines in sight and hearing, which afflict many elderly people especially hard, will almost certainly dent linguistic skills. A decline in physical health may also lessen old people's visits outside the home to shops and libraries, thereby lowering exposure to fresh reading materials. Such increased social isolation will probably also cause a decline in conversational skills. However, although these factors affect a greater proportion of the old than the young, these are not problems unique to old age. More interesting in this respect are changes in reading habits – the elderly seem on the whole to prefer lightweight reading, such as newspaper or magazine articles, rather than heavyweight literature, such as 'classic' fiction or textbooks. It is tempting to conclude that this is because the elderly can no longer cope with the intellectual demands of the latter. However, there is no strong proof for this assertion, and equally plausible is that old people cannot be bothered to wade through turgid fiction because they no longer have to prove to themselves how well read they are. Thus, the changes in reading patterns could be for motivational reasons. However, for whatever cause, this change means that old people receive 'poorer quality' reading practice than the young. This change can in part explain the decline in reading skills, but more important factors are level of (fluid and crystallised) intelligence and chronological age itself. Concentrating on specific linguistic skills, such as word recognition, syntactic processing and story recall, it can be seen that there are age-related declines, but the extent of the fall is heavily dependent upon other factors such as degree of distraction, type of test materials used, cohort effects, and so forth. Perhaps the biggest criticism is that many reading tests are highly unrealistic – normal people do not spend their time learning short stories verbatim, pronouncing obscure words or deciding if a string of letters form a word or not. Thus, a loud note of caution needs to be sounded over these results, since the measures used probably do not correspond to real life experiences.

Recommended reading

Light & Burke's (1988) edited collection of papers on ageing linguistic skills is probably the most comprehensive review currently available (see reference for Hartley 1988). However, there is a great deal of repetition between chapters, and many authors assume a detailed prior knowledge of linguistics and/or psychology. Kemper (1988, 1992) provides an excellent overview of her own work and of recent advances in the field. In her 1992 paper, she also presents a survey of probable future areas of research in this field. Given the complexity of the topics, she provides a very readable account. There are also a number of interesting studies in Poon *et al.*s (1989) *Everyday Cognition in Adulthood and Late Life* (see reference for Stine et al 1989). For those interested in the general mechanics of reading, Ellis (1984) is warmly recommended.

CHAPTER 5

Ageing, Personality and Lifestyle

Introduction

This chapter considers how the elderly present themselves to others. This will be principally examined by looking at age-related changes in personality, but the related issue of the lifestyles which elderly people elect to follow will also be examined. 'Personality' can be defined in many ways, but a useful general definition is:

> 'the individual characteristics and ways of behaving that, in their organization or patterning, account for an individual's unique adjustments, to his or her total environment.' (Hilgard, Atkinson & Atkinson, 1979)

Elsewhere in this book, the efficiency of the psychological skills under discussion can usually be measured by a simple scale. For example, how many questions are correctly answered, how syntactically complex an utterance is, how many list items are correctly recalled. Personality assessment is less clear-cut, since how can one judge what is a 'good' or 'bad' personality? Obviously, people who behave like Mother Theresa or, conversely, Adolf Hitler, are easily categorised, but most people fall into a 'grey area' between. Most exhibit a mixture of attractive and quite unappealing behaviours. To complicate matters further, what is appealing to some is appalling to others. For example, someone who is the life and soul of the party to one group of people may be seen by others as a loud-mouthed airhead. Accordingly, a single, objective measure of personality 'goodness' is impossible to construct. The best one can hope for is to look for qualitative differences between the personalities of individuals, and, where possible, to measure these against 'real life' behaviours.

Because personality measurement is relatively resistant to objective measures, much work in this field is descriptive and resistant to abbreviation. The solution to this problem is either to devote an entire textbook to the subject or to present a general overview in the form of a thumbnail sketch.

For obvious logistical reasons, the latter solution is adopted here. However, the reader should be aware that, behind many of the apparently simplistic arguments presented, lie often sophisticated theories and descriptions. A further reason for erring on the side of brevity is that much of the work in ageing personality research draws heavily from research in other areas (particularly sociology) and thus falls outside the ambit of this book.

Trait models

Perhaps the area of personality research with the strongest links to main-stream psychology is the study of the **personality trait**. This may be defined as an enduring characteristic of a person's personality which is hypothesised to underpin his or her behaviour. The concept sounds com-plicated but, in fact, it is often used in everyday life. For example, if one is told that a person is 'very nervous' then one can predict how he or she will behave when watching a horror film (i.e., one assumes that the trait of 'nervousness' will cause that person to display a characteristic behaviour pattern). A number of trait models, which seek to explain behaviour by means of a few predisposing factors, have been developed by psychologists. The best known example is probably Eysenck's measure of **extroversion–introversion**, **neuroticism** and **psychoticism** (e.g. Eysenck & Eysenck 1969). Eysenck argues that people's personalities are principally determined by the degree to which they display these three traits (Eysenck prefers to refer to them as 'dimensions', but the difference in terminology is unimpor-tant). The extroversion–introversion (**E**) trait measures the degree to which a person is outgoing and assertive. Someone who tends towards these characteristics is said to be an **extrovert**, and the stronger they possess these characteristics, the more **extroverted** they are said to be. Conversely, someone who is shy and retiring is an **introvert** and, again, the more pronounced these characteristics, the more **introverted** they are. Eysenck argues that the extroversion–introversion measure is a continuum: people are never purely extroverted or purely introverted – instead, they possess features of both attributes, although overall they tend to be of one kind or the other. Thus, for example, a person who is an extrovert and can go to a karaoake bar without the slightest worry may nonetheless be racked with embarrassment in using a public changing room. The psychoticism (**P**) trait measures the degree to which a person is emotionally 'cold' and antisocial, and the neuroticism (**N**) trait the degree to which a person is anxious and has rather unstable emotions. High scores on the P and N scales do not mean that an individual is mentally disturbed, but rather that, under stress, they are likely to display psychotic or neurotic characteristics. Eysenck measures the E, P and N traits using the **Eysenck Personality Questionnaire (EPQ)**. Subjects are asked to give 'yes' or 'no' answers to a series of statements designed to elicit how strongly the subject identifies with each particular trait. For example, one of the questions designed to assess the strength of extrovert tendencies is, 'Are you a talkative person?' (Eaves *et al.* 1989, Appendix B).

E, P and N alter as people get older, and gender also has an important influence. P (psychoticism) declines with age, but the rate of decline is much greater for men than women. At 16 years, male P scores are almost double those of females but, by the age of 70, this difference is practically non-existent. More curious is the change in E (extroversion–introversion). Both men and women become more introverted as they get older. However, males in their late teens are more extroverted than females, but thereafter show a more rapid decline in their extroversion, so that by their sixties, the males are more *introverted* than the females (the cross-over point, where the two sexes are equally extroverted, occurs in the forties). The changes in N (neuroticism) are less spectacular. There is a decline in neuroticism for both sexes, but at all age groups women score appreciably higher on the N scale than do men (Eysenck 1987, Eysenck & Eysenck 1985). Eysenck (1987) argues these findings predict that older people should be less prone to violent swings of mood and, hence, should be calmer. Note that he is not arguing that people should necessarily be happier in old age. If anything, older people should tend to be more *indifferent* about the world, with only relatively small swings of mood in either direction. At an ideal best, such indifference might be cultivated into a calmness and serenity, but equally, an undesirable apathy and sloth might be produced. Eysenck argues that personality changes across the lifespan are primarily the result of physiological changes altering levels of excitation within the central nervous system. This argument is disputed by other psychologists, and a plausible case can be made for changes in lifestyle being the prime cause of shifts in the level of E, P and N. For example, old people may become more introverted, not because of changing levels of neural excitation but because, as they age, society becomes less geared to their needs. This causes the elderly to withdraw upon themselves, and this in turn engenders feelings of reserve and hence, increased introversion. Because men, more than women, define themselves by their role in society (see below), men should show a disproportionately bigger loss of assertiveness as they age, and this is shown in the greater decline of their extroversion scores.

The argument for an influence of lifestyle on personality change receives guarded support from other trait studies. Kogan (1990) reviewed a number of longitudinal studies of changes in personality traits across the life span. His general finding was that in many instances there were significant shifts in personality which were commensurate with changing lifestyles (e.g. the transition from college to paid employment). However, he also found that, generally, there was less change in the latter half of adult life. Most studies in Kogan's review found that individuals retain the same personality strengths relative to the rest of their age group. In other words, if a woman was more extroverted than 20 per cent of her age group when she was 20, then she was likely to be more extroverted than 20 per cent of her age group when she was 60. However, this does not mean that personality 'strengths' are as stable across the life span, and some researchers have found major changes. Thus, the woman at 20 might have an E score of 40, but at 60 this score might only be 10 – it is the fact that the rest of her age group has also shown a decline in scores which enables her to keep the same relative position within the group. Other researchers have failed to find such major shifts in personality traits. For example, Butcher *et al.* (1991) found no appreciable changes in the pattern of personality scores on another common measure – the **Minnesota Multiphasic Personality Inventory (MMPI)**. Longitudinal studies of self-report personality measures have similarly recorded relatively little change, even though subjects often feel that their personalities have changed dramatically (Perlmutter & Hall 1992). Kogan concludes that this discrepancy in findings may be due to researchers using completely different tests and analysis methods.

This failure of trait research to produce clear findings should not perhaps be surprising, because the area of study has been heavily criticised. The principal argument is admirably summarised by Davis (1987, p 614):

> 'the results of research in this field [personality trait tests] have had little impact on the development of psychology, whether in the laboratory or in the clinic. One reason for this has been the relatively low reliability (i.e. reproducibility) of the data; another, the controversial nature of the statistical techniques. There are formidable difficulties too in generalizing from responses made in the miniature situation of a test to make predictions about behaviour in the complex social setting of real life'.

Psychotherapy and the ageing personality

The earliest attempts to codify the ageing personality came from **psychotherapy**. It is difficult to give a concise and all-embracing definition of psychotherapy. However, in its usual sense, it means any treatment regime which is based upon an integrated theory of mind. Often these theories are named after their author (e.g. 'Freudian' after Sigmund Freud, 'Jungian' after Carl Jung). Strictly speaking, **psychotherapy** is not part of psychology, and many psychologists have questioned its efficacy (e.g. Eysenck 1952). However, from a historical viewpoint at least, a brief examination is necessary. The founding father of psychotherapy, Sigmund Freud, was skeptical about the value of psychoanalysis being administered to older patients, because they had relatively little remaining life in which to enjoy the benefits of treatment. The crux of Freud's theory is that personality is made up of a mixture of three components – the **id**, **ego**, and **superego**. The id describes basic appetitive urges, the ego people's rational selves, and the superego a set of moral dictums (often unrealistically harsh). For reasons too complex to describe here, Freudian theorists felt that the id's efficiency and strength were drawn from the state of a person's smooth (i.e., involuntary) muscle, whilst the ego's strength is dependent on the state of the CNS. Because the CNS declines more rapidly in old age than does smooth muscle, the ego becomes relatively weaker than the id. A tenet of Freudian theory is that the ego strives to keep the id in check. To prevent the id gaining the upper hand, the ego starts to conserve its energy by rationalising resources. In psychoanalytic terms, this means adopting a relatively unvarying and conservative set of attitudes and responses, even though they may not be entirely appropriate to the situations the elderly find themselves in. This perceived inflexibility of the elderly is specious, however. For example, Pratt *et al.* (1991) found no age differences on measures of moral reasoning, and as shall be seen below, the ageing personality varies greatly across individuals (i.e., there is not a typical 'old personality'). It is also worth noting that, although he did little formal work on ageing, in his private life and correspondence Freud appears to have had a very melancholy and illogical attitude towards ageing (Woodward 1991).

Erikson (1963, 1983) felt that personality developed throughout the lifespan – unlike other psychoanalysts, who felt that it was essentially determined by childhood habits. He argued that, at different ages, different conflicts had to be resolved. For example, in infancy, individuals must resolve the conflicting impulses to trust or to mistrust by developing a sense of trust. There are eight of these conflicts to resolve, of which only the final one occurs in old age. This is the conflict of **integrity versus despair**. The goal of this final stage is **ego integration** – the acceptance that earlier goals have been satisfied or resolved, and there are no 'loose ends'. A person who feels that not everything has been achieved can feel a sense of despair because, with death approaching, it is too late to make amends. Thus, the despairing individual also comes to fear death, and he or she ends life feeling anxious and depressed. A criticism of Erikson's theory might be that, taken simplistically, it portrays successful ageing as a passive preparation for death. However, this is not what Erikson intended. He viewed the final stage of development as a learning process, and in 'such final consolidation, death loses its sting' (Erikson 1963, p 268).

Peck (1968) expanded on Erikson's theory, and argued that in old age, three conflicts needed to be resolved. The first of these is **ego differentiation versus work-role preoccupation**. Many working people (particularly men) establish their status and self concept through their work. Thus, a professional person may develop a high self-esteem simply because they have an occupation which society regards favourably. However, when a person retires, this status disappears with the job. Thus, retirees must find something in themselves which makes them unique or worthy of an esteem previously conferred on them simply by a job title. The second conflict is **body transcendence versus body preoccupation**. For most individuals, ageing brings a decline in health and general physical status. If an elderly individual over-emphasises bodily well-being in extracting enjoyment from life, then disappointment will almost inevitably result. Successful ageing involves an ability to overcome physical discomfort, or at least finding enjoyable activities where bodily status is relatively unimportant. The third of Peck's conflicts is **ego transcendence versus ego preoccupation**. This essentially means that a person comes to terms with the fact that he or she will inevitably die. This is obviously an unpleasant thought, but Peck argues that, by attempting to provide for those left after a person has died, and continually striving to improve the surroundings and wellbeing of loved ones, an overweening concern for the self and the self's fate can be overcome.

Levinson's view of ageing is akin to Erikson's and Peck's but concentrates rather more on the role of the aged individual in family and society (e.g. Levinson 1980). Changing physical and occupational status means that in the early to mid sixties (the **Late Adult Transition**), people must come to terms with the fact that they are no longer the prime movers in either work or in family life. To remain content, the elderly must therefore learn to shed leadership and take a 'back seat'. This does not mean that all cares and duties can be avoided, since aside from assuming the role of wise counsellor to family and younger friends, the elderly must come to terms with their past (in a manner similar to that described by Erikson). Levinson refers to this process as the **'view from the bridge'**.

Do these theoretical personality types really exist outside the confines of a psychotherapist's office? Reichard *et al.* (1962) interviewed 87 American men aged 55–84, half of them in retirement, and half in full- or part-time employment (note that for many jobs in the USA there is no compulsory retirement age). Many points raised by Reichard *et al.* support the psychoanalytic theories. For example, subjects approaching retirement seemed to be particularly 'on edge' and self-deprecatory, indicating that the period in question was perceived as being one of change and of anxiety. Overall, five main personality types were identified. **Constructiveness** is akin to the optimal resolution envisaged by Erikson's and Peck's theories – subjects possessing this trait had come to terms with their lives, and were relatively free from worries, while striving to interact with others. The **dependent** or **'rocking chair'** trait created some contentment, but individuals were dissatisfied with products of their own efforts, and relied on others to help or serve them, regarding old age as a time of leisure. The **defensiveness** or **'armoured approach'** trait is essentially neurotic. Subjects possessing it carried on working or were engaged in a high level of activity, as if to 'prove' that they were healthy and did not need other people's help. The fourth trait, **hostility**, involves blaming others for personal misfortune. Subjects unrealistically attributed failures throughout their lives to factors other than themselves. In part this sprang from a failure to adequately plan. The final trait identified by Reichard *et al.* was **self-hatred**. The self-hating individuals were akin to the hostile trait possessors, except that they turned their hatred and resentment inwards. Reichard *et al.* found that people possessing the first three traits were well adjusted towards old age, whilst the those having the last two were less successful. However, given that the researchers' personality descriptions contain implicit value judgements of quality of lifestyle, this is not a surprising finding.

Continuity of personality across the lifespan

Reichard *et al.* also observed that people's personality types had developed long before the onset of old age. In other words, the types are not a result of the ageing process; it follows from this that, in order to enjoy old age, one must prepare for it. This argument is somewhat supported by the findings of a longitudinal study reported by Haan (1972). Subjects were studied from their teens to the onset of middle age. Various personality types were identified, but these can be principally divided into: the stable and secure; those akin to Reichard *et al.*'s defensive personalities; and the insecure who blamed others for their misfortunes and who often had disorganised lifestyles. These types are remarkably similar to those found in studies of the elderly, and it is reasonable to conclude that the traits of old age are probably those which have been there since early adulthood (Kermis 1986). However, this may not be entirely true. In a review of the literature,

Aiken (1989) notes that whilst some of the more stable personality types may not alter much over the lifespan, the less stable traits may be more labile in response to age changes. Again, it can be shown that they become more inward looking (Neugarten 1977). This is not necessarily surprising. Unstable personalities might be expected to change, and stable people may always have been stable because circumstances have always been consistent and rewarding. Old people may become inward looking, not because of an intrinsic compulsion, but because the death of friends and a world which caters primarily for the young leaves few attractions for the outward-going elderly.

It is interesting to note that some personality types may be better adapted to early rather than late adulthood and vice versa. **Type A personalities** are very hard edged, competitive types who find it difficult to relax – in modern parlance, they are ideal 'yuppie' material. **Type B personalities** are the opposite – easy going, carefree, and so forth. It might be expected that Type As will be best suited to young adulthood when there are the greatest chances to exhibit competitiveness in career chasing, sport, and so forth. Old age should not suit Type As because of its emphasis on a sedentary, relaxed lifestyle. For Type Bs, the reverse should hold true. Strube *et al.* (1985) measured the psychological well-being of a group of people aged 18–89, and found that in general Type A and B personalities fulfilled this prediction, although the results were mediated by factors such as the social environments of individuals.

Returning to studies of the measurement of personality types within old people, Neugarten *et al.* (1961, 1968) studied a sample of people in their seventies. Four principal personality types (with subdivisions) were identified, which bore great similarity to the traits uncovered by other studies already mentioned. The most desirable trait was the **integrated personality**. People in this category were either: **reorganisers** (as one activity became physically impossible, another was found); **focused** (activities were limited to a small set of feasible and highly rewarding ones); or they were **disengaged** (the deliberate abnegation of many responsibilities). Another major trait was the **armoured–defensive** personality. People in this category were either **holding on** types who felt that they could stave off decay by maintaining a high level of activity; or they were **constricted**, and dwelt on what they had lost as a result of ageing. The armoured–defensive individuals were less satisfied than those with integrated personalities. A third group possessed **passive–dependent personalities**. Like Reichard *et al.*'s dependent/'rocking chair' types, such people relied on others to help them (the **succourant seeking**), or they withdrew from interaction with others as much as possible (the **apathetic**). The fourth and final group comprised the **disorganised personalities**. These unfortunate people had serious problems (possibly early dementia?) and could not be classified as functioning normally.

As has been noted, there is much similarity between the various personality type studies. All emphasise that personality is largely fixed long before the first grey hairs appear and that, essentially, the elderly can adjust their personalities but not alter them radically. There is more than one way to age successfully, but all essentially involve accepting limitations and renouncing responsibilities without suffering a feeling of loss. A slightly less successful strategy is to maintain a fear of the ravages of old age, and to fight them by keeping as active as possible. However, as this involves a failure to come to terms with ageing, it is ultimately a less satisfactory strategy. The worst option is to have no strategy at all and to blame all the wrong factors for one's present state. Many commentators have arrived at similar conclusions (e.g. Aiken 1989, Kermis 1983, 1986, Turner & Helms 1987, Whitbourne 1987). However, the argument presented is a generalisation and a potentially misleading one. Successful ageing involves accepting limitations and abnegating responsibility, but this may be because of societal pressure to hand over the reins of power. Accepting this change willingly may be akin to surrendering gracefully to a stronger opponent on the principal that if one is going to lose, one may as well do so with the minimum of hurt. In other words, the successful aged have not gained a philosophical insight so much as grasped a point of pragmatics. Another important consideration is socioeconomic class. The 'unsuccessful' aged may rant and rail about external forces precisely because their social position has yielded them fewer privileges and 'lucky breaks' (often researchers note that such individuals are downwardly socially mobile). In contrast, someone who has known 'all the glittering prizes The cars, the hotels, the service, the boisterous bed' (Auden, 1979), will be more likely to have a relaxed view of life. Accordingly, the aged personality may be as much a product of social and economic circumstances as of any internally motivating factors. This consideration does not refute the theories described, but one should be careful not to consider personality as a purely internally-driven entity.

It will not have escaped the reader's attention that some researchers have argued for the relative stability of personality across the lifespan, whilst others have argued that it changes. There are several possible reasons for this. The first is that it is due to differences in measurement techniques (Kogan 1990). This is plausible, but it hardly bodes well for research if a factor as important as personality can behave so capriciously when measured. However, it is worth noting that many longitudinal studies have only found personality changes when the subjects are compared over several decades – relatively short periods do not yield large changes. Also, there may be a cohort effect – older subjects may be less 'open' about their responses than younger people, not because of their personalities *per se*, but because they wish to be 'polite' (Stokes 1992). A further factor is that different studies have measured different aspects of personality. Personality cannot be measured on a single scale as intelligence can be gauged by the IQ measure. Which of a wide range of measures are taken as representative of the personality and at what level (e.g traits versus types) may lie behind many of the discrepancies between studies. As was noted above, personality theory has been heavily criticised, and hoping to find reliable ageing changes when the measures are in such dispute may be a forlorn task.

Self-image and life satisfaction in old age

General changes

It follows from the caveat just given that, to understand personality in old age, external forces impinging on old people's self-image and life satisfaction must also be considered. A general consideration is the effect of the stereotype of a 'typical' old person. As was noted in Chapter 1, society expects people to behave appropriately for their age. Kite *et al.* (1993) found that stereotypes of the elderly are stronger than those of gender differences, and that stereotypical 'masculine' attributes are particularly felt to decline in old age. Because the label of 'old' or 'elderly' is usually derogatory in western culture, it is small surprise to discover that in one study, only 20 per cent of people in their sixties and only 51 per cent of those in their seventies labelled themselves as being 'old' (Ward 1984). The author of this study also notes that, ironically, old people are often hoisted by their own petard, since when they were younger they formed the illogical stereotypes of what it is like to be old which now haunt them. Stereotyping seems to affect the elderly's confidence and, generally, the more old people believe in stereotypes, the lower their self-esteem (Ward 1977). However, given that many elderly are likely to be more inward-looking, might it not be the case that they come to think that everyone of their age is like themselves, and thus the lower their opinion of others, the lower their self-regard? Again, perhaps self-image and stereotypes are self-reinforcing, creating a vicious circle. At present the exact relationship remains unclear but, for whatever reason, for the majority, self-image declines in old age (Aiken 1989). This is reinforced by a more recent study by Ryff (1991). She asked young, middle-aged and older adults to rate their past, present and future selves and well-being. She found that the young and middle-aged adults tended to see themselves on a path of self-improvement – they were better than their past selves, and in the future would get even better. The elderly, on the other hand, saw themselves on a plateau looking at the oncoming fall – that is, they saw themselves as maintaining the level they had experienced in the past, but that in the future they foresaw a decline.

It is important, however, to note that a lowered image of importance is not simply nor uniquely something which occurs in old age. Graham & Baker (1989) examined two groups of (Canadian) subjects: a group of old people (mean age 67 years) and a group of students. Subjects were asked to grade imaginary people of different ages (e.g. '40-year-old man') for their level of status in society. The researchers found that, for both groups of subjects, children were graded at a low level, status then rose through the teens, twenties and thirties, and then began to decline once again, so that 80-year-olds were perceived to have roughly the same status as five-year-olds. However, although older subjects gave the same pattern of judgement as younger subjects, the difference between the highest and the lowest ratings was significantly less. Thus, although different generations have the same view of ageing and status, the old are apparently 'slightly more egalitarian than the young' (Graham & Baker 1989, p 255).

Causes of change in self-image

Physical changes, from the relatively minor (e.g. grey hair) to the more serious (e.g. arthritis) can all cause a reevaluation of self-concepts (Ward 1984). Modern cosmetics and medical treatments can often alleviate these, but other changes – in societal roles and relationships – are irrevocable. Probably the biggest of these are retirement from full-time employment, and widowhood.

Work and retirement

Herzog et al. (1991) studied older adults who were working or were in semi-retirement. They found that well-being was not related to how *much* work they did as to whether the work they did was what they wanted to do. This finding was the same for a group of slightly younger workers (aged 55–64 years). With regard to retirement, it has been noted that people approaching retirement tend to be more apprehensive and self-deprecatory, but in most instances, once people have stopped working, the experience is pleasurable. There are some instances of people suffering serious psychological problems because they no longer feel useful. For example, Swan et al. (1991) reported in their study of American retired persons that those who felt that they had been 'forced' to retire had generally lower levels of well-being, and (perhaps not surprisingly) that people with Type A personalities were more likely to complain that they had been 'forced' to retire. However, it is difficult to exclude the possibility that such people would have suffered problems in any case. For the majority, retirement brings little change in satisfaction with life. Indeed, there may be an increase among very healthy retirees (Parnes 1981). White collar workers tend to enjoy retirement more than blue collar workers, but this can probably be attributed to better health and financial security (Bengtson & Treas 1980, Ward 1984).

Widowhood

Widowhood (loss of one's partner of either sex) more commonly affects women than men, because of the differing life expectancies of the two sexes. There is some evidence that the impact of the loss depends upon how expected it was. For example, Eisdorfer & Wilkie (1977) found that the loss was less stressful if the deceased had been ill for some time. In addition, the elderly tend to have a lesser reaction to loss than do younger people (Cook & Oltjenbruns 1989), because the elderly are better primed to accept the death of a partner. In the majority of cases, adjustment to loss is reported as being at least satisfactory, though there are some residual signs of grief and other negative feelings 30 months after bereavement (Thompson *et al.* 1991), and a sizable proportion (20%) of widowed persons report a failure to cope adequately (Lopata 1973). Carey (1979) noted that men are better able to adjust than women. This may be because in traditional sex(ist) roles, a married woman's status is determined by the presence of her husband, while the reverse does not apply as strongly. Also, a widowed man is likely to be financially more secure, and may have greater opportunities to find another partner. Other studies, however, have contradicted this viewpoint (Cook & Oltjenbruns 1989), possibly because more men than women are inept at looking after themselves, and also because widowhood is primarily a woman's experience. Thus, on the available evidence, the question of which gender suffers the more cannot be settled. Perhaps in any case the current societal reevaluation of gender roles may eradicate whatever differences there are.

Other factors

Although retirement and widowhood are the two principal factors influencing self-image, other events, such as the death of friends, troubles of or with younger relatives, and so forth, can also influence a person's well-being

(Kermis 1986). Krause *et al.* (1991) demonstrated that financial problems (common in many of the elderly) are a prime factor in reducing feelings of self-worth and in increasing depressive symptoms (the study found the same findings in samples of both American and Japanese older people). The level of social support received by the elderly can also have an effect. In a longitudinal study, Russell & Catrona (1991) found that the less social support the elderly person experienced at the start of the study, the higher his or her depressive symptoms after one year (and the greater his or her experience of 'daily hassles').

However, the extent of these events' influence is mediated by a person's personality type and socioeconomic situation. For example, a well-integrated individual can cope with stress far better than someone who is disorganised. Conversely, an individual in bad health and with poor finances may be better able to cope with the declines of health and wealth because they are already used to it (Ward 1977, 1984). In other words, the effect an event will have very much depends upon the individual. It is also worth noting that intellectual changes can dent self-esteem. For example, in Chapter 3 it was noted that a high self-report of memory lapses is correlated with level of depression. Perlmutter *et al.* (1987) note that this may create a vicious circle – an old person who perceives his or her performance on a memory task to be poor may suffer a lowering of morale, which may further hamper his or her abilities.

It is also important to note that specific episodes in a person's past can impinge upon their attitudes in old age. Obviously, decisions about careers, relationships, whether to have children, and so forth, directly affect old people's material state, but other experiences can also have a direct impact. For example, Caspi & Elder (1986) examined feelings of life satisfaction in a group of elderly women who in their thirties had experienced the American Great Depression. Middle class women who endured hardship at this time now had demonstrably higher ratings of life satisfaction as a result. However, the reverse applied to working class women in the same situation – they suffered a lowering of satisfaction. Perhaps this is because the middle class women had demonstrably 'won through' to a better lifestyle, while the working class women perceived themselves as still being 'at the bottom'.

Personality and disease

One of the most extreme effects of personality on life expectancy is the rise in the suicide rate among the elderly. For example, in the USA, white elderly males are the most likely section of the population to kill themselves.

Furthermore, suicide attempts by the elderly in general are more likely to be successful than younger people's efforts, where there is over a 50 per cent 'failure' rate (Cook & Oltjenbruns 1989). It is tempting to interpret this information as reflecting a despair with age and its attendant effects. However, this will not suffice, because black males and elderly women do not show this increase in suicides (in fact, if anything, there is a decline). The most parsimonious explanation is that white men are more accustomed to power and a high standard of living, and a loss of, or a decline in these is too much for some individuals to cope with (e.g. Miller 1979).

Other research has considered rather less immediate health changes. It is important to note that one aspect of personality is how one chooses to live, and this includes choices of diet, exercise, smoking, and so forth. The link between smoking and reduced life expectancy and the (more tenuous) relationship between diet, exercise and health are too well-known to need re-iterating here. In any case, the area of study is more properly the preserve of dieticians and medics, and thus is outside the scope of this book. Also, people rarely take up 'bad habits' in old age (e.g. elderly smokers have usually been abusing their bodies for several decades) and, accordingly, unhealthy lifestyles are not just a problem of old age. It might be supposed that the elderly would find it harder to change their habits than younger people but, in fact, the two age groups respond to health education equally well (see Elias *et al.* (1990) for further discussion). Another important caveat is exercise – undoubtedly peak physical performance declines with age, and this is more pronounced for activities requiring sudden bursts of energy (e.g. athletics throwing events) than for activities requiring lower, but sustained, levels of energy (e.g. middle- and long-distance running). However, several (though not all) studies have found that old people who follow an exercise regime have faster reaction times and better psychomotor performance (Spirduso & MacRae 1990). This is not surprising, but of greater interest is that well-exercised old people's performances would put many people in their twenties to shame (see the excellent review by Spirduso & MacRae, 1990, for further details). Thus, if an old person chooses to, they can considerably improve their life expectancy and physical and (in part) psychological well-being.

Considering a more direct relationship between personality and health, there appears to be a positive link between mental and physical well being. Studies have found a high correlation when old people's self-reports are considered, and a somewhat lower correlation when objective measures of physical health are taken (Whitbourne 1987). Whether physical well-being actually causes a person to feel content – or *vice versa* – is open to debate. Kermis (1986) raises the point that depression and/or stress can cause a worsening in health (e.g. by suppressing the immune system). Taking the reverse direction, it is clear on *a priori* grounds that poor health and physical disability can have a bad effect on a person's psychological state. However, an important caveat needs to be raised. Maas & Kuypers (1974) observed that many senile illnesses are preceded by related physical complaints earlier in the lifespan. In other words, physical changes may occur before old age begins. This means that, in many instances, if there is a personality change in response to illness, it may not 'just' be the illness which is causing this (since the same complaint was there prior to old age). A plausible explanation is that it is a combination of an ageing body (perhaps no longer able to cope with the pain), an awareness that the illness may be there until death, and the illness itself which causes the change in personality.

Following from this argument, one can raise the hypothesis that physical and mental changes can exacerbate each other, forming a vicious circle. However, the links between physical illness and personality can be exaggerated. For example, the Type A personality has been associated with a significantly higher heart attack rate. However, a review by Elias *et al.* (1990) observes that whilst this may be true for younger people, having a Type A personality *after* the age of 65 does not increase the risk of coronary problems (the finding cannot be simply attributed to most people with Type A personalities dying before they reach old age). Again, old people are often unaware or dismissive of their physical health (Costa & McCrae 1985), indicating that the link between illness and level of self-image may be less clear-cut than first supposed.

A related topic is that of **hostility** and ageing. Hostility can be defined as 'a negative orientation toward others that has cognitive, affective and behavioral manifestations' (Barefoot *et al.* 1993, p 3, derived from Barefoot 1992). Some studies have reported higher levels of hostility amongst young adults and the old elderly, with a drop in hostility during middle age and early old age (see Barefoot *et al.* 1993). This may in part be adaptive, because a healthy cynicism is arguably a useful tool for both young adults first finding their way in the world, and for older people in increasing dependency on health care and social welfare services. However, as many commentators have argued, it can also be disadvantageous, because high hostility levels are associated with an increased risk of heart disease and other illnesses. This research is still in its infancy and, as with many personality measures, there is little correlation between different measures of hostility (Barefoot 1992). Therefore, firm conclusions should perhaps not yet be drawn.

Marriage

Generally, elderly married couples are found to be as happy or even more content than young married adults (Cunningham & Brookbank 1988). Levenson *et al.* (1993) assessed younger (40–50 years) and older (60–70 years) married couples on a variety of measures. They found that the older couples displayed greater equanimity of aims and sources of pleasure (and fewer sources of disagreement) and also tended to have more equal standards of health. These results are encouraging, in that it would appear that older married people are not simply clinging to the wreckage because the prospect of living apart is financially and/or emotionally too awful to contemplate. In another sense, the results are uninformative, because they do not indicate whether happily married older couples have always been happily married or whether today's happiness is the result 'of a process in which old wars are diminished' (Levenson *et al.* 1993 p 312) to the point where a truce has been called. As the authors acknowledge, their 'preliminary snapshot' (Levenson *et al.* 1993 p 312) calls out for a fuller longitudinal study.

Sexuality and ageing

It is a commonplace observation that the media portray sex as being for the young and slim, and ageist humour dictates that older people wanting a sex life are either 'dirty old men' or ugly and desperate. Even those older people whom the media have labelled as 'sexy' are chosen because, generally, they do not 'look their age'. Accordingly, the elderly do not receive support from everyday sources that wanting a sex life is normal and healthy. Tangential to this, many elderly people were brought up in less 'permissive' times, and are not accustomed (and indeed may lack the vocabulary) to talk about sexual issues. Surveying the history of studies of sexual activity in the elderly, Gibson (1992) observes that the more recent the study, the more often the elderly admit to having sexual relations.

There are a variety of problems associated with studying sexuality in the later years. One is the possible cohort effect just mentioned – different groups may have different levels of willingness to talk about what is, after all, a rather personal matter. Non-compliance is a traditional problem with sex surveys (conversely, subjects who are rather *too* willing to participate may also provide biased data). Therefore, older groups may provide less information than the young, not because they have sex less often but because they are less willing to talk about it. Another problem often cited by researchers concerns what constitutes 'sex'. If penetrative intercourse is taken as the only measure of sex, then the elderly may show a greater decline in sexual activity than if a wider range of activities is considered. A further problem is one of opportunity. Since women live longer than men (see Chapter 1) there are many more elderly women than elderly men. Accordingly, for women, the opportunities for heterosexual contact are diminished, and activity may stop not because of lack of capability or willing, but because there are not the opportunities. For men, the biggest problems are usually inability to sustain an erection and/or lacking the physical strength to have intercourse. Extrapolating from Gibson (1992), between 10 and 20 per cent of elderly men and 35 per cent (or more) of elderly women have no sex life (though figures vary enormously across studies). Generally, the level of sexual activity is dependent upon the level of activity in early adulthood (e.g. Martin 1981). This implies that, once again, the state of one's old age is determined by one's behaviour in earlier life. However, it is worth remembering that sexual drives differ markedly between individuals (e.g. Masters & Johnson 1966), and it is wrong to assume that there is a 'correct' level of activity or indeed, that sexual activity is necessary at all, for successful ageing to occur.

Preferences for lifestyle

So far, the elderly personality has been conceived principally in terms of changes *within* the individual. In this and the following section, attention is turned to the question of how the elderly choose to interact with others. It has been tacitly acknowledged that part of ageing is a preparation for death. Nowhere is this more explicitly stated than in the **disengagement theory** of Cumming & Henry (1961). This argued that as people got older, their contact with the world lessens. At one level this is through a decline in the senses. At a social level, the loss of spouses and friends, and other social estrangements (e.g. retirement) cause the elderly to disengage from contact with others. This was seen by Cumming & Henry as a rational process, initiated by the elderly individual and aided and abetted by societal conventions. It is as if the elderly are preparing to die by shedding links with the physical world. The theory can be criticised (and indeed was) for presenting the behaviour of passively waiting for the Grim Reaper as a good role model for the elderly. This is perhaps being a little harsh on Cumming & Henry, who were talking about relative not total disengagement. Later evidence indicated that disengagement was largely confined to individuals who were always reclusive (e.g. Maddox 1970b). In other words, the phenomenon may be a 'natural' extension of a particular personality type, not a universal feature of ageing. Another criticism is that disengagement is a very rare phenomenon in many 'Third World' cultures, where the elderly are kept in an active role in community life (e.g. Merriman 1984).

Subsequent researchers argued that the best policy for the elderly is to keep as active as possible. Their argument is roughly as follows. The elderly usually want to keep active, and life satisfaction is found to be greatest in old people with an active involvement. People who disengage from society have probably been doing so for most of their adult lives – in other words, it is not purely a response to old age (Maddox 1970a). In its extreme form this **activity theory** is as unattractive as the argument it tried to replace. The image of hordes of social workers forcing the elderly to mix with others 'for their own good', with compulsory whist drives and so forth, is not a pleasant one. The modern consensus is that disengagement and activity theories describe the optimal strategy for some but not all elderly individuals, and which is the better depends upon a variety of factors, such as: financial circumstances (e.g. can one afford an active lifestyle?); health (e.g. does one still have the vigour for some hobbies?); and personality types (e.g. a lifelong introvert may hate an active lifestyle). It is also worth noting that a number of studies have found increased social involvement only appreciably to improve feelings of well-being in lower income groups (Caspi & Elder 1986, Larson 1978).

The role of the family

Many people, given the choice, would probably like to combine aspects of both the disengagement and the activity lifestyles. This is shown in research on preferences for family relationships. It would appear that in western nations at least, the elderly prefer to live independently, but also to have their offspring or close relatives living nearby. In about 80 per cent of cases, elderly parents live within 30 minute's travel of at least one of their offspring (Bengtson & Treas 1980). Thus, the elderly seem to like to combine the opportunity for activity through interaction with family members with disengagement through the privacy of their own homes. This can be a double edged sword, however. In a masterly review of the literature, Bengtson & Treas observed that while family members were the usual and preferred source of comfort and help in a crisis, the elderly were more depressed the greater their expectations of assistance from their offspring. In other words, expect too much, and disappointment will almost inevitably follow (although note that the proportion of the elderly with unrealistically high expectations is relatively low).

As was noted in Chapter 1, in westernised nations at least, the proportion of the population aged over 60 has risen dramatically over this century. At the same time, for a variety of reasons the birth rate has dropped. This means that old people today have fewer relatives to seek support from than did the elderly at the turn of the century (though about 80% of the elderly have at least one living son or daughter). However, does this mean that the elderly's plight (if there is one) has worsened? The answer is probably not. First, because the general improvement in living standards and pension schemes means that the elderly can be self-sufficient more often than could their counterparts in 1900. The workhouse, the refuge of the working class elderly, no longer looms like the dire punishment it did only a few decades ago. It is also worth observing that the extended family (where three generations live under the same roof) was the exception rather than the rule in pre-twentieth century Europe (e.g.Laslett 1976). In short, there has not been a 'golden age' in the past where greater personal care was given to the elderly.

The position of old people in their families can be a mixed one. It can be easily supposed that, in relevant cases, they will find a positive role as grandparents. However, this ignores the fact that the majority of people become grandparents during middle age and, thus, this is not usually purely an experience of old age. It is clear that, where kin live within close proximity, the elderly expect them to be a source of aid. However, Bengtson & Kuypers (1986) have observed that when a crisis does occur and aid is needed, this may damage familial relations, because family members may feel that they have not adequately coped, and hence are incompetent at looking after the elderly relative.

A detailed model of how the family can intervene and care for an elderly relative in times of crisis is McCubbin & Patterson's (1982) **double ABCX model**, where A is the event causing the crisis, B the familial resources for coping with the event, C the familial perception of the crisis and X the perceived stress. Variations in A, B, C, and X will determine the overall level of stress the family and elderly person experience. Gatz et al. (1990) create a similar model, comprising a sequence of event-stressor-appraisals-mediators-outcomes. The event is the crisis (e.g. serious illness), and the stressor is the deleterious effect of the event (e.g. the person is in pain, the effects on the family's lifestyle). Appraisals refers to the process whereby the family caregivers decide the degree to which they can control the situation, and the mediators is the availability of aid and caring skills. The outcomes process refers to the degree to which the family feel stressed and/or adapted to the change in the situation.

Both these models of family care in a crisis are essentially descriptive, and there is a considerable research literature available to describe each stage of either model. The tone of this is rather uniform – most aspects of caring and adaptation are potentially stressful and have deleterious effects (see Chapter 6's section on caregiving for demented patients). Detailed reviews are provided by Gatz *et al.* (1990) and Wenger (1990). A caveat to these observations is that the majority of caregiving duties fall on the spouses or offspring of elderly patients (Qureshi & Walker 1989) – thus, most caregivers are elderly or late middle-aged. Accordingly, caregivers themselves may experience physical problems in nursing sick patients, and increased incidences of ill-health in caregivers have been reported (see Gatz *et al.* 1990).

It is also important to remember that findings on the role of familial support can vary according to the social class of the family. For example, Sundstrom's (1986) Swedish study notes that the geographical distance between elderly parents and their offspring tends to be greater in the middle- than in the working-classes (although when this is controlled for, level of care is little different between the classes). This is perhaps accounted for by the finding from Qureshi & Walker's (1989) English study that members of 'higher' social classes tended to use the phone and postal services more frequently. Other class differences are perhaps due to material opportunity rather than motivation. For example, Qureshi & Walker also found that the 'upper' and 'middle' class elderly were more likely to visit other members of the family. However, measures of level of 'emotional closeness' between family members were roughly the same across all classes.

Cross-cultural differences in ageing

Societies differ in their attitudes to the elderly, and the study of this topic is known as **ethogerontology**. The traditional division between West and East has often been commented on (in the Far East, old age is revered to a greater extent than in the West). Tangential to this, in general, relatively 'primitive' non-industrialised societies have a higher regard for old age, according it a special status. This may be because old age is relatively rare in such groups, and in peoples lacking a written language system, the elderly may be especially valued for their memories of the past. The very old, however, are often regarded less favourably (see Perlmutter & Hall 1992).

Within westernised nations, ethnic minority groups tend to have a higher proportion of multigenerational households, and closer-knit families. In addition, for some ethnic minorities (e.g. black Americans) the church may play a greater role in providing social support (Jackson *et al.* 1990). However, it is dangerous to overgeneralise such arguments, and confounding factors, such as the fact that ethnic minorities tend to have a lower socioeconomic standing, are difficult to tease apart (see Rosenthal (1986) for a discussion of the methodological implications of ethnicity research).

Notwithstanding these comments, the elderly within an ethnic minority face what has been termed the **double jeopardy** – the problem that not only will they be treated prejudicially because they are old, but also because of their ethnic identity. Norman (1985) states the case more strongly, and argues that many elderly members of ethnic minorities are in fact faced with a **triple jeopardy** because, in addition to the aforementioned problems, they also, through the prejudice of others, and often through communication problems, cannot get the help they need and deserve from the local or state authorities. Norman makes a strong case based on the practical problems faced by elderly ethnic minorities in claiming services and amenities. However, other measures, such as well-being and living conditions provide more equivocal support (see Perlmutter & Hall 1992). This is not surprising, since many of the effects of the 'host' country will be ameliorated by the practices of the particular minority to which the elderly belong (this does not mean, of course, that effort should be spared in assisting older people).

Summary

This chapter encompasses changes in the elderly's personality in the widest sense – not only how the elderly's predispositions to certain types of behaviour can alter, but also how their interactions with other people can be affected. The findings of research in these areas is varied. Findings on personality types indicate that the elderly essentially 'receive' their personalities in early adulthood, and any changes thereafter tend to be a diminution in the strength of feelings and attitudes, rather than any major change in the balance of traits. Thus, there is not a personality type unique to old age. On the other hand, some types of personality enable people to cope with old age better than others. The identification of these types comes primarily from psychotherapy rather than mainstream psychology, but there is considerable empirical evidence to support these. However, these arguments must be weighed against the considerable criticisms of personality testing and research methodologies. Again, it would be unwise to place too much emphasis on the taxonomies, because there are implicit value judgements loaded into the classifications. For example, a successfully ageing person is held to have a placid and almost stoic attitude towards life. However, this conforms to the stereotype that old people should be placid wisdom-dispensing archetypal grandparent figures. Therefore, are the successfully aged those individuals who cause the least fuss and still make themselves available for others? This may be morally the best way to age, but equally efficient (if less justifiable) is to be selfish and squander money on oneself, arguing that 'you can't take it with you', and leaving nothing for one's dependants. In short, are the successful aged those elderly who provide for younger people?

Having acknowledged that personality traits are largely born in early adulthood, and that some traits are better than others at coping with old age, the elderly still have a number of methods at their disposal for improving their lot. Taking a definition of personality as meaning 'lifestyle', the elderly can improve their health through changes in diet, exercise, and smoking habits. The relationship between lifestyle and well-being is more complicated than might first appear, however. Socioeconomic class, ethnicity, widowhood, and familial relations, among other factors, interact to provide a complex chain of events and pressures whose effects are far from fully mapped. Considerably more research is needed before any definite answer can be provided.

Recommended reading

Bengtson & Kuypers (1986) and Gatz *et al.* (1990) are excellent on ageing and changing familial relations. Kermis (1983) provides an excellent general introduction to the models of ageing personalities. Ward (1977) is very good on societal attitudes to the elderly. Gibson (1992) provides an intelligent overview of sexual and emotional changes. Perlmutter & Hall (1992, Chapter 16) provides an excellent overview of ageing in American ethnic minorities. The appropriate sections of Birren & Schaie's (1990) *Handbook of the Psychology of Aging* (see reference for Gatz *et al.*) provide an admirable introduction to more advanced aspects of these areas of research.

CHAPTER 6

The Dementias

Introduction

Dementia describes the global deterioration of intellectual function resulting from atrophy of the central nervous system (CNS). Many textbooks give the impression that it has only a few causes; in fact, about 50 have been identified (Haase 1977). However, the majority of these are extremely rare. Many laypersons assume that dementia is a punishment for growing old. Indeed, the word 'senility' which means 'old age' has become synonymous with 'dementia'. *It is not.* Dementia can occur at any time in adult life: only the *probability* of becoming demented increases with age. Indeed, as will be seen, some forms of dementia most commonly occur before the onset of old age; despite this, most textbooks persist in considering it as a disease of the elderly. It is also important to note that the level of incidence of dementia means that most old people will never contract it. White *et al.* (1986) estimate that, as a rule of thumb, about one per cent of non-institutionalised 60-year-olds have dementing symptoms, and this figure doubles every five years (i.e., 2% at 65, 4% at 70, 8% at 75, etc). It is worth bearing in mind that many individuals only show fairly mild symptoms, and, cold comfort as this is, they will probably die from other causes before the disease has gained a firm hold. Figures on the duration of the illness vary widely between studies, but a reasonable estimate is that the illness takes 5–10 years to run its course (Hart & Semple 1990). Within western societies, approximately five per cent of the elderly are institutionalised, and of these only about 50 per cent (i.e., about 2–3% of the total elderly population) are there because of dementing illness (Kermis 1984). Thus, old people's fears of becoming 'ga-ga', 'senile', 'mad', or any of the other charming epithets, are largely unfounded.

Although an individual old person's fears may be unrealistic, this does not mean that dementia is not a serious problem. From a demographic viewpoint, the illness poses a challenge to developed nations. As was noted in Chapter 1, both the actual number of old people and the proportion they form of the total population are increasing. This means that the number of cases of dementia is also rising. Some commentators have spoken of an 'epidemic' of dementia, but this is misleading because it implies that the illness is spreading at a greater rate through the elderly population, which it is not. However, certainly there are more demented patients than ever before, and the numbers will (barring a cure) keep pace with the 'greying' of the population. This will lead to increased health care resources having to be devoted to psychogeriatric care, more specialised medical and para-medical staff recruitment, and so forth.

The principal concern, however, beyond the degree to which health services will be affected, is that dementia is a hideous way to die. The patient is, after the early stages of the illness, usually mercifully unaware of his or her condition. On the other hand, the effect on those left to look after the patient can be devastating. Usually, until the terminal stages of the illness, patients are not fully institutionalised. This means that the burden of care falls on the patient's spouse or children. These caregivers (whom, it should be remembered, are often not in their physical prime, being either elderly or middle-aged) have the task of tending the needs of someone who has no memory, is frequently incontinent, and subject to temper tantrums and other irrational behaviours. As an added bonus, many demented patients cannot even recognise their own spouse, children, or close friends. Thus, the reward for a lifetime's love, affection and sharing can be to tend for a grotesque parody of a human being, who bears the outward appearance of a loved one, but within whom any semblance of a recognisable sentient being has disappeared or is, at best, intermittent. No one deserves to die in such an undignified fashion, and no one should have to witness it happen to someone they have loved. Such an end would be tragic if it lasted several weeks, but for most patients the decline is gradual and takes place over three or more *years*.

Dementia is thus a cause for major concern, doubly so given there are no known cures for its principal forms. An understanding of the illness is important if attempts are to be made to combat it. In this chapter, the psychological aspects of the dementias will be examined. First, the major forms of the illness will be discussed. Lengthy details of the diagnostic procedures involved have been avoided. This is because, first, they would occupy a disproportionately large part of the text; second, they are not central to an understanding of the psychological features of the illness and third, there are already a number of excellent textbooks covering this area (e.g. Kermis 1986, Wasylenki 1987). A consideration of illnesses easily confused with dementia is also given. The chapter continues with an examination of specific aspects of the dementing process, before conclud-ing with a brief examination of the effects of caring for a demented patient.

Classifying dementias

Identifying the handicap

The first step in diagnosing dementia is to discover the extent of the handicap suffered by the patient. The state of the patient upon referral may be influenced by several factors, of which the two commonest are the following. First, the age of the patient plays an important role. Younger patients (in their fifties) will probably present themselves earlier because their symptoms are incompatible with being in the 'prime of life'. Older subjects may have more advanced symptoms because the onset of the illness can be insidious, and initial memory loss and/or intellectual impairment can be easily dismissed as simply part of 'growing old'. As has been noted in previous chapters, the elderly expect their physical and mental abilities to decrease as they get older. Also, relatives and friends can retard or accelerate referral. For example, if they are critical of the patient's perform-ance, then he or she may seek help earlier than usual. Alternatively, relatives

Table 6.1 Memory questions used in the Mental Status Questionnaire (Kahn *et al.* 1960)

1. Where are you now?
2. What is this place?
3. What day is this?
4. What month is this?
5. What year is this?
6. How old are you?
7. When is your birthday?
8. In what year were you born?
9. Who is the president of the United States?
10. Who was the president before him?

> Score of 0–2 = no or mild impairment
> Score of 3–8 = moderate impairment
> Score of 9–10 = severe impairment

may attempt to cover up the patient's problems, blocking attempts at what they (mis)perceive as outside interference.

The general level of the patient's handicap is usually assessed by a few simple memory tests and a questionnaire about the patient's behaviour. Perhaps the widest used British test of this type is the **Blessed Dementia Scale** (Blessed *et al.* 1968). In the USA, the equivalents are the **Mental Status Questionnaire** or **MSQ** (Kahn *et al.* 1960) and the **Mini-Mental State Examination (MMSE)**. These ask the patient such memory questions as: 'who is the current Prime Minister/President?'; 'what is the day today?'; and 'what is your name?'. In short, these are memory questions which no normally ageing person, however stupid, should get wrong (in fairness, some questions are more searching). The ten memory questions asked in the MSQ are shown in Table 6.1. The questionnaire on the patient's behaviour is usually given to the caregiver, for the obvious reason that the patient usually cannot remember what he or she has done recently. Questions ask whether the patient is still functionally independent, or whether they now need help with some activities, such as getting dressed. This has the dual advantage of not only assessing the patient's current state, but also of indicating the level of nursing care the patient will require if he or she is to be institutionalised. Scales such as the Blessed and the MSQ can also be used as the illness progresses, to keep a useful check on the general status and needs of the patient.

A more detailed method of describing the level of functioning of the demented patient is provided by Reisberg *et al.*'s (1989) Functional Assessment Stages, or **FAST**. The method was originally designed to describe the functional status of Alzheimer's Disease patients (see below). Patients are placed into one of seven categories, with stages 6 and 7 divided into substages. Stage 1 describes normal functioning. In Stage 2, there are subjective feelings of loss of intellectual power, although these are not perceived as serious by other people. In Stage 3, intellectual impairment (particularly in mnemonic skills) is evident in complex tasks which previously posed no problems, and in Stage 4 this has extended to relatively complex everyday tasks (e.g. 'ability to handle finances'). Stage 5 is defined as 'deficient performance in choosing the proper clothing to wear', and in Stage 6, the patient is no longer able to dress him- or herself or properly to attend to personal hygiene (the stage is divided into five hierarchical substages, ranging from problems with dressing through to faecal incontinence). Stage 7 describes the loss of motor and speech skills (six substages, beginning with the loss of speech through to 'loss of ability to hold up head'). The authors also place estimates of the length of time a patient is likely to remain in a particular stage if he or she does not die during it

(Stage 3 = 7 years; 4 = 2 years; 5 = 18 months; 6 = 2 years 5 months; 7 = 6 years +). A slightly simpler assessment is provided by the **Clinical Dementia Rating (CDR)**, which is a checklist of level of functioning on a variety of tasks (e.g. memory, orientation, behaviour in the home). Based on the scores, the patient is graded as having no dementia, or 'questionable', 'mild', moderate' or 'severe' forms of the illness (Berg 1988).

Memory and functional impairment alone do not define dementia, however (although they are a key part of it). The American Psychiatric Association periodically produces a taxonomy of mental illnesses. The most recent edition of this is the third edition of the **Diagnostic and Statistical Manual of Mental Disorders (DSM III-R** (American Psychiatric Association (1987)). This is a highly influential publication, and not just in the USA. The criteria for a classification of dementia can be summarised as:

(1) A loss of intellect sufficient to interfere with everyday activities.

(2) Memory loss (although note that, in some instances, memory loss is not the initial cause of referral).

(3) A change in at least one of the following: abstract thought, judgement, one or more aspects of higher cortical functioning, or personality.

(4) The patient behaves like this when fully awake and with no evidence of intoxication (e.g. from alcohol or drugs).

The illness is also graded by its functional effect: *mild* (no supervision necessary), *moderate* (some supervision necessary) or *severe* (constant supervision required).

The different types of dementias (sometimes called dementias of different **aetiologies** or **etiologies**) all fall within this general definition, but each has its own unique pattern of dysfunction. Below the general characteristics of the most often encountered forms of dementia are described.

Dementia of the Alzheimer Type (DAT)

This is the commonest of the dementias, accounting for between 50 and 70 per cent of all cases of dementia (Cohen & Dunner 1980). It was first described in 1907 by Alois Alzheimer, in a case study of a 51-year-old woman. The illness is known by several similar names – Alzheimer's disease (AD) and senile dementia of the Alzheimer type (SDAT) are both in common use as well as **dementia of the Alzheimer type (DAT)**. For the sake of convenience, only the latter term is used in this textbook. It is worth noting also that in some older textbooks, DAT is used to describe cases of dementia arising before the age of 60, and **senile dementia** for those arising after this age. This is because at one stage it was felt that the pre-senile and senile forms of the disease were different entities and thus merited different names (although Alzheimer himself did not support this view). However, it has since been found that this division is specious (e.g. Sulkava 1982, Sulkava & Amberia 1982). Some caveats must be added to this statement. Usually the illness progresses faster through the early stages in younger patients (Reisberg, Ferris, Franssen *et al.* 1989) although, perversely enough, they survive longer in the later stages of the illness (e.g. Nielsen *et al.* 1977). Also, there is a tendency for linguistic abnormalities to be more pronounced in pre-senile patients (Seltzer & Sherwin 1983). However, overall the similarities outweigh the differences, and young and old patients are now generally considered to be suffering from the same illness.

There are several possible causes of DAT. Many commentators devote a great deal of space to discussing which is the 'correct' explanation. This is probably a fruitless exercise, since there is no reason to suppose that DAT could not arise from several completely different origins. To think otherwise would be like arguing that red spots can only be caused by the *rubella* virus (see Hart & Semple 1990, Chapter 2). Undoubtedly there is a genetic component in *some* cases of DAT, probably caused by the unfortunate combination of several genes rather than just a single aberrant gene (Kidson & Chen 1986). The search for the aberrant genes is an area of active research. Some researchers (e.g. St. George-Hyslop *et al.* 1987, Schweber 1989a) have found a flawed structure in chromosome 21, at a location close to that of the damage found in patients suffering from Trisomy 21, the commonest cause of Down Syndrome. Many commentators have noted that Down Syndrome patients develop DAT-like symptoms in middle age, and that the neuropathology of the patients' brains is very similar to that of DAT patients (e.g. Schweber 1989b).

However, although there may be a genetic component to DAT, this does not mean that this is the sole cause. For example, if DAT develops within a family, then transmission of the illness is *not* automatic. If the son or daughter of a DAT patient develops dementia, then there is approximately a 50 per cent chance that his/her siblings will do likewise. These cases are likely to develop at a pre-senile age (<60 years) and develop faster (Heston *et al.* 1981). Thus, DAT can develop in people with a particular genetic makeup, but it would be wrong to move further from this position to argue that people with 'DAT genes' will *inevitably* become demented. It can be shown probabilistically that more people in DAT-ridden families have 'DAT genes' than will actually become demented. A more immediate demonstration is that there are recorded instances of only one of a pair of identical (monozygotic) twins developing DAT. Since identical twins have identical genetic structures, clearly more than just genes must cause the disease to occur. The most likely explanation is the **threshold model of dementia**. Namely, that a person's genetic makeup may make him or her more *susceptible* to the illness, but it requires something in the environment to push him or her past a particular point where the onset of the illness becomes inevitable.

A number of candidates for this lurking menace in the environment have been proposed. In recent years, aluminium has been suggested as the likely culprit. This is because brain cells in DAT patients have been found to have 'ingested' minute fragments of aluminium, causing loss of cell function or even death. This has led some worried people to stop using aluminium cooking utensils: a probably futile gesture, because the metal is a very common element, and is present in a great many 'natural' things and foodstuffs. Why DAT patients are especially susceptible to aluminium is still unknown. It may be the case that the aluminium uptake is a symptom rather than a cause of the decline. In other words, the decaying brain absorbs aluminium because the brain's defence mechanisms have broken down, but if aluminium were not so abundant, it might just as well have been another metal which was absorbed. Wisniewski & Sturman (1988) found that cells which have died from aluminium poisoning have an appearance different from that of the affected cells of DAT patients (see also Wisniewski 1989). Another proposal is that the illness is caused by a slow acting virus. It is known that some dementing illnesses, such as **kuru** (which affects a few native tribes in Papua New Guinea), can be caught by handling diseased nervous tissue. These explanations may be valid (and the genetic, aluminium and viral theories are not mutually exclusive). However, whatever the true cause transpires to be, it is unlikely to be a simple one. As will be seen below, damage to DAT patients' brains tends to be restricted to particular sections of the brain. It is difficult to see how a virus or aluminium could affect some pieces of nervous tissue and spare others. In short, a more sophisticated explanation is needed.*

The neuropathology of DAT is complex. However, in broad terms, the illness is characterised by atrophy. There is considerable cell death, and senile plaques and neurofibrillary tangles (see Chapter 1) are present in much greater abundance than in normal ageing. Cell loss is fairly selective, and is concentrated in the cortex (although with the occipital lobe relatively undamaged), and some subcortical regions, principally the amygdala, the hippocampus and brain stem (Moss & Albert 1988). It is worth noting that

---

* *Readers unfamiliar with brain anatomy are advised to consult the appropriate section of Chapter 1 before proceeding.*

some areas of the CNS are spared, however, notably the cerebellum, the basal ganglia, and the spinal cord (Petit 1982). Output of neurotransmitters from the cholinergic system is heavily depleted (Kermis 1986, Moss & Albert 1988). Since it is known that deliberately suppressing cholinergic activity reduces mnemonic efficiency in humans and animals, it is tempting to pin the cause of DAT patients' ills on lack of this transmitter. This is called the **cholinergic hypothesis**. However, there is ample evidence that cholinergic depletion does not usually cause all the types of memory loss shown in DAT (Moss & Albert 1988). Furthermore, neurotransmitters other than those in the cholinergic system are also known to be significantly depleted (Rossor & Iversen 1986). Therefore the cholinergic hypothesis cannot provide a full explanation. Having thus briefly considered the causes of DAT, what are its symptoms? Below is a description of the principal criteria used to arrive at a diagnosis of DAT. The information is derived from the references so far cited in this chapter and from the author's own notes on patients.

DAT can occur at any age from about 50 onwards, although the probability of developing the disease rises rapidly from the mid seventies. About 25 per cent of people in their mid eighties or over display some symptoms of DAT. There are some very rare instances of DAT patients in their early forties. Generally, the older the patient, the more advanced is the illness when he or she first presents for treatment (the reasons for this have already been examined in the Introduction). In terms of general demeanour, a mildly demented DAT patient can on the surface appear normal: social skills usually remain intact. Often the only indication of something amiss is a strange glassy stare or a certain indefinable deadness in the eyes. Often the patient's initial complaint is of severe memory problems beyond the scope of normal experience, such as getting lost in very familiar surround-ings (e.g. the local shopping centre, or streets near home). Generally, memory is described as poor or appalling by people close to the patient. Mnemonic tests at this time will usually show a gross failure to remember anything new for more than a few minutes or even seconds (i.e., an apparent failure to transfer from short- to long-term memory). Short-term memory (STM) measures, such as digit span, may show a decline. Sometimes, though not inevitably, patients show a loss of ability to perceive using certain senses. For example, they may display **apraxia** (inability to recognise by touch) or **visual agnosia** (inability to recognise by sight). In some cases, these alone are the cause of the original referral – the patients' mnemonic abilities may be relatively unscathed. Language may seem to be intact, although some-times vocabulary can appear to be rather impoverished. Patients may have difficulties producing the appropriate words, and may fail to comprehend abstract phrases, such as proverbs. Patients' responses to their symptoms vary. Some are depressed, others are apathetic and unconcerned. Some develop a mild paranoia that people are deliberately hiding things, while others make strident attempts to gloss over their problems. All these reactions are common. In general, however, their declining intellectual skills mean that the patients have little insight into the surrounding world.

As the illness progresses, so the severity of the above symptoms increases. Memory for new items is now severely curtailed, often even for items in STM. Memory for remote events, encoded before the onset of the illness, also worsens. Recognition worsens, even (to the obvious distress of relatives) to the point of being unable to recognise friends and family. Language worsens considerably and **aphasia** (language failure) becomes a key feature of the later stages of DAT. The patient can have problems producing speech (**Broca's aphasia**), understanding speech (**Wernicke's aphasia**), or both. Speech can be reduced to a few words and a series of garbled speech-like sounds, or can consist of recognisable words produced in a nonsensical order. Sometimes, the ability to read aloud is, remarkably, preserved. Patients can read aloud very well, observing intonation and punctuation marks, but have not the vaguest idea about what they have read (**demented dyslexia**). The external appearance of the patients reflects their inward decline. Without the aid of dedicated helpers, the patients' grooming and general demeanour inevitably worsen. Movement begins to appear crabbed and awkward. A shuffling gait, characteristic of **Parkinsonism** (see Glossary) becomes commonplace. In the terminal stages of the illness, the patient usually falls into an uncommunicative state. Incontinence becomes habitual. Often patients display **Kluver-Bucy syndrome**. This is a set of bizarre behaviours, including **hyperorality** (the urge to put everything seen into the mouth) and the associated problem of **bulimia**, the urge to eat vast quantities of food (practically any food, from cream cakes to brown sauce). The other symptoms of Kluver-Bucy syndrome are visual agnosia, **hypermetamorphosis** (the compulsive need to touch everything) and a loss of **affect** (emotion). Death occurs on average five years after the presentation of the first symptoms (although quite large variations either side of this figure are possible). The DAT patients' demise is usually from either a major failure of a bodily function or from infection. The description of the stages of development has been deliberately kept loose. There is immense variation between patients in the severity of their symptoms, the relative sparing of individual functions, and the length of time patients remain in each stage of the illness. However, a DAT patient who progresses to the terminal stage of the illness will at some stage endure all the listed stages.

THE DEMENTIAS / 141

A diagnostic test, specifically designed for DAT is provided by the **NINCDS-ADRDA criteria**. The initials refer to the 'National Institute of Neurological and Communicative Disorders and Stroke' and the 'Alzheimer's Disease and Related Disorders Association of America', the two bodies who jointly devised the scheme. It provides three levels of certainty about the diagnosis: 'probable', 'possible' or 'definite'. The final judgement can only be given when there is physiological proof from a biopsy or autopsy, so most researchers content themselves with a 'probable' diagnosis (Nebes 1992). The 'probable' diagnosis requires, amongst other factors, proof of functional handicap (e.g. as measured by the Blessed Dementia scale), mnemonic loss, 'deficits in two or more areas of cognition', and an absence of indicators of other causes, such as tumour, acute confusional state (see below), and so forth. Katzman *et al.* (1988) note that the DSM-III-R diagnostic criteria are probably equivalent in accuracy.

Multi-infarct dementia (MID)

As noted in Chapter 1, infarcts ('miniature strokes' which cause the death of surrounding tissue) are found in the brains of most elderly people. However, in **multi-infarct dementia (MID)** they occur in much greater abundance, to the extent that a demented state is induced in the afflicted patient. The infarcts occur relatively randomly throughout the brain, although the cortex and other areas controlling 'higher' function are especially badly affected. The identification of MID as a syndrome distinct from **stroke** (where the patient suffers one or a few larger haemorrhages) is relatively recent (Hachinski *et al.* 1974). It is worth noting, however, that misdiagnosis of MID patients as stroke victims and *vice versa* is not unknown (Funkenstein 1988). The causes of MID are not fully identified. Not surprisingly, patients often have a history of cardiovascular **(CV)** problems, and there may also be some familial tendency of MID or stroke. It is also known that a number of CV illnesses can be the trigger for MID (Funkenstein 1988). The illness can occur at any age from about 55 onwards. The average age of onset is about 65, some ten years earlier than DAT (Kermis 1986).

A popular method of testing for MID is the **Ischaemic Rating Scale**, also known as the **Hachinski Ischaemic Score (IS)**, after its inventor (Hachinski *et al.* 1975). This awards points to the patient based upon the number of symptoms they display, with particularly salient symptoms being weighted to reflect their greater importance (e.g. if the patient has had a history of strokes, and shows a stepwise progression of deterioration, then these symptoms are awarded two and one points respectively). A score of seven or more indicates MID.

Infarcts occur quasi-randomly in MID and, because of this, the course of the illness is difficult to predict, and symptoms vary greatly between patients. To quote one commentator, 'there are few findings that can be considered *consistent with* a diagnosis of MID' (La Rue 1992, p 236; author's italics). This is because the areas of the brain controlling different mental functions may decay at different rates (according to where the infarcts most often strike). Accordingly, psychological abilities will display a differential decline between and within patients. To take an example, suppose there are areas of the brain called *A, B, C, D,* and *E,* which control abilities *X, Y, Z, P,* and *Q* respectively. One MID patient may show a decline in areas *A, B,* and *C,* and thus in abilities *X, Y* and *Z*. Another patient may have well preserved areas *A* and *B,* but show decline in areas *C, D,* and *E,* manifesting itself as a decline in abilities *Z, P* and *Q*. Thus, two patients with the same illness can have radically different symptoms. It will not have escaped some readers' notice that, because infarcts strike fairly randomly, in some instances the damage they inflict will be in the same areas affected by the atrophying processes of other dementias. In other words, MID may by chance mimic the effects of dementias of other aetiologies. For example, if the infarcts strike particularly heavily in the cortex and the hippocampus, then a reasonably good imitation of DAT might be created. Because of this problem, diagnosis of MID can be problematic and estimates of the incidence of the disease in the dementing patient population vary between 5 and 15 per cent (Moss & Albert 1988). However, it is important to note that some patients display psychological and physiological symptoms of MID *and* DAT simultaneously, in a condition known as **AD-MID**. Alafuzoff *et al.* (1989) suggest that patients with AD-MID display symptoms which are more than just a combination of DAT and MID, but it is possible that the more pronounced of these symptoms are simply the products of an interaction between the two conditions.

Nonetheless, there are aspects of 'pure' MID which make it distinguishable from other dementing disorders. For example, the onset of symptoms can in some cases be quite sudden: there may not be the insidious development seen in dementias of other aetiologies. However, some MID patients display a gradual onset, so this is not an infallible distinguishing feature. In some instances the intellectual deficits displayed are **lacunar** in nature. In other words, there are gaps in the intellect – some skills are missing, while the remaining ones are relatively intact. However, as just noted MID can mimic other forms of dementia with widespread deficits, so this also is not a reliable diagnostic criterion. The cardinal difference between MID and other forms of dementia is in the development of the illness. While patients suffering from other dementias show a steady rate of decline, MID patients display a stepwise, jerky degradation. They tend to stay at one level of competence for some time (weeks or months) before suddenly and precipitously worsening. This process then repeats itself, with each drop removing more of the patients' intellectual powers. Presumably this is caused by the infarcts slowly destroying segments of the brain until a critical point is reached and a particular area can no longer adequately function given the quantity or quality of neuronal tissue that remains. Because infarction is relatively random, which faculties are lost at which time cannot be predicted but inevitably, as the disease progresses, the range of intellectual functions the patient is capable of becomes more curtailed. Memory is almost always an early victim. Eventually the patient is reduced to a vegetative state. Paralysis is much commoner in MID than in the other dementias. Death usually occurs from a CV related illness (e.g. heart attack) or opportunistic infection, on average about four years after the onset of the first symptoms.

Pick's disease

Pick's disease (named after its discoverer) is not commonly a disease of old age. It is rarely encountered in the over-sixties, and virtually never in anyone aged 70 plus. On average, onset is in the late forties. However, because Pick's patients are sometimes used as comparative groups in experimental studies of 'old age' dementias, a brief examination of the disease is necessary (as are the examinations of the other 'young' dementias which follow). The stages of development of Pick's disease are relatively well-defined. Atrophy of the neural tissue begins in the frontal lobes, and progresses inexorably 'backwards' across the brain, with all the attendant changes in mental functioning this involves. At a cellular level, neurons often degenerate into **Pick's bodies**, which have a characteristic swollen appearance. Some patients can have the general pattern of atrophy of Pick's disease (damage principally in the frontal and temporal lobes, etc) but lack Pick's bodies. Whether these patients should be classified as suffering from the disease or from a separate syndrome is still open to debate (Moss & Albert 1988).

The Pick's patient usually first presents with problems expected of frontal lobe damage, such as loss of planning skills, ability to think in the abstract, and so forth. Kluver-Bucy syndrome usually manifests itself early in the course of the illness (as opposed to the late stages of DAT). It may also incorporate compulsive sexual behaviour, often without regard for social propriety. As the disease progresses, dementing symptoms akin to DAT begin to manifest themselves. Often language is more impaired than memory, but this is not an infallible rule. Pick's patients are also more prone to confabulation (i.e., trying to cover up their mistakes), something rarely seen in MID or DAT patients. In the terminal stages, patients are reduced to a vegetative state, as with the other dementias. Death usually occurs about four years after the onset of the first symptoms.

Creutzfeldt-Jakob Disease (CJD)

This is a very rare illness, affecting approximately one in a million people. It is caused by a virus, and it is the only known dementia (other than the aforementioned kuru) which is infectious. In Britain there is some media concern that a strain of CJD might be contracted from eating meat from cattle suffering a bovine form of the illness (**bovine spongiform encephalopathy (BSE)** or 'mad cow disease'). As yet there is no scientific evidence to support this. Indeed, recent suggestions for the cause of BSE have placed the blame for the illness on pesticides, as opposed to the original theory that the cows contracted it from feed infected with scrapie, a sheep disease. However, the issue is still one of heated debate. CJD, like Pick's disease, is not an illness of old age. Most people developing the disease are in their fifties and sixties, but cases from all ages from the twenties upwards have been reported. Initial symptoms are usually of motor disturbances (of gait, balance, feelings of dizziness, etc) with dementing symptoms following. The development of CJD is very rapid: death is usually within nine months of the appearance of the first symptoms.

Huntington's disease

Huntington's disease (also called **Huntington's chorea**) is not considered to be a dementia by all commentators. Like CJD, it is relatively rare, but it tends to cluster in families, indicating a strong genetic component (which in recent years has been identified). Also like CJD, the early symptoms of the illness are disturbed movements, often taking the form of writhing and twitching. Subsequently patients develop general dementing symptoms, although the intellectual decline can also mimic schizophrenia (Kermis 1986). Huntington's disease lasts longer than the other dementias: life expectancy after the first symptoms appear is usually about 15 years. The illness does affect the elderly, but the commonest age of onset is middle age, and child patients are not uncommon.

Other dementias

As was mentioned in the Introduction, there are about 50 known types of dementia. Most are mercifully rare. However, it is worth noting that some illnesses can cause dementia or dementia-like symptoms. Principal among these is **Parkinson's disease (PD)**. This is chiefly a motor disease, causing tremors, a characteristic shuffling gait, and so forth. However, there is a higher than average risk that PD patients will develop general dementing symptoms (about 10–15%: Moss & Albert 1988). It should be also noted that many DAT patients develop PD-like symptoms (Parkinsonism) as their illness progresses. The most salient difference between PD and mild, early stage DAT is that linguistic functioning is considerably better preserved (or unaffected) in PD (La Rue 1992).

Lennox *et al.* (1989) note that many PD patients' brains contain **Lewy bodies** (small round 'clumps' of dead filaments contained within brain cells). They propose that the damage caused by these is responsible for the dementing symptoms, and accordingly suggest a new disease category of **Lewy body disease**. This categorisation has not yet been widely accepted, however.

Another cause of dementia is syphilis. If the illness is untreated, then it can, up to several decades later, create a general atrophy of the CNS, leading to a demented state. Syphilitic dementia may well decline in frequency over the next generations because of improved treatment of venereal disease, greater public awareness of health matters, etc. Other causes of dementing syndrome include tumours, AIDS, long term exposure to solvents and other toxic chemicals, and **normal pressure hydrocephalus** (where cerebrospinal fluid gets trapped in the brain instead of draining away, putting destructive pressure on CNS tissue).

The cortical and sub-cortical dementias

Dementias can be divided into those where the atrophy is principally in the cortex (the **cortical dementias**) and those where it is principally in the sub-cortical regions (the **sub-cortical dementias**). By this reckoning, the commonest cortical dementias are DAT, MID and Pick's disease, while the commonest sub-cortical dementias are PD and Huntington's disease. Since the cortex is principally concerned with higher intellectual functions, and the sub-cortex with control of motor actions, emotion, and so on (see Chapter 1), there should be a functional division between the two classes, and indeed this is what is found. The primary feature of DAT *et al.* is a decline in intellectual functions, whilst PD and those of a similar ilk first manifest themselves as a disturbance of motor skills. Sub-cortical dementias tend to strike before the onset of old age, and many commentators do not consider them to be 'true' dementias. There is an excellent review of sub-cortical dementias by Peretz & Cummings (1988).

Illnesses which can be confused with dementia

There are two principal conditions which afflict the elderly which can successfully mimic dementia. Both, unlike the dementias, are treatable, and thus their accurate diagnosis is essential (they are also sometimes called the **reversible dementias**). The first of these is **pseudodementia**. This can arise in elderly people who suffer severe depression, and it should be noted that for the young elderly, depression, not dementia, is the commonest cause of referral for psychiatric treatment (Post 1982). In becoming depressed, the old person loses motivation, and this is reflected in very poor scores on tests of mnemonic and other intellectual functions. This, and their general lack of interest in their surroundings, can provide an excellent impersonation of dementia.

The prime differences between pseudodemented and truly demented patients are threefold. First, pseudodemented patients are usually well oriented in time and space (i.e., they know where they are, the day of the week, why they are being tested, etc). Second, pseudodemented patients often perform better in the middle of the day than in the morning and, third, they are usually aware that they have performed badly on a test (unlike most truly demented patients, who are blissfully unaware of their failings). The intellectual performance of pseudodemented patients usually improves as the depression is treated (Jenike 1988, La Rue 1992). However, it is important to note that in one study, 57 per cent of elderly patients referred for treatment for depression subsequently developed true dementia (Reding *et al.* 1985). Generally, it has been found that 20–30 per cent of demented patients are depressed (e.g. Marsden & Harrison (1972) – although note that patients may report themselves as less depressed than the ratings given by their caregivers: Teri & Wagner (1991)). Thus, the depressive state may in some cases be a reaction to cognitive failings rather than the reverse.

The other major impersonation of dementia is **acute confusional state (ACS)**, also known as **delirium**. ACS is usually very rapid in onset (i.e., a matter of hours or days). The age groups most vulnerable to it are children and the elderly. Delirious patients display poor intellectual and mnemonic skills, and they also tend to be either excessively languid or, alternatively, hyperactive. Rambling or incoherent speech is also a common feature. To this extent, they resemble many demented patients. However, a major difference between ACS and dementia is that many delirious patients suffer from **illusions** (i.e., distorted perceptions of the real world about them). Illusions are very rarely encountered in the dementias, despite some popular stereotypes of 'senile' people. Delirious patients often also have an alarmingly short attention span. ACS is caused by a general disturbance of CNS metabolism. There are many possible causes. Some of the commonest are: fever; infection; drug intoxication (because the elderly body cannot excrete (legally prescribed) drugs, thus causing an overdose); stroke; and inadequate diet (particularly a deficit of vitamin B12). Most cases of ACS are reversible by the successful treatment of the underlying cause. The syndrome is difficult to confuse with dementia because the onset is so sudden. However, sometimes no information prior to referral may be available (e.g. a reclusive elderly patient is found unconscious in the street), in which case the diagnosis may not be as clear-cut, although there are diagnostic tests available which act as a checklist of symptoms (e.g. the **Delirium Rating Scale (DRS)**). It is also important to note that, although ACS is separate from dementia, this does not stop demented patients contracting it, and cases of delirious demented patients are relatively common.

Problems with diagnosis

Clinicians tend to diagnose dementia by default. A diagnosis of dementia is arrived at after all other possibilities (depression, fever, tumour, etc) have been ruled out. Thus, it is not that dementia has any unique features, it is simply that the changes cannot be attributed to anything more tangible. Diagnosis of the type of dementia a patient is suffering from is even more fraught with problems, and accuracy is moderate to poor, with 30–50 per cent of misdiagnosed cases being not unknown (Gurland & Toner 1983, Roth 1979). The problem is principally one of time. The major dementias possess the same general set of symptoms: memory loss, poor intellectual functioning, odd behaviour, and so forth. They only appreciably differ in the way they develop: MID is the only one to progress discontinuously: Pick's disease nearly always begins with a personality change before any mnemonic loss takes place, and so forth. However, deciding what sort of dementia a patient possesses from the way the illness develops will obviously take months. The relatives of the patient may be able to give some record of the development of the symptoms, but this will probably be vague and lack the details necessary to pinpoint the precise nature of the problem. This is understandable: relatively few people are well acquainted with the symptoms of dementia, and a justifiably high level of emotion about the patient's state of mind may well cloud the relatives' judgement. Thus, the clinician (beyond maybe knowing that the patient has been 'acting oddly' for the previous few months) has to start from scratch in his or her examination. This is a problem, since different dementias share the same symptoms. For example, suppose that the patient has language problems – is this early stage Pick's disease or later stage DAT? Again, the patient might have all the hallmarks of DAT, but might this be a case of MID masquerading as DAT? Diagnosis of dementia type is thus usually performed by searching for a symptom or symptoms which occur more frequently in one kind of dementia than in others. For example, a history of CV illness may consign a patient to the MID category, personality problems to Pick's disease, and so on. Note that clinicians are not searching for symptoms unique to particular dementias, since none has yet been found. Often a diagnosis of DAT is arrived at because typical features of other common dementias have not been found. Given this probabilistic method of diagnosis, it is not surprising that the rate of misdiagnosis is so high.

It is highly probable that, within a few years, accurate physiological measures will become available (one hopes in tandem with cures). However, at present, a more immediate and attainable goal would be to improve understanding of the psychological aspects of the dementias, which may point the way to more accurate diagnostic criteria. In recent years, many studies have been performed on psychological aspects of the dementias (particularly DAT). In part, these have sought to identify psychological deficits unique to particular types of dementia, as opposed to the rather broad concepts of 'intelligence', 'memory' and 'language' outlined above. In addition, by concentrating on specific aspects of intellectual functioning, these studies have attempted to identify how the dementing mind continues to operate. In the next section, some of these assessments of 'specific' skills will be examined.

Specific psychological deficits in dementia

The studies which have examined specific aspects of demented intellectual functioning have tended to heavily concentrate on DAT, since it is by far the commonest of the dementias. Accordingly, the most parsimonious approach this review can take is to examine issues primarily from the perspective of DAT, noting dementias of other aetiologies when research has been directed at them.

General test batteries

Some researchers have given subjects batteries of tests, in the hope that different types of dementias may display different patterns of dysfunction. For example, suppose that DAT and MID patients show a decline in skills *A, B, C, D, E,* and *F,* but that DAT patients are especially bad at *A* and MID patients at *E*. This has useful diagnostic implications, because two demented groups can be distinguished on their different patterns of ability. Some studies have noted this pattern. For example, Fuld (1984) noted that a sizeable proportion (45%) of the DAT patients in her sample scored in a particular pattern on the Wechsler Adult Intelligence Scale (WAIS). Namely, the average of their scores on the 'Information' and 'Vocabulary' subtests was higher than their average score on 'Similarities' and 'Digit Span', which in turn was better than the 'Object Assembly' score. The average 'Digit-Symbol' and 'Block Design' score was lower than the 'Similarities' and 'Digit Span' *and* the 'Object Assembly'. Other researchers have tended to echo these findings (La Rue 1992), but since the pattern only describes some DAT patients, and some members of other patient groups also display this pattern, the practical utility of the finding is questionable.

Vitaliano *et al.* (1984) tested normal elderly controls and groups of DAT patients who were mildly or moderately impaired. The subjects were assessed on a number of measures, including attention, calculation, recognition, recall, and orientation. Vitaliano *et al.* found that normals and early stage DAT patients were best discriminated between on recall and orientation measures, while the biggest differences between the mildly and moderately demented DAT patients were on measures of recognition and attention. However, most studies have failed to find such a neat pattern of dysfunction. For example, researchers have noted that DAT patients are always worse than normal elderly controls on a wide range of cognitive measures (e.g. Brinkman *et al.* 1983, Leli & Scott 1982, Rosen *et al.* 1984). Perez *et al.* (1975) noted that DAT patients were worse than MID patients on the WAIS test. Bucht & Adolfsson (1983), however, found that their sample of MID patients had a lower level of cognitive performance than DAT patients. Thus, DAT patients' intellectual performance is worse than normal controls' (no surprise) and may or may not be worse than MID patients'. This latter anomaly is probably due to the selection of demented subjects. Whether one demented group is brighter or duller than another depends upon the stage of the illness the patients are in. Accordingly, choosing early stage DAT patients, and MID patients with more advanced symptoms, will mean that the former will probably outperform the latter. If the severity of the patient groups was reversed, this would probably create the opposite result. Therefore, finding quantitative differences between demented groups' general performance levels is unlikely to be informative. Other factors further cloud the issue. For example, Bucht & Adolfsson (1983) noted the tremendous variability of symptoms between the DAT patients when compared to the MID group. Breen *et al.* (1984) also found this, and in addition observed that depression coexisting with the dementia can cause a further significant decline in cognitive functioning.

Thus, the majority of work on test battery performance has shown that demented groups are worse than normal controls. This is uninformative, since this is part of the definition of dementia. Attempts to show which demented group suffers the greatest level of handicap are similarly uninteresting from a theoretical viewpoint, because it is practically impossible to find any common term of reference upon which to base the comparison (i.e., it is impossible to judge if two demented groups are at the same relative stages in their illnesses and/or if they have been demented for the same length of time). Vitaliano's findings of differences between normal controls and DAT patients at differing stages of the illness are interesting, but probably of little diagnostic use. While it is possible to demonstrate differences in *average* levels of performance of *groups*, this does not mean that *individual patients* will behave in this way. Given the findings on the immense variability in symptoms between DAT patients, this seems a plausible argument.

Physiological correlates

Given that dementia is caused by a deterioration of brain tissue, an obvious research policy is to examine possible links between the degree of atrophy (or other signs of physical dysfunction) and psychological abilities. There is certainly ample evidence that demented patients have suffered considerable brain damage, and there is a good correlation between degree of psychological handicap exhibited when alive and post mortem discovery of infarcts, senile plaques, and other forms of dementing damage (e.g. Blessed *et al.* 1968). However, such studies obviously rely on the patient being dead, and thus are limited in their usefulness. There are two basic options for examining atrophy in living patients. The first is a biopsy (the extraction of brain tissue by surgical operation), which is hazardous. The second is to scan the patient's brain electronically. Until a few years ago, scanning was too inaccurate to detect atrophy until it was very well advanced. Accordingly, studies reported a low or non-significant correlation between changes noted by scan and the patients' intellectual status (e.g. Berg 1988, Feher *et al.* 1984). However, in recent years, as scans have improved so have the strengths of the correlations (Moss & Albert 1988). It is highly likely that in the next few years, as scanning techniques become yet more refined, that it will be possible to map changes in intellectual functioning onto specific areas of atrophy. However, a word of caution needs to be sounded. Neuropsychological research has shown that some sections of the brain can withstand much greater damage than others before the functions they control are affected. Hence, there must be a cautious interpretation of information from scans which show a good correlation between atrophy and level of intellectual handicap. Some sites of damage may be more important than others, and this information will be masked if only general correlations are considered.

Psychomotor skills

Demented patients show a marked decline in **psychomotor skills**: that is, the degree to which they can control their movements and the speed at which they can do this. A popular test of psychomotor skills is the **Gibson Spiral Maze**. This is a paper and pencil test which requires the subject to trace a pencil line around a spiral shaped path as quickly as possible. Gilleard (1979) demonstrated that demented patients are slower and make more mistakes on this test than do depressed patients and normal elderly controls. In a subsequent study, Gilleard (1984) demonstrated that the performance of relatively young demented patients (aged 60–70) was characterised by an abnormal slowing, while older patients (70–89) were more notable for their poor accuracy, when compared with non-dementing controls. Another common test of psychomotor skills is the **peg board**. There are several variations of this test, but the central feature is that the subject is required to place pegs into holes in a board as quickly as possible. Miller (1974) found that pre-senile demented patients are slower than controls, but the principal cause of this slowness was a retardation in movement speed, rather than in deciding when and where to move. A similar effect was discovered by Vrtunski *et al.* (1983) in assessing demented patients' RTs (reaction times). The researchers found a slowing in all aspects of RT performance, which, they argued, represented 'a virtual psychomotor disintegration'. However, the speed at which subjects moved seemed to be especially badly affected.

Interesting as the above findings are, they add little to the overall understanding of dementia. This is principally because the subjects are clinically not clearly differentiated into dementias of different aetiologies. In any case, finding that demented patients are slower and less accurate than normal controls is precisely what would be predicted by the general definition of dementia as a gross impairment of intellectual function.

*Memory**

Given that severe memory loss is a cardinal feature of dementia, it is not surprising that much research has been devoted to this topic. Mnemonic measures alone can usually distinguish between demented patients and controls and may be used as an initial rough guide to the degree of handicap (e.g. Blessed *et al.* 1968, Branconnier *et al.* 1982, Whelihan *et al.* 1984). Even on a simple STM span test, most demented patients have significantly reduced spans and, usually, dementing patients' mnemonic skills dispropor- tionately worsen the harder the memory test is (e.g. Nebes 1992). For example, demented patients are usually more disadvantaged the longer they have to retain TBR items in memory, and they are worse at recall than recognition tests (Moss & Albert 1988). It can be shown that the ability to transfer information from short- to long-term memory is also handicapped. This has been demonstrated by Miller (1973), using a **supraspan learning** technique, which is performed as follows. First, the experimenter finds each subject's memory span. Suppose one subject is found to have a digit span of five numbers. She is then given a sequence of six numbers to learn (i.e., her span+1). This is beyond the capacity of her short term store, but one would expect the subject to learn the list given a couple of practices. It is argued that this is done by the subject transferring the numbers to long term memory (which is supposed to have a practically limitless capacity), and then recalling them from there. One might also predict that if the subject was given longer lists (i.e., span+2, span+3, etc) then these would take longer to learn, until an upper limit was reached, where no amount of practice would enable her to learn the list (presumably because her brain could no longer cope with the processing demands). Miller gave such a supraspan task to a group of DAT patients, and compared them with a group of patients suffering from specific damage to the hippocampus. Patients with hippocampal damage are known to suffer severe amnesia (see Chapter 1). There was little difference between the average digit spans of the two groups. However, on a supraspan task, it took the hippocampal group an average of two trials to learn a span+1 list, and four to learn a span+2 list. The DAT patients, on the other hand, took seven trials for a span+1 list, and most had not learnt a span+2 list after ten trials. It is well documented that DAT patients suffer hippocampal damage, but clearly they are suffering from more than this, otherwise the two groups' performances would be identical.

---

* *Readers who are unfamiliar with psychological theories of memory are advised to consult Chapter 3 (particularly the Introduction) before proceeding.*

Several commentators have argued that the principal source of DAT patients' mnemonic deficits is probably an encoding problem (e.g. Kopelman 1985, Miller 1973, Wilson *et al.* 1983). This has been demonstrated by Kopelman (1985), who compared DAT patients with normal elderly controls and a group of patients suffering from **Korsakoff's syndrome**. This latter condition (usually caused by long term dietary deficiencies coupled with alcohol abuse) is characterised by a relatively intact STM, but a very poor long term memory (i.e., there is a failure to transfer newly-acquired information from a short- to a long-term store). First, Kopelman established that the DAT patients had significantly shorter spans than the other two groups. This difference also held for a working memory task in which the subject had to remember a three word sequence while counting backwards from 100 in twos or threes (this type of task is sometimes called the **Brown-Peterson task**, after its inventors). Then, Kopelman gave subjects a visual recognition task (the subjects were given a set of pictures to look at, and then asked which they had seen before from a set of targets and distracters). The Korsakoff's and DAT groups' recognition scores were significantly worse than the normal group's, so they were given extra practice at this task, until their recognition scores were roughly on a par with the normal subjects' after *they* had seen the pictures once. Kopelman examined how many pictures the subjects could recognise ten minutes, one day, and one week after their initial presentation. He found that the rate at which the pictures were forgotten over this time was the same for all three groups. Thus, if the patients were given more opportunities to encode than the normal group, they could retrieve memories just as effectively. Becker *et al.* (1987) found a similar pattern of results. They tested DAT patients and normal controls on their memories for items 30 seconds after exposure, and again half an hour later. The researchers found that, although the DAT patients forgot more than the controls after 30 seconds, the amount of extra information they forgot in the 30 minutes after that was the same as for the controls.

A logical consequence of this is that the reason why DAT patients have poor long term memory measures is because their encoding abilities are especially handicapped, and they need longer than normal for them to operate effectively. Their retrieval mechanisms, surprisingly, are relatively intact. However, it should be noted that Kopelman used DAT patients in the relatively early stages of the disease. It is probable that as the illness becomes more severe, then retrieval process may also be affected, as the research on remote memory outlined below will demonstrate (see also Miller 1975). It should also be noted that other dementias besides DAT demonstrate particular problems with encoding. For example, Martone *et al.* (1984)

found comparable results in a study of Huntington's disease and Korsakoff's patients, and normal elderly controls. Pseudodemented patients, however, behave like normal controls, although overall they have lower memory spans (e.g. Gibson 1981, Miller & Lewis 1977).

Researchers have also cited another major problem in DAT patients' memories – namely a failure of certain aspects of the working memory system, although other aspects of the model may remain relatively well preserved. For example, the principal store for verbal memories is the phonological loop, which is thought to behave rather like 'a voice in the head' speaking onto a tape loop. In the same way that the spoken voice can be 'tripped up' by lists of similar sounding words (e.g. tongue twisters like *the sixth sheik's sixth sheep is sick*), the phonological loop can be forced into errors be being given lists of items which sound similar. Thus, a list of letters such as *B,C,V,D,G* should be harder to remember than *H,W,J,Y,E* and, indeed, this phenomenon has often been observed in normal subjects (Baddeley 1986). If DAT affects the phonological loop, then this effect should disappear, and the patients should be equally good (or bad) at remembering similar and dissimilar sounding lists. However, DAT patients are, relatively speaking, just as prone to confusion over similar sounding items as are normal controls (Morris 1984). If the slave systems are functioning normally (and Baddeley (1986) surmises that this is the case) then what is causing the appalling memory loss in DAT patients?

The answer probably lies in the central executive. Baddeley *et al.* (1986) present evidence supporting this view. They gave DAT patients and non-dementing controls the task of remembering lists of numbers while tracking a randomly moving square on a computer generated display with a light pen. DAT patients' performance disproportionately worsened when they had to perform both tasks concurrently. Furthermore, Morris (1986) found that if the distracting task in a working memory test is made more difficult, then the memory span disproportionately declines for DAT subjects compared with normal controls. These findings strongly suggest there is a serious deficit in central executive functioning, since one of the functions of this mechanism is to control and coordinate intellectual and mnemonic tasks (Morris & Kopelman 1986). Beyond working memory, a further role of the central executive is felt to be to control the general organisation of cognitive functions, and it is possible that the decline in the central executive alone could account for much of the intellectual decline observed in DAT patients (Baddeley 1986, Morris & Kopelman 1986). There is some tentative evidence that the central executive may be anatomically based in the frontal lobes (Baddeley 1986, Chapter 10), an area known to be badly affected in DAT. However, such a theory in its basic form has difficulty explaining why Pick's disease patients, whose handicap is principally in the frontal lobes, should not display the same degree of memory loss.

An important caveat to the above concerns the apparent similarity between dementing and normal ageing effects on working memory. In both cases, a decline in capacity seems to be attributable to failings in the central executive. It is thus tempting to conclude that DAT is a form of exaggerated ageing. However, as Baddeley (1986) and other commentators have pointed out, the decline in normal ageing is only quantitative – that is, all the processes work in the same manner as young people's, the only difference being that they are less efficient. In the case of DAT patients, the differences are quantitative and qualitative (i.e., the patients behave differently as well). This qualitative difference can be clearly seen in research on visuo-spatial STM. One of the most popular methods of testing this is the **Corsi blocks** task (Corsi 1980). The experimental apparatus consists of an array of wooden blocks, which the experimenter taps in a particular order, with the subject then attempting to replicate the same sequence. The number of blocks tapped increases on each trial, until the maximum span a subject can reliably remember is reached. DAT patients are extremely bad at this task, even compared with patient groups suffering from amnesia or from dementias of other aetiologies, who have been matched on other mnemonic measures, such as word or digit span (e.g. Cantone *et al.* 1978, Grossi *et al.* 1977).

Stuart-Hamilton, Rabbitt & Huddy (1988) tested subjects on a visuo-spatial task based on the Corsi test. In their version, instead of blocks, shapes printed on a large sheet of card were used. There were two conditions. In the first, all the shapes were black squares, whilst in the second, each shape was unique in outline and colour (e.g. an orange triangle, a turquoise star). The researchers found that MID patients and non-dementing but low IQ elderly controls found sequences on the coloured shapes easier to remember than the black squares, whilst for the DAT patients the reverse was true: they found the black squares relatively easier to remember than the coloured squares. It is easy to see why the coloured shapes condition might be advantageous – the shapes look different from each other, and hence should be easier to distinguish between when trying to remember a sequence. In the black squares condition, all the shapes (obviously) look the same, and thus tapping movements have to be remembered by patterns of movement alone. The researchers concluded that the DAT patients simply get distracted by the extra range of shapes and colours in the coloured shape condition, and this distracts them from the movements of the experimenter, and hence they fail to encode the sequence adequately. This was reinforced by a further experiment by the authors. This was a visual search task, in which the subject had to point to the picture of a named object (the target) surrounded, though not obscured, by geometric shapes (the distracters). The target picture was always of a familiar object (a candle, an apple, etc), and the distracters were geometric shapes, either very similar in outline to the target (e.g. a candle surrounded by rectangles, an apple surrounded by circles) or dissimilar (e.g. an apple surrounded by crosses, rectangles, squares). Normal and MID patients performed faultlessly on this task. DAT patients, however, performed badly. Surprisingly, they made more mistakes when the target was surrounded by dissimilar shaped distracters. Thus, the DAT patients' problem was not that they had difficulties telling the difference between the target and the shapes (otherwise there would be more mistakes when the distracters looked similar). Instead, it appears that the DAT patients' problem was that, given a varied visual display, they simply could not cope with the extra processing involved, and suffered an 'information overload', and this is reflected in a decrement in performance. Furthermore, DAT patients' performance on the visual search task correlated well with their performance on the memory task, indicating that the same handicap governed their failings on the two tasks. Thus, the principal deficit in DAT patients' visuo-spatial memory may not be memory *per se*, but the processes feeding it, particularly a failure to attend to the target items and to exclude distractions. However, it is worth noting that other research on attention in DAT patients has produced ambiguous findings, and the nature of the deficit is not clear-cut (Nebes 1992). It is possible that attentional problems are limited to only some DAT patients, with others remaining relatively unaffected (Freed *et al.* 1989).

The above may be another example of central executive failure, but it should be noted that Cantone *et al.* (1978) found a poor correlation between DAT patients' visual and verbal memory scores. In a similar vein, Wilson *et al.* (1982) recorded a poor correlation between memory for faces and verbal materials. Therefore, without further investigations, it is not possible to judge whether a central executive failure underlies both verbal and visuo-spatial STM. Aside from this issue, it is also important to note that the Stuart-Hamilton *et al.* study showed that DAT patients behaved in a qualitatively different manner from a normal control group, thereby providing evidence that DAT is not just exaggerated ageing.

Another aspect of the mnemonic process is remote memory. A common stereotype of the dementing patient is that he or she is quite happy and able to live in the past — it is the present which is impossible to cope with. Indeed, until their linguistic abilities decline, demented patients can often provide the researcher with long strings of reminiscences. However, such observations cannot be taken at face value, since many reminiscences may be confabulations, or they may be attributable to the rehearsal of a few choice anecdotes. Formal laboratory studies have supported this argument, showing that demented patients' remote memories for famous names and events are significantly worse than non-dementing elderly controls (e.g. Corkin *et al.* 1984, Stuart-Hamilton *et al.* research note 2, Wilson *et al.* 1981).

Some studies have found that memory is better for more distant events and names than it is for recent ones (see Nebes 1992). However, Corkin *et al.* (1984), Stuart-Hamilton *et al.* and Wilson *et al.* (1981) found non-dementing elderly subjects remembered more recent than remote names, whereas DAT patients displayed a 'flat' (i.e., equally low) level of recognition for names from any time period (i.e., recent and very remote names were recognised equally badly). Whether a flat response or one biased towards older items is found may be a product of the test materials used. Stuart-Hamilton *et al.* used the Famous Names Test (FNT), and, as in an earlier study of non-dementing elderly (Stuart-Hamilton, Perfect & Rabbitt 1988), they calculated the probability of the DAT group recognising each name on the FNT (see the 'Remote Memory' section in Chapter 3). This creates a 'league table' of popular names, with the most often recognised names at the top down to the least recognised at the bottom. It was found that individual names on the FNT occupied the same league positions for DAT patients and normal controls (as well as a group of MID patients). This implies that dementia destroys the memories of all but the most famous names, regardless of when they were 'in the news'. It is a chance artifact of the FNT that the very best remembered names are spread fairly evenly across the time period covered by the test (see Chapter 3 for further discussions of the FNT's design), thus yielding the 'flat' response observed by researchers. A similar argument can explain a bias towards more remote names.

The results of remote memory studies belie the argument that storage and retrieval mechanisms are intact in demented patients, and that the principal deficit is encoding. There is no reason to suppose that prior to the onset of the illness, demented patients' encoding abilities were any different from anyone else's. This means that memories of famous names were accurately encoded. Indeed in qualitative terms, the same 'memorability value' seems to have been assigned to individual famous names by demented and normal subjects alike, indicating the same basic encoding process at work. However, the dementing subjects have significantly lower remote memory test scores, indicating that they can no longer retrieve these memories from storage. This means that either memories have decayed while in storage to the point where they are now irretrievable, and/or that the retrieval mechanism is faulty. Hence, dementing memory declines because old memories cannot be retrieved, and new memories cannot be created.

An obvious question is whether the demented patients' mnemonic problems can be alleviated. Several possibilities arise from the work discussed so far. The first, arising from the discussion of visuo-spatial memory, is to make visual materials intended for DAT patients as unvaried as possible, so there is less to distract them. However, Backman *et al.* (1991) attempted to improve DAT patients' memories for pairings of faces and names by getting them to concentrate on just one part of the facial features. However, this did not improve recall. A second suggestion is that, in general, demented patients' problems worsen the more they have to cope with at once – hence, tasks should be kept as simple as possible. Another approach is to examine whether demented patients' performance can be improved by **priming**. 'Priming' has several meanings, but essentially it involves giving the subject a hints about items he or she is trying to remember (e.g. giving the first letter of a word – **initial letter priming**). Both dementing and non-dementing subjects improve if given initial letter priming, and the latter group's span may even match the former's (e.g. Davis & Mumford 1984, Miller 1975). However, other, less direct priming methods, such as giving a word semantically related to an item, do not aid demented subjects (e.g. Davis & Mumford 1984). Similarly, if non-dementing subjects are given lists of semantically related words, they remember more of them, because their conceptual similarity makes them easier to remember. Dementing subjects, on the other hand, are not aided (e.g. Weingartner *et al.* 1981, 1982). Diesfeldt (1984) found that semantic structure only aided demented patients when the rationale was explained to them *and* they were also given priming.

Why demented patients should be unaided by all but the most blatant priming is still disputed. Some commentators (e.g. Miller 1975) have argued that it reflects a failure of retrieval – that is, unless the dementing subject is practically told what he or she has in the memory store, then it cannot be recognised. Others (e.g. Martin *et al.* 1985) have suggested that the problem is in encoding – demented subjects do not encode enough information about items for all except the unsubtlest of primes to retrieve them from memory. There is an excellent review of this (as yet unresolved) debate by Morris & Kopelman (1986).

Visuo-spatial skills

It has been noted that DAT patients are especially bad at a visual search task (and also visuo-spatial memory) and that this is attributable to a decline in attention. Other research has similarly found a severe handicap in visuo-spatial skills. For example, Grossi & Orsini (1978) noted that demented patients were bad at reproducing a spatial arrangement of eight crosses. However, alone among patients with dementias of many different aetiologies, DAT patients were the only group not to improve on a second trial. Brouwers (1984) found DAT patients to be worse then Huntington's disease patients on a range of visuo-spatial tests (barring those involving knowledge of personal space). DAT also appears to create an especially severe handicap for **iconic memory**. This is the memory for items which appear for a very brief time (i.e., fractions of a second), and which disappear from the subject's sight before they there is time for them to be fully processed and recognised. Therefore, if the subject can subsequently identify the item, it must be from a memory of its appearance, since it is no longer in the subject's sight to be analysed. Iconic memory is usually tested using a technique called **backward masking**. The TBR (to-be-remembered) item (usually a letter) is flashed on a computer display screen for a fraction of a second, and is immediately replaced by a **mask**, which is designed to interfere with the memory of the item. The mask take various forms, from a simple burst of light, to a complex pattern. Masking usually makes identification of the TBR item harder. This can be seen by the fact that, in order for it to be correctly recognised, the TBR item has to be presented for a longer time when it is followed by a mask than when it is presented alone. This increase in exposure time is called the **stimulus onset asynchrony (SOA)**. It is also known that different masks exert their effects at different parts of the visual processing system. For example, some ingenious experiments (see Morris & Kopelman 1986) have shown that a simple mask of a flash of light interferes with processing at the start of the processing chain (i.e., before the signal has reached the cortex). On the other hand, a pattern mask, such as one made out of letter fragments (which look like real letters 'cut up') exerts its interference further along the processing chain, in the cortex. There is considerable evidence that DAT patients have poor iconic memories (e.g. Coyne *et al.* 1984, Moscovitch 1982, Schlotterer *et al.* 1984). DAT patients need significantly longer exposure times before they can identify items with the same accuracy as non-dementing controls. DAT and normal groups have the same SOAs for simple light flash masks (Moscovitch 1982), implying that the early stages of DAT patients' visual processing mechanisms are qualitatively normal (this has been confirmed by related work by Schlotterer *et al.* 1984). When a pattern mask is used, then DAT patients' SOAs become disproportionately larger than normal controls' (e.g. Coyne *et al.* 1984, Moscovitch 1982). This points to the principal deficit lying in the cortical processing of iconic memory. It is unlikely that this deficit is in the basic visual processing of the image, because the occipital lobes (which are principally responsible for visual perception – see Chapter 1) are relatively spared.

This leads one to conclude that the problem probably lies in the interpretation of the visual image. There is some evidence to support this view. For example, Moss & Albert (1988) noted that DAT patients find it especially hard to draw an item to command. For example, they have difficulty in obeying the instruction 'draw a clock and set the hands to ten after eleven'. Yet the same patients have no or little difficulty in copying a drawing of such a clock. Other researchers have reported similar findings (e.g. Hecaen & Albert 1978, Rubens & Benson 1971). In short, DAT patients may see what is there, but they cannot work out what it is. What causes this deficit (**visual agnosia**) is still uncertain. Warrington (1975) has uncovered a strong link between the complaint and a general failing of semantic memory, and the issue will be examined more fully in the discussion of anomia below. However, it would be unwise to assume that visual processes survive completely intact in DAT patients. Individual cases of poor vision, and of atrophy concentrated in the occipital lobe have been reported and, generally, visual contrast sensitivity (see Chapter 1) declines in DAT patients (Nissen *et al.* 1985).

Linguistic abilities

As was noted earlier, demented patients in general and DAT patients in particular suffer language difficulties which grow in stature until the patients become mute in the later stages of their illnesses. Berg *et al.* (1984) noted that if DAT patients initially present with particularly severe linguistic difficulties, then the development of the illness is likely to be significantly more rapid than usual. Many linguistic skills decline in dementia, but usually the first problem to present itself is **anomia**, or the failure to name objects (Appell *et al.* 1982). Indeed, when compared directly with other dementing groups (Huntington's disease, PD, MID), DAT patients are especially bad at naming (Bayles & Tomoeda 1983). Martin & Fedio (1983) found DAT patients to be worse than normal controls at naming, and also at producing words (i.e., verbal fluency). The researchers found that when DAT patients misnamed an object, they tended to substitute a word from the same semantic category (e.g. 'clock' instead of 'watch'). Furthermore, in general, DAT patients gave proportionately more general category names (e.g. 'dog', 'cat') than specific names (e.g. 'Alsatian', 'Persian'). This echoes the finding by Warrington (1975) that demented patients could correctly answer questions about the category to which an item belonged, but could not reliably answer questions about its features. Warrington and Martin & Fedio took their findings as evidence that, as DAT patients lose their vocabularies, they tend to lose words for specific things, leaving a residue of more general words. Schwartz *et al.* (1979) reported a similar loss in a single patient case study. It is as though DAT patients' language loses its fine detail.

However, other researchers (e.g. Nebes & Brady 1990) have found that if DAT patients are given the names of attributes and asked to match them to an item, then they display much more normal patterns of response. It would appear that the patients can passively recognise a connection between an item and its features, but if asked actively to process such information (e.g. by naming an attribute rather than simply recognising the connection between an item and an attribute), then ability declines markedly (see Nebes 1992).

Aside from these considerations, the bulk of the evidence points to anomia being a problem of confused semantic classification rather than a simple perceptual failure (e.g. Bayles & Tomoeda 1983, Martin & Fedio 1983, though see discussion in Hart & Semple 1990, Chapter 9). It will not have escaped some readers' attention that anomia and visual agnosia are similar conditions, and indeed Warrington (1975) noted a strong link between them in several case studies, suggesting that anomia can result from a failure of verbal memory and/or visual memory. Martin & Fedio (1983) attributed the anomic symptoms of the patients in their study to a failure to match the required word to the right semantic concept. However, given the wide variability of symptoms in DAT patients, samples of patients can probably be found to display many different patterns of response.

Another characteristic of dementing language is the high proportion of **intrusions** and **perseverations**. Intrusions occur when the subject gives an inappropriate response which is a repeat of a reply to an earlier question. These contrast with perseverations, where the subject inappropriately says the same phrase twice or more in succession. Shindler *et al.* (1984) examined the language of patients suffering from DAT and other dementias, as well as that of aphasics (i.e., brain damaged patients whose problems are solely linguistic) and normal controls. The researchers found that perseverations were common to all the abnormal groups, a finding echoed by Bayles (1985a). However, errors of this type were most frequent in hydrocephalus and Wernicke's aphasia patients. Intrusion errors were commonest in DAT and Wernicke's aphasia patients (this is not necessarily surprising, because many DAT patients develop Wernicke's aphasia – Appell *et al.* 1982). Another aspect of demented patients' linguistic failings is there is often a high degree of **circumlocution**. In other words, because patients can no longer find the *mot juste*, they attempt to talk around the subject. This can be seen as a logical reaction to a loss of word finding ability, a problem known to be common, especially in DAT patients (e.g. Huff *et al.* 1986). Generally, demented patients have problems in generating words (see Hart & Semple 1990), but detailed comparisons between dementias are probably unwise, because it is difficult to match patients for levels of illness (see 'Problems with research methods' below).

However, although the semantic content may be severely depleted, other aspects of demented language are remarkably well preserved. For example, **phonology** is fairly intact. This can be defined as an awareness of speech sounds, and many demented patients (particularly DAT) can spot and correct errors in their pronunciations (e.g. Appell *et al.* 1982). Similarly **morphology** (knowledge of word structure) is well preserved. Knowing that words have the same root (e.g. *farm-farmer-farming*) seems to be reasonably intact, since patients make few morphological errors. Syntax and general intonation of speech are also preserved (Bayles 1985b, Moss & Albert 1988).

However, having acknowledged these areas of preservation, the fact remains that demented patients' language is often devoid of meaningful content. Given that semantic abilities are so poor, this is not surprising, and the handicap is multiplied in the comprehension and production of longer and more complex utterances. This especially displays itself in a failure to understand pragmatics. An obvious effect of this is that one must be extremely careful that in testing demented patients (particularly DAT patients, who develop linguistic problems earlier than most – Bayles 1985b), they understand the instructions. Part of the failure of patients on the tests described may be due to their being unsure about what the experimenter wants, and worrying about this may mar their performance. An analogous situation would be to test a monoglot Englishman's digit span in Serbo-Croat, giving all test instructions in Serbo-Croat as well. The test score thus attained would make him look very retarded indeed. However, the failure would be not one of memory, but of communication.

Problems with research methods

An obvious problem with the studies mentioned so far is that they should help improve the diagnosis of dementia types, but researchers (the present author included) seem content to test patients assigned to their groups by methods known to be ineffective, and to find differences between groups which cannot be due to all the members of each group having the same disease in common. In fact, numerous researchers comment on the heterogeneity of their samples of patients (particularly when they are suffering from DAT), but they do not seem then to act upon this information. The reason for this is not ignorance nor laziness. For statistical reasons, to attempt an accurate regrouping of patients, very large sample sizes are needed, and these are well beyond the resources of many researchers. Furthermore, a large sample study would only be worthwhile if some new measure showed some promise of distinguishing between dementia types. The research reported here has shown that a dementia of one aetiology produces severer deficits than another, but all the dementias produce the same general range of deficits – it is all a question of degree. It has *not* been shown that some deficits are unique to one type of dementia. Thus, the only reliable diagnostic option is to wait and see how the illness develops (although even this is inaccurate). This is not to say that the findings are not theoretically interesting. The research has been very useful in showing how and why different symptoms of dementia develop. Again, it has shown that dementia (and DAT in particular) is a failing of intellectual processes and of interpretation of memories and perceptions, rather than a sophisticated form of amnesia, as was once thought. Such findings, however, draw one no nearer to a cure for the disease.

Another problem concerns the choice and interpretation of tests used in studies. Showing that demented patients are less intellectually gifted than normal elderly controls is uninformative, because it is simply restating the basic definition of dementia. The illness is Murphy's Law applied to intellectual functioning – in other words, whatever can go wrong, will. A deficit in an ability is only interesting if it is significantly greater or less than the general level of decline. Thus, if one ability is better preserved than others, then this is informative, because it implies that the brain mechanism controlling it is also relatively spared. Similarly, a disproportionate loss indicates the reverse. A skill which simply declines at the same rate as the general pattern of loss is uninteresting because it is simply part of the general decline, and is behaving exactly as predicted. To gauge the relative decline of a skill, the subjects must be tested on several skills, and the correlations between them calculated. Unless a skill correlates weakly with the others, then it is part and parcel of the general decline, and hence in theoretical terms it is uninteresting.

A final concern is the use of controls (i.e., groups of subjects with whom the demented patients are compared). When 'normal' controls have been used, they have usually been matched with demented patients by age alone. Some researchers have been more sophisticated, and have also matched by the estimated **pre-morbid IQ** of the patient (i.e., the level of intelligence that the patient is estimated to have had prior to the onset of dementia).

Neither of these two approaches is satisfactory. This is because the people chosen for such control groups will, by the laws of probability, be an average cross-section of the population in general, and as such the groups will have average IQ scores. But showing that groups of demented patients perform worse than average elderly subjects is once again simply restating the obvious. A more satisfactory option is to select a group of non-dementing elderly controls who have very low IQ scores. This is for two reasons. First, because it would enable one to demonstrate differences between genuine dementing change and harmless senescent changes in the very stupid – an issue of some clinical importance. A second reason is that it may be possible to match demented patients and the very stupid for level of IQ. If so, it would then be feasible to show what changes are due to dementia and what are simply due to a generally low level of *g*. Another problem is that often a demented group is only compared with a normal group – that is, two or more groups of demented patients are not compared. This seriously weakens the value of a study, because it is impossible to judge if the failings of a demented group are due specifically to the *type* of dementia they suffer from, or whether they are held in common with dementias of other aetiologies. For example, suppose it was shown that a DAT group performed less well on tests X and Y than did a group of normal controls. If a MID group also behaved less well on tests X and Y, then the failure might be attributed to a general dementing decline. However, if the MID group did not exhibit a decline on test Y, but only on X, then a qualitative difference between DAT and MID would have been shown. This might be developed into a diagnostic measure. However, no-one will know if the difference exists or not unless two or more groups of demented patients are tested on the same measures.

The effect on caregivers

There is ample evidence that caring for a demented relative usually results in significantly higher levels of depression, stress, and other related health problems (e.g. Coppel *et al.* 1985, Kennedy *et al.* 1988, Morrissey *et al.* 1990). The reasons why this should be so are obvious. Of greater theoretical interest are the findings by Morrissey *et al.* (1990) that the caregivers' (in this study, always spouses') social role may be crucial in determining the level of depression that is felt. If the caregiver did not have paid employment (a 'homemaker'), then the lowering of social contact and the disruption to household chores, as well as the degree of handicap of the spouse, were cited as the prime causes of depression. For spouses who still went out to work, the severity of the spouse's handicap was cited as less serious, and the disruption of household chores as more serious. More intriguingly, the presence of a large number of friends and relatives helped to alleviate the depression for homemakers, but exacerbated it for the workers. Morrissey *et al.* concluded that, for the latter, 'friends' included workplace colleagues who may inadvertently add stress (because although they provide opportunities for interaction, they are not necessarily sources of help). However, for whatever reason, caregivers are depressed, and level of depression helps determine the level of outside assistance the caregiver may be willing to accept, and more alarmingly, increases the risk of suicide (Fry 1986).

Schulz & Williamson (1991) conducted a two-year longitudinal study of caregivers of DAT patients, and again found that levels of depression were strongly correlated with the number of problems created by looking after the patient. More interestingly, the researchers found that, for female caregivers, the level of depression tended to remain the same throughout the period of the study, whilst for male caregivers, the level of depression increased. The researchers add a cautionary note that, because the levels of depression prior to the onset of DAT are not known, it is difficult to judge how much of the depression is a reaction to the illness. However, Dura *et al.* (1991) measured their sample of caregivers before the patient (a parent suffering from dementia) arrived at the home, and then measured them a year later. Compared with controls, there was no difference in incidence of mental illness prior to the arrival, but a year later 34 per cent of the caregivers had developed depression or an anxiety disorder as defined by the DSM-III-R (this compared with 8% of the controls).

The degree to which caregivers experience negative emotions is mediated by several factors. The availability of assistance (or lack of it) is an often-cited example (although note that Rivera *et al.* 1991 found no difference between depressed and non-depressed caregivers in their level of satisfaction with received support). So are financial security and coping strategies (e.g. Pruchno & Kleban 1993). The caregiver's attitude to the patient may also be of importance. A study by Cicirelli (1993) on daughters caring for their elderly mothers found that strong feelings of emotional attachment lowered the perceived burden, whilst strong feelings of obligation increased it.

Summary and overview

In closing this chapter, it is worth noting that the severity and awfulness of dementing symptoms can lead one to an exaggerated view of dementia's prevelance. Thus, it is worth repeating that only 5–6 per cent of all the elderly develop dementing symptoms, and many are only mildly demented at death, thus allowing a relatively dignified end. It is also inaccurate to think of dementia as being a disease of old age, as though it was an inevitable consequence of ageing. As has been seen, all the dementias can begin prior to old age, and some, indeed, are rarely seen past the age of 65–70. Furthermore, the psychological performances of demented patients are qualitatively different from those of the normal elderly, thereby demonstrating that dementia is not a natural extension of the normal ageing process.

Dementia is a progressive loss of mnemonic, intellectual and linguistic functioning, usually accompanied by radical changes in personality and sometimes in motor skills. Symptoms vary markedly between patients but, generally, the different dementias are distinguishable by their patterns of development. Neurophysiologically, dementias of different aetiologies are distinguishable (although usually only at post mortem) but all share the same general symptom of gross atrophy of CNS tissue. Several illnesses can masquerade as dementia, most notably pseudodementia and delirium, but these are usually distinguishable by concurrent depressive symptoms and very rapid onset respectively. A survey of studies of specific aspects of the dementing intellect reveals some interesting and important theoretical insights, but little of fresh diagnostic worth. Perhaps the most important finding is that dementia (particularly DAT) is probably primarily an intellectual and interpretive handicap rather than merely a severe form of amnesia (although of course demented patients also have serious memory problems). However, these arguments are drawn from research methodologies which are often seriously flawed, and thus conclusions must often be guarded. Finally, it must not be forgotten that dementias affect not only the patient but also his or her family and friends, and depression and other related illnesses are significantly higher among caregivers.

Recommended reading

Aside from the books on diagnosis of dementia recommended in the Introduction (Kermis 1986, Wasylenki 1987), there are several other notable texts. Hart & Semple (1990) is strongly recommended as a general introduction to the effect of dementia (and particularly DAT) on psychological functioning. La Rue (1992) is an excellent overview of the diagnostic criteria and psychological characteristics of dementia and related illnesses. For the more specialist reader, Morris & Kopelman (1986) provides a masterly survey of memory deficits in DAT and Moscovitch (1982) does likewise for changes in visual processes in ageing and dementia. Bayles (1985b) is couched in slightly less technical language, and handles the conceptually difficult topic of linguistic deficits very well. Also of note is Fry's (1986) textbook on general aspects of stress, adaptation and coping in the elderly. An ingenious novel by Bernlef (1988) presents the 'autobiography' of a patient succumbing to dementia, and is a useful adjunct to the above works.

CHAPTER 7

What is the Future of Gerontology?

Introduction

In previous chapters, the current state of the psychology of ageing has been examined. The first section of this chapter takes an overview of this research to highlight problems with existing research methodologies, and possible future directions which gerontological research might take to amend these. In the second section of the chapter, potential new forms of psychological changes in the elderly themselves will be assessed. Existing knowledge about the psychology of ageing will be used to predict how the elderly are likely to respond to changes in technology and society.

The view from without

Simone de Beauvoir (1970) divided her classic study *Old Age* into two main sections: one is the view from without, and the other is the view from within old age. This book has taken the view from without for the simple reason that research on gerontology is almost solely carried out by the young, or at least the pre-retired. In reading many works on the psychology of old age, one might well ask why the research was done, since the elderly are described in terms of decaying or defective mental functions: the *person* seems to have been lost, as has the relevance of the observed changes to everyday life. There are two obvious rebuttals of this charge. First, that it is necessary to take a rather distant approach in order to gain an objective view of the situation. Second, that knowledge has to be built up incrementally, and thus although the interests of individual experiments may appear to be rather esoteric, they all help to build up a coherent picture. It would also be grossly unfair to accuse researchers of being *morally* uninterested in age decrements. Nonetheless, there is an unvoiced belief, running through the gerontological literature that the elderly form a group distinct from the cohort of researchers. This is understandable, if not desirable, since, as mentioned already, researchers are nearly always aged under sixty, and often considerably so. (A random sampling by the author of the researchers cited in the bibliography found the majority to be in their thirties and forties.) The voice of age apartheid has probably slipped into this book. While every effort has been made not to address explicitly only a young (pre-60) readership, undoubtedly slips have been made, if only because it is difficult to escape this *zeitgeist* of gerontology.

There is no justification for age apartheid, even though it may have arisen, in part at least, from laudable motives. It is undoubtedly true that most old people show decrements in intellectual and physical functioning. From this it may be surmised that they often require greater health care, and may need extra consideration for their physical and mental comfort. However, having a greater call on resources does not make the elderly into radically different people. This may seem to some readers to be stretching an argument. However, consider a statement such as 'this is what one would expect of old people'. This seems to be a reasonable phrase, and one which a lot of people make with the best of intentions. One is, after all, merely identifying that old people are likely to behave in a particular manner. Substitute 'black' for 'old' in the above statement, and one gains some insight into the sort of global stereotyping which is being made. Thus, while it is right to identify the special needs of the elderly, and to note that the majority of them might behave in a particular manner, it is quite another matter to treat *all* old people as a unitary and distinct group. The above arguments in any case assume that old age is an easily defined and radically different state of being, which a person suddenly receives, rather than slowly enters into. However, the strangest aspect of age apartheid is that, unlike racism, the perpetrators are almost certain to become that which they attack. The xenophobe has the secure knowledge that his or her skin and nationality will stay the same, but everyone who remains healthy and accident-free grows old. It is not even that the 'symptoms' of old age arise on a person's sixtieth birthday – the signs of ageing are there from early adulthood if one looks closely enough.

Two main solutions to this problem present themselves. The first is that researchers make a greater effort not to write about and discuss the elderly as if they were interesting specimens and useful fodder for experiments. Occasionally recalling that they are discussing their own futures might be a salutary exercise. Another consideration is that the people best qualified to test old people are old people. Research has largely concentrated on those aspects of psychological functioning which young researchers think are central to the elderly's mental lives. There would be consternation if the elderly alone could decide what aspects of young adults' behaviour were researched. However, people seem quite happy to accept the reverse. This is not an attempt to displace psychologists and related professionals from their posts – the services of people well versed in research and analysis techniques are obviously essential. However, it might prove informative to allow the elderly to determine what is examined, and use the expertise of (younger) professionals to ensure that a sufficient degree of scientific rigour is maintained over the enterprise. The latter solution is open to a host of potential problems (e.g. what constitutes the best advice from the elderly on this matter?). However, it is hoped that the main point of this argument is appreciated – namely, that researchers cannot continue supposing explicitly or implicitly that old people are there to be tested and judged as if they possessed a condition which the testers stand no chance of contracting.

Are the psychological tests valid measures of real life skills?

Throughout this book, psychological tests (intelligence tests in particular) have been presented as if they were 'pure' measures of intellectual skills. If this is so, then one would logically expect psychological tests to correlate highly with abilities at 'everyday' skills. For example, intelligence test scores should be very good predictors of scholastic ability, salary, job status, ability at chosen job, and so on. However, this is not the case. An old psychological chestnut is that the best correlation ever found between IQ and a real life measure was 0.7. The real life measure was the number of real (as opposed to false) teeth possessed by the subjects. Usually, IQ tests are poor predictors of real life performance – correlations are usually of the order of 0.2–0.3: in other words, about ten per cent of the variance on the real life measure is predicted by IQ. This is not to say that intelligence tests are useless. Even their detractors acknowledge that they are good at identifying extremes of ability. Thus, IQ tests can identify the very bright and the very stupid (though it can be argued that one doesn't need an intelligence test to do this). What intelligence tests cannot do is identify the strength of ability at a real life function for the majority, who fall between these two extremes. This raises an uncomfortable question for gerontological research – if intelligence tests are not an accurate reflection of everyday skills, then of what value is the bulk of the work on senile intellectual changes?

Salthouse (see Chapter 2) provides one answer to this question: namely, that although intelligence is a poor predictor of absolute ability, it is vital as a control process. This may be so, but one might still wonder why psychologists have indulged in so much research on measures which have at best only a minor relevance to everyday intellectual functioning. An uncharitable view might be that, although IQ tests are poor predictors, they are the still the best measure available, and thus they continue to be used, until, to quote the song, 'the real thing comes along'. By this reckoning, the psychology of ageing is now very well versed in what happens to ten per cent of the elderly's intelligence but, like the iceberg, 90 per cent of it remains hidden. This is too severe a judgement, however. At a *general* level, IQ tests are probably perfectly adequate indicators of intellectual changes. Throughout this book, it can be seen that changes in specific mnemonic, linguistic and intellectual skills are correlated with a decline in IQ test performance. Admittedly, the correlations have often been small, but nonetheless they have been statistically significant and have fallen in the expected direction. For example, there have been no instances where the old have got higher intelligence test scores than the young, or where memory has improved the less intelligent the experimental subject has been. IQ tests are quite adequate at signifying trends.

The real failure of predictions has occurred when psychologists have attempted to be more specific about the nature of this decline. This can be seen, for example, in the supposed dichotomy between fluid and crystallised intelligence, outlined in Chapter 2: crystallised intelligence ('wisdom') is supposed to remain unscathed by the normal ageing process, whilst fluid intelligence ('wit') falls. However, on several occasions it has been demonstrated that crystallised intelligence worsens in old age (e.g. that the elderly's reading ability worsens, or that they are significantly slower to answer crystallised IQ test questions). Accordingly, this division, while theoretically convenient, has at best ambiguous experimental support. One is therefore left with only a general description – changes in intelligence level are *associated* with much of the decline in mnemonic and intellectual ability, and this in turn is probably explained by a slowing in neural transmission. However, with only a few debatable exceptions, gerontology has failed to uncover *how* this change takes place.

It would be unfair to blame gerontology for this failure to find the IQ test of more than general descriptive use. The problem is one which has beset **psychometrics** (the study of psychological differences) since its inception. What is at stake is convenience. In an ideal psychometric world, subjects could take a single IQ test, and their score would perfectly predict their ability on any intellectual task they could ever encounter. A single test score would tell one all one needed to know about a person's intellectual capabilities. Unfortunately for psychometricians, this test does not exist, and it is virtually impossible that one could ever be devised. The reason for this is that psychological research has shown that intellectual skills are not determined by a single factor, but rather by several different intellectual skills, each of which is at least partially autonomous of the others. The general intelligence test is really only an expression of the aggregate of performance on all these sub-skills, and hence can only hope to give an overall impression of an individual's abilities.

The situation is akin to predicting the performance of a football team. A team consists of different players with different abilities. A league table gives an overall gauge of how good an individual team is, by showing its position relative to other teams. However, league position tells one little about the abilities of individual players in the team. Of course, good teams will tend to have more good players than bad teams, but this is not an inevitable rule. For example, a particular side might have the best forward in the history of the game, but the side may be languishing at the bottom of the league because the rest of the team is poor. In a similar manner, the overall score on an IQ test can give an indication of the overall intellectual performance of an individual, but it cannot accurately predict how well a person will perform at a specific task. Nor can it be said that measures of sub-skills are necessarily more informative. There is a double bind in psychometrics which is as follows. General intelligence measures are poor predictors of everyday skills. Measures of sub-skills give better predictions, because they assess abilities which are more akin to those used in 'real life'. However, there is a danger that the tests of sub-skills may be so like the real life problems that one might as well cut out the middle man and use the real life ability as a measure. Thus, at one extreme a measure fails because it is too general, while at the other it flounders because it is too specific.

The remainder of this chapter could be spent outlining the pros and cons of specific versus general IQ tests, but this would be misleading, because a future trend in psychometrics may be to sidestep this debate, and instead concentrate on how the interaction between subskills creates the overall level of performance. To return to the footballing analogy – instead of considering how well the team performs or, alternatively, analysing the abilities of each player individually, one instead considers how the players interact with each other, and how their relative strengths and weaknesses combine to create the team's overall performance. In other words, information on sub-skills performance is combined to explain why an individual is gifted in the way he or she is. Those readers with some knowledge of psychology will appreciate that this will require the synthesis of two previously disparate areas of the science – namely, cognitive modelling and psychometrics. Rabbitt (1988c) has noted that psychometrics has been concerned with what makes two individuals different without being overly concerned to find out if the source of this difference is due to individuals having completely different mental processes. Conversely, researchers in cognitive modelling and related disciplines have been interested in constructing models of intellectual functioning, while assuming that all individuals will possess the same model (i.e., think in the same way). These approaches are logically flawed. It is like noting the time taken for several individuals to travel from one place to another, and assuming that some people were slower than others because everybody walked, but that some people are faster walkers than others; thus conveniently ignoring the possibility that some individuals may have used alternative methods of transportation. What is needed is a new synthesis, in which differences between subjects are examined to see if the difference in abilities is due to the same skills being used more efficiently by some than others, or that different people have different methods for tackling the same intellectual tasks, but that some methods are intrinsically more efficient than others.

One may question what relevance this issue has to the study of ageing, and the answer is that much of the ageing intellect may be cast into a new light if this new synthesis is adopted. It is known that intellect changes in old age. However, at the moment, this is seen in fairly simplistic terms of a general decline in some skills and a general sparing of others. The reason for this, and the one adopted in this book, is because, adopting Occam's razor, it is the most straightforward explanation. However, this parsimony may be occluding a more complicated truth. Suppose that, in old age, some mental processes decline more than others. This is a reasonable assumption, given the evidence presented in earlier chapters. It is known that different intellectual tasks are reliant on different subskills. For example, reading is heavily reliant on linguistic subskills, but does not place any great emphasis on visuo-spatial reasoning. In solving a chess problem, the reverse would apply. When a subskill declines, this is potentially damaging to all the processes which use it. For example, a decline in the speed to identify word meanings might have a detrimental effect on reading. However, one cannot guarantee this. It could be the case, for example, that an elderly person circumvents the problem by creating a new method to do the same task. Thus, a decline in word identification speed might be compensated for by increasing the reliance on using contextual cues to anticipate what is coming up, thus making words more predictable and hence easier to process. To return to the footballing analogy, it is akin to a team switching to a more attacking role because the goalkeeper is injured.

This means that the changes which take place in ageing cannot be taken at face value. Old people's mental functioning may be qualitatively the same as it was in their youth but, equally, there may have been changes in thinking style as well. (Perhaps dementia only becomes apparent when all alternative thinking styles to compensate for the losses being suffered have been exhausted.) This presupposes that there is only one type of youthful process and one type of elderly. The situation will of course be much more complicated if there is more than one of each. Another possibility is that there are several styles appropriate to the general intellect. For example, high IQ individuals think in one manner, middle IQ people in another, and low IQ people in yet another. Perhaps a general decline in IQ in old age causes a qualitative shift to a manner of thinking appropriate to the IQ band the elderly now find themselves in. Again, perhaps the elderly retain the same thinking methods, but as their general level of ability declines, their neural transmission rates are no longer efficient enough to cope, thus resulting in a disproportionate decline.

The above are several possibilities from a much longer list. It may well transpire that the explanations of senile changes in intellect which are published over the next decade prove too complicated to be easily assimilated into simple explanations. Thus, ironically, measures of g (general intelligence) may well be retained because, for all their imprecision, they at least give a simple concept to picture. To return to the football analogy – although one can see and appreciate the abilities of individual players, and to a certain extent one can see how they can interact with each other, in comparing different teams, one ultimately has to consider the performance of the team as a whole, even though this means losing sight of the individuals who are responsible for the team's performance. One needs a convenient 'overview' measure, even if one loses a lot of accuracy in the process.

So far, ageing intelligence has been discussed in fairly absolute terms – that is, how much 'better' or 'worse' are test scores, and so forth. This may well be (subconsciously) derived from the 'prejudice' outlined above that the elderly constitute a discrete group. Given that the elderly are part of a continuum, perhaps it is a mistake to pursue research methods which show that the old are different from the young. An alternative is to reject existing research methods and instead couch experiments in terms of describing the process of continual change. This, however, is rather too fey a concept. On average, there is too considerable a change in intellect for it to be swept under the carpet in this manner.

Will psychological tests always be the best measures?

It is unlikely that psychological discoveries can in themselves do much to alleviate the problems of ageing. Psychological therapies cannot cure dementia, they cannot remove the signs of ageing, nor can they directly reveal how cures for these various ills can be found. The best that therapies can do is help the elderly cope with their problems – an example, cynics would argue, of papering over the cracks. Solutions to many of the problems of ageing are likely to be physical (particularly medical and pharmacological) rather than mental. Therefore, is there a future for psychological research and psychological assessment?

The answer to this question is probably 'yes', and in much the same form as at present. For example, it is highly likely that, in the next decade, cures for at least some of the dementias will be found. Psychological research will in part have assisted in the research towards these goals, and undoubtedly psychological assessments will be used to gauge the mental status of the patients. One is unlikely to initiate a physical treatment without first ascertaining that there is a psychological problem and, similarly, the only valid manner in which a patient might be judged to be cured of dementia is by the state of their psychological health.

A similar picture can be presented for other areas of gerontology. Undoubtedly, physical measures will present researchers with clearer insights into the physical workings of the mind. For example, the accuracy of brain scans improves yearly, and it is tempting to think that with a clear picture of the brain one has an insight into the mind it represents. However, the advent of a brain scan which can literally read minds is certainly at least decades away, and in the meantime, a psychological assessment will be required when studying the ageing intellect and personality.

Will the elderly's psychological attributes change in the future?

In the final half of this chapter, the ways in which the elderly will be react to and be treated by a future, possibly more technologically-driven society are considered. This will be done by bringing to bear existing knowledge about the ageing mind, described in earlier chapters.

What will constitute being old?

At the current time, judgements about what makes a person 'old' are based on several criteria, including appearance, attitudes, and amount of leisure time. However, a variety of developments is likely to change all of these in the future.

Appearance may well be the most fundamental factor to be affected. Already, plastic surgery and (for women) hormone replacement therapy can 'remove' a decade or more from a person's appearance. These are largely cosmetic changes. There is little reason to doubt that techniques in this field will improve and possibly become more affordable, so that a wider range of people can avail themselves of them. This is aside from the possibility that advances in medical science may find further ways of retarding the ageing process. It is already well established that some animals (rats for example) can be made to live much longer by simple manipulations of their environment and diet. The leap from this to humans is not a simple one, but at some point the change will almost certainly come, and the over-sixties will no longer look 'old' by the current understanding of the word. However, will this necessarily change matters? Might it not be the case that people will look for subtler signs of the ageing process, so that whereas at one time wrinkles and grey hair signified ageing, the telltale sign now becomes the dullness of the eye? It can be demonstrated that cultures differ in what is a key physical attribute in other respects – erogenous zones, for example. Heterosexual males of different nationalities might be most attracted by breasts, buttocks, legs, or the nape of the neck. Why should the prime indicator of age not similarly shift across cultures separated by time? Alternatively, age retardation may be very successful, so that no-one can tell how old an adult is. This raises a series of possible dilemmas. Will some individuals deliberately elect to grow old 'naturally' and choose to make themselves outcasts? Again, perhaps anti-ageing treatments will be very expensive, and accordingly only the very rich will be able to afford them. There may then arise a new neurosis, of individuals 'trapped' in a body too young for their thoughts and attitudes. Perhaps treatments might delay the onset of the ageing process, but nonetheless it will inevitably arrive, albeit at a later age. Might this physical change (which an individual has taken deliberate steps to avoid) be more traumatic than for a person who has aged naturally and passively allowed his or her body to undergo the ageing process? Before voting too hastily in favour of anti-ageing treatments, it would be wise to consider the potentially serious psychological effects.

Attitudes are supposedly a good indicator of age. The popular conception of the elderly person is that he or she is conservative and cantankerous – an erroneous view, as was noted in Chapter 5. However, there is a further reason for doubting this. There has been a radical sociological shift in the past 50 years towards a far more liberal and permissive society, which has allowed young adults to express and celebrate being young, rather than attempting to become carbon copies of their parents' generation as quickly as possible. The first generation of these 'teenage rebels' is now in its mid-fifties (or older) and looking retirement in the eye. The hippies and flower people are already in their forties. The full ramifications of these changes are complex and more properly dealt with by a sociological text, but an important psychological prediction emerges from this. Namely, that the old people of the future are unlikely to fit into the niches which have been established by societal expectations with quite the same willingness as previous generations. They have seen that conventions can be flouted without the world crashing down. Accordingly, the old themselves may force society to change its views.

A final consideration surrounds leisure time. Perversely enough, in westernised societies, where leisure is treasured, an excess of it is usually greeted with distaste, since it often indicates unemployment or retirement. However, the increased automisation of work (particularly computerisation) may well change this attitude. Shorter working weeks, and an increase in 'home offices' may lead to more people of working age spending a much greater amount of time in their homes than in traditional workplaces. This means that retired persons, marked out because they are at home all day, will no longer stick out so obviously.

The elderly and the technological society

It is a cliche to note the immense changes in lifestyles of people in westernised nations, which have resulted from the technological and scientific advances of this century. It is tempting to imagine that the elderly will become swept up in this tidal wave of changes, and this raises the question of how well they will cope.

Intuitively, one might suppose that the greatest impact will be in medical and pharmacological care. One's immediate thought might be that people will live longer. However, as was pointed out in Chapter 1, this is not necessarily so. Although a greater *proportion* of the populace will reach old age (circa 20% by the year 2000 by some estimates) life expectancy for *individual* adults is not that much greater than it was at the turn of the century. Furthermore, the older a person is, the less this difference becomes. Thus, as mentioned in Chapter 1, while a 20-year-old in 1900 might have several years' less life expectancy than a 20-year-old today, this difference diminishes to little more than a few months when comparing 70-year-olds. This suggests two points. The first is that the reason why more people live longer is that they are surviving illnesses in their young adulthood, not that they have a healthier old age. The second, and related argument, is that since the life expectancy difference diminishes the older the cross-time age groups being compared, modern medical intervention is less effective the older the age group. In other words, modern medical care can carry more people into old age but, once there, it seems to be little better at prolonging life than it was at the turn of the century. There are several reasons for this. More people are surviving into old age because previously lethal infections have been successfully combated using a combination of antibiotics, widespread inoculation, and a less hazardous environment. However, several types of illness (particularly some forms of cancer and cardiovascular complaints) remain incurable. Although these are not exclusively the preserve of the elderly, the probability of their occurrence increases as people get older. Accordingly, several of the major diseases which cause death in old people are as incurable today as they were in 1900 (although various medical treatments can alleviate some of the symptoms, and thus the afflicted individuals may now survive a little longer). In other instances, treatments may be available for a complaint, such as chemotherapy or surgery. However, these are financially costly and require a physically robust patient. When faced (as is often the case) with more patients than hospital beds, medical practitioners will be less willing to treat the elderly than younger adults, since: (a) they (i.e., old people) are likely to have fewer remaining years in which to reap the benefits of treatment; and (b) they may in any case be too weak to withstand the treatment. A final consideration is the physical state of the elderly person. It has been noted elsewhere in this book that old people suffer from general physical deterioration and that, usually, the degradation in function is disproportionately higher the more bodily systems are involved. It can also be noted that, in younger adults, a defect in one organ is not necessarily indicative of a widespread physical deterioration. However, in the old (and especially the very old), if one function breaks down, it is usual for several others to be simultaneously teetering on the edge of collapse. This further militates against the treatment of the elderly – it can be argued that there is little point in using valuable resources to treat an ailing heart if the liver is simultaneously failing.

Because of these considerations, it is unlikely that those aged 70 or above are likely to demonstrate an appreciable rise in life expectancy in the near future. This is simply because, although cures for individual illnesses might be found, methods of overcoming widespread senile degeneration will have to be discovered before much benefit can be reaped. This raises a further, more controversial issue – will there be the impetus to pursue this? The increasing proportion of the elderly in the population is potentially a serious financial burden on governmental resources, not only in terms of pensions, but also with regard to social welfare provisions and health care. Any moves to increase the length of time an old person is alive, and thus needing to be provided for, are likely to carry a heavy financial cost. There is also a moral issue – if a method is found to prolong life, it carries with it the question of whether the quality of the life makes the effort worthwhile. If, for example, life-prolonging drugs have serious side-effects, then many people might choose not to take them, and have a shorter but less painful existence. However, will they be given this choice? At present, most countries have declared euthanasia to be illegal. Will refusal to take a life-prolonging drug be classified as voluntary euthanasia? Mercifully, such questions can for the foreseeable future remain the preserve of science fiction writers (e.g. John Wyndham's (1960) excellent *The Trouble With Lichen*), as the advent of life-prolonging drugs remains unlikely for many years.

Another major impact of technological change is in the automation of tasks. It is a commonplace notion of science fiction to envisage a time when all manual tasks will have been superseded by machines. This process has already begun, and the marked decline over the past 20 years in the proportion of the population employed in 'blue collar' work is a testimony to this. However, what is not so readily appreciated is that many 'white collar' jobs are also likely to be superseded. The advent of word processors greatly reduces the need for copy typists, for example. The changes are not likely to be limited to routine clerical careers, however. The use of 'expert systems', which seek to emulate the diagnostic abilities of a specialist, is also likely to come to the fore. Large investment and banking firms already use computers to monitor changes in stock market prices and can automatically initiate the buying and selling of shares. In the future, it may be possible to consult a computerised doctor, which will perform the same role as a general practitioner by analysing the patient's responses to a series of questions, using algorithms based on the diagnostic thought processes used by human doctors.

The impact of automation is too vast a topic to be encompassed in this chapter and, in any event, much of it is more properly the preserve of demographics and sociology. Nonetheless, aspects of these changes will undoubtedly affect the elderly. One of the most basic issues (and one already touched on) concerns shifts in working practices. There will undoubtedly be changes in the socioeconomic backgrounds of retired persons. As noted in Chapter 5, social class and occupation type are predictive of attitudes towards retirement and old age and, accordingly, these may alter. The retired people of the future are also likely to be more highly educated. The rapid expansion of tertiary education from the 1960s onwards means that, in about a decade's time, the first appreciable mass of university graduates will begin drawing their pensions. Also, as noted earlier in this chapter, as the concept of 'work' changes, the functional differences between the employed and the retired are in any case likely to diminish. These arguments are highly speculative, however, and a perusal of 1960s textbooks on the future impact of technology provides a suitable warning. Then there were predictions that, by the 1990s, everyone would either have died from pollution, nuclear war, famine and/or overpopulation, or otherwise they would be living a life of luxury, with every need catered for by robots. It is highly probable that these predictions will be similarly inaccurate. Humanity has a strange habit of finding more work to do when employment opportunities in one area are replaced by automation.

Of greater interest to the psychologist are the likely direct effects of technology on old people. The effects of this can be somewhat anticipated from the impact of previous technological innovations. The by now almost ubiquitous telephone, television and radio allow the elderly access to an outside world which would have been unthinkable for all but the very wealthy 40 years ago. Modern household appliances take much of the strain out of cooking and general housework. These items are financially available to most if not all old people, and undoubtedly they are immensely advantageous. For example, refrigeration and better methods of preserving food reduce the risk of food poisoning when an old person's senses become blunted to the point where they cannot detect food becoming rotten. In shaping leisure activities, the impact of television on modern life cannot be underestimated. Besides being entertaining, television enables old people to see places, plays and concerts which they perhaps are no longer physically or financially robust enough to attend in person. Often, the elderly (especially those living alone) use the television or radio as a comforting background noise without especially attending to the broadcast programme (Stuart-Hamilton & Rabbitt, unpublished). However, there are disadvantages as well. The programmes on the television and radio are primarily geared to the needs and demands of the young. Programmes may either be presented in a manner too lurid for an old person's tastes, or possibly even the basic content may be unappealing (e.g. pop music programmes). This may help to reinforce the impression that the world is generally unsympathetic to the needs of the old. Added to this, media presentation of crime may lead many of the elderly to suppose that the environment is far more hostile and threatening than it really is. Several possible solutions suggest themselves. The most extreme is that television will cease to dominate people's leisure time. Some other form of entertainment may come to supersede it, in the same manner that television once supplanted the radio. A more plausible suggestion is that advances in broadcasting technology will open the way for smaller, more community-oriented broadcasting stations. In this manner, a local station might have a 'box and cox' arrangement, with programmes aimed specifically at the elderly being broadcast during the daytime, with evening viewing being reserved for a younger audience. Arrangements similar to this already exists in some American television companies, with a fair degree of success. Looking further ahead, there is the possibility of two-way interactive broadcasting. Each participant has a camera in their own home, and group discussions and similar participative events can be arranged. Trials of such a system in a small Pennsylvanian community have met with great success (Burns 1988). The advantages of interactive television are obvious for elderly people who are housebound or otherwise fairly immobile. There is also the opportunity to experience media presentations which are specifically geared to old peoples' tastes. However, there are also disadvantages. The first is that for obvious reasons the number of participants has to be kept small, and this may lead to a rather socially claustrophobic feeling. A bigger potential worry is that interactive television may discourage mobile and active elderly people from getting out and about, because while they previously had to travel to meet people, they can now do this without making the effort to leave their own homes. There are obvious advantages to this, but the danger is that this may encourage the healthy elderly to be less active than is good for them.

Other technological changes might also bring mixed blessings. It is tempting to see the advent of computers and other microchipped devices as being a boon to the elderly. Indeed, several ingenious devices are already available. For example, trials of a microchip-controlled pill dispensing device have been carried out. The time at which some drugs are taken is vital for their effectiveness, and because some old people are forgetful, this automated pill box emits a beep at the appropriate time. One can easily envisage a small LCD screen being attached to the box to indicate which pills should be taken. There is of course one minor snag with the device, which is that it relies upon a forgetful person remembering to carry the box with them at all times, because otherwise they might not hear the beep. This is a problem which pervades most gadgetry designed to help the forgetful or otherwise mentally enfeebled elderly – they have to remember to use it. Aides-memoires, be they beeping pill boxes or simple electronic diaries, clearly fall foul of this problem. The problems old people face from a declining prospective memory (see Chapter 3) show the magnitude of the issue facing designers.

Some prospects for the future seem quite benevolent, such as the expert systems packages outlined earlier. However, expert systems require a computer, and where will the computer be located? If elderly people have to make the effort to travel to their doctor's surgery, they will surely want to be treated by a flesh and blood doctor as a reward for their efforts. Alternatively, it is possible that computers may become more widely available, and that old people will be persuaded to have one installed in their home. This in itself is a big assumption, because the majority of uses for a computer are unlikely to fall within the ambit of retired people's interests. For example, they are unlikely to need to do massive numerical calculations or to do a lot of word processing. Equally, the prospect of playing computer games is unlikely to entice many of the elderly. Computers will therefore have to be sold to the elderly on the basis of specific programmes. Will old people really want to buy (potentially expensive) software to deal with being ill? Given that many illnesses will in any case require treatment (and hence human intervention) it is unlikely that the computerised doctor will be anything more than a hypochondriac's toy. Also, the prospect may also seem to many old people to be unjustifiably morbid. Assuming, however, that computerised expert systems are made available to the elderly, there is a further problem that if old people choose these systems, they do so in a dangerous manner. To return to the computerised doctor example. It was noted in Chapter 5 that many old people deny that they are old, and play down the extent of any illnesses they have. A similar air of refusal might pervade their answers to a computer's questions about their condition. Thus, some physical symptoms, which may be indicative of a serious disease, might be glossed over or even denied. A human doctor might detect this from visual cues given by the patient, but a computer cannot do this. Therefore, the system is open to potentially serious abuse.

A further consideration is that much of the new technology is designed for younger adults. Miniaturised electronic gadgets are no doubt a tribute to the designer's art, but they are often too small for an old person to see or to handle efficiently. In Chapter 1 it was noted that the elderly perceptual system loses its ability to process fine detail in any sensory modality, and it thus appears as if many pieces of modern technology are designed to handicap the older person.

Accordingly, technological advances are a mixed blessing to the elderly. While they promise great hope, many of the details of their operation have not been sufficiently thought through. Machines which are designed to help save labour may be impossible to operate or create more harm then good. Medical advances may help cure some illnesses but still leave the elderly vulnerable to others. A medical breakthrough which could delay the ageing process is a mixed blessing because it invites people to extend the time in which they can suffer as well as enjoy life. To imagine that the elderly will automatically be made happier by many of these advances is probably foolishly optimistic.

Conclusion

A view of the future almost inevitably stems from a criticism of the present, and many of the predictions and arguments presented in this chapter are fuelled by the current problems with gerontological research and with the lot of the elderly. However, it would be unfair to conclude from this that something is rotten in the state of the psychology of ageing. The area shows a healthy growth and an agreeably wide range of interests. The predictions presented in this chapter can be divided into two sorts – those which ought to come true and those which might. In the former camp fall those born of criticisms of existing research methods. Researchers *must* stop treating old people as if they are a race apart. Not only is it unscientific, but it is also patronising and divisive. On a milder note, attempts should be made to examine changes in the ageing brain as a complex interactive process. Examining changes in single systems, divorced from the context in which they usually operate is creating at a best an over-simplified and at worst a completely erroneous view. The present approach is analogous to the old chestnut about three blind men examining an elephant – depending upon which part of the animal they felt, the men identified the animal as being like a snake, a tree or a bird (there are other, often ruder versions of the same tale, in case this one is unfamiliar to the reader). Inevitably changing to a multifactorial analysis will lead to problems, and a simple single figure result is unlikely to suffice. However, as the inestimable Mr Wilde wrote, the truth is never pure and rarely simple. The second set of this chapter's predictions concerns possible future changes in technology and attitudes, and how these might affect the elderly. It is improbable that many of the changes described will be readily apparent for several years at least. It is always tempting to think that technology will inevitably shape lives. A possibility rarely considered is that people may simply choose to ignore it. Old people may resist new inventions and gadgets, not because of any inbuilt conservatism (which in any case Chapter 5 showed to be ageist stereotyping) but simply because they cannot see the worth of adopting new practices which are likely to be of only limited use. Perhaps in many ways this is the most optimistic vision one could have of future generations of pensioners – old people standing up for what *they* want, rather than what younger adults are foisting on them 'for their own good'.

If there is a message to be taken from this book it is this:

> *Whether an old person is clever or stupid, content with life or suicidal, healthy or housebound, principally or solely depends upon the genes he or she was born with and how he or she behaved earlier in life. A content old age is a reward, but it is not an automatic right. It can only be reached by approaching the prospect of*

ageing with a clear and open mind. The only psychological aspect which cannot be efficiently controlled is the ageing intellect. Of course there is mental degradation for some (but by no means all) individuals, but not enough to mar a happy and productive retirement. For those who are unmoved by this argument, and still insist on stereotyping the elderly as a homogeneous, inferior group, there remains a final thought. All elderly people are survivors; this is an accolade which a third of younger people will not live long enough to claim. That fact is the only one which describes every old person.

Glossary of Technical Terms

The Glossary contains definitions of all the technical terms printed in bold type in the main body of the text. In addition, it includes definitions of other terms in common (or relatively common) use in the gerontological literature.

An italicised word within a definition indicates that it has its own entry in the Glossary. An entry in bold italics indicates that the term is defined within the definition being read, and that the term's own entry will simply refer the reader back to the definition currently being read.

A-68 Protein found in abnormally high concentration in patients with *dementia of the Alzheimer type*.

AAMI *Age associated memory impairment*.

acceptance of prospect of dying stage See *Kubler-Ross's stages of dying*.

accommodation (vision) The ability to focus at different distances.

acetylcholine Type of *neurotransmitter*.

acquired dysgraphia A profound difficulty in writing (particularly spelling) resulting from brain damage.

acquired dyslexia A profound difficulty in reading resulting from brain damage.

ACS *Acute confusional state*

active life expectancy The average number of years remaining in which members of an *age cohort* can expect to lead an active life.

activity theory The counter-argument to *disengagement theory*, which argues that elderly people should be kept involved and active in the community.

acuity (vision) Ability to focus clearly.

acute brain disfunction *Acute confusional state*

acute brain disorder *Acute confusional state*

acute confusional state (ACS) A major disturbance (usually temporary) in intellect and perception resulting from a general deleterious change in the central nervous system's metabolism (e.g. through fever, intoxication, drug overdose). Can be confused with *dementia*, but its very rapid onset is in itself a sufficiently distinguishing feature. Usually encountered in children and the elderly.

acute crisis phase (of dying) See *Pattison's stages of dying.*

AD *Alzheimer's Disease.*

AD-MID A *dementia* in which the patient displays symptoms of *dementia of the Alzheimer type* and *multi infarct dementia* simultaneously.

ADL *Assessment of daily living.*

aetiology The origin and causes (particularly of disease).

affect Emotion.

afferent (neurons) Carrying signals from the *peripheral nervous system* to the *central nervous system.*

age-appropriate behaviour *Social age.*

age-as-leveller The argument that old age diminishes the perceived differences between socio-economic/ethnic groups.

age associated memory impairment (AAMI) Normal memory decline in old age.

age bias *Age discrimination.*

age cohort A group of people born and raised in the same period of time/history.

age discrimination Unfair bias against a person because of his/her age.

age-equivalent scale Test scores expressed in terms of the proportions of an age group who typically possess them. Thus, whether a person is advanced or retarded for their age can be assessed.

age grading The societal pressures which determine what is considered appropriate for different *social ages.*

age norm The mean score on a test for a given age group, and hence the score one would expect an average member of that age group to achieve.

age normative effect A factor which influences the majority of people at the same point in their lives.

age scale *Age-equivalent scale.*

age set *Age cohort.*

age-specific mortality rate Proportion of people in an age group likely to die before they get too old to be in the said age group.

age stratification Dividing the lifespan into a series of *social ages.*

age x complexity effect The phenomenon that the difference between old and young adults gets disproportionately larger the more complex the task set. See *age x treatment interaction.*

age x process interaction *Age x treatment interaction.*

age x treatment interaction The phenomenon that some psychological skills decline more than others in old age (see *differential preservation* and *preserved differentiation*). Thus: if skill 1 requires mental process X and skill 2 process Y, but skill 1 declines disproportionately more than skill 2 in old age, then process X must be more affected by ageing than is process Y. This is not the same as the *age x complexity* effect, which argues that changing the complexity of items which the same skill has to process has a disproportionate effect on older subjects.

AGECAT A computerised package for assessing the mental state of elderly patients.

ageing Process of change occurring with the passage of time. Usually restricted to changes (often perceived as negative) which occur after adolescence. See *anatomical age, biological age, carpal age, chronological age, distal ageing effects, physiological age, primary ageing, probabilistic ageing, proximal ageing effects, secondary ageing, social age,* and *universal ageing.*

ageing/aging Either spelling is acceptable. However, citizens of the USA tend to use 'aging' and UK inhabitants 'ageing'.

ageism *Age discrimination* (usually refers to discrimination against the elderly).

agerasia Having a *biological age* considerably younger than would be predicted from one's *chronological age* (loosely, looking 'well preserved').

aging See *ageing/aging.*

AIDS dementia *Dementing* symptoms found in some patients in the terminal stages of acquired immune deficiency syndrome (AIDS).

alcoholic dementia (1) Old (and misleading) synonym for *Korsakoff's syndrome.* (2) A *dementia* resulting from long term alcohol abuse, and similar to *Korsakoff's syndrome* although with a different neuroanatomical pattern of decay (this distinction is controversial and not universally accepted).

alexia A complete failure to read or to recognise words or letters (in *dyslexia* there is a partial ability). Only usually seen in brain-damaged individuals.

alpha waves A pattern of electrical activity detected by *EEG* with a frequency between 8 and 12 Hz.

aluminium theory of dementia of the Alzheimer type Brain cells of Alzheimer patients show unusually large concentrations of aluminium, and the incidence of the disease appears to be higher in areas where there is a greater concentration of aluminium in the water. This has led to the theory that the principal cause of *dementia of the Alzheimer type* is the 'poisoning' of the brain with aluminium contamination. However, recent work suggests that this may be an artifact of the manner in which the cells are analysed.

alumni education US term for education schemes for former students (alumni) of an institute of higher education. The courses are intended for intellectual enrichment, rather than for specific postgraduate qualifications, such as a Masters or PhD degree.

Alzheimer-type dementia *Dementia of the Alzheimer type (DAT).*

Alzheimer's Disease (AD) *Dementia of the Alzheimer type.*

ambiguous loss Phenomenon usually encountered in severely *demented* patients, that the afflicted individual exists only physically – there is no sign of a sentient being occupying the body.

amenity migration Moving from one country or area of the country to another because there are better amenities/lifestyle, etc. The term is often used to describe retired people moving to a 'nice place in the country'.

amnesia A failure of memory. Usually arises as a result of *stroke*, head injury, illness (e.g. *dementia*), or poisoning (e.g. chronic alcoholism). Amnesia usually is fairly specific in its effects – e.g. causing a failure to remember events which have occurred after the onset of the illness, or alternatively, a failure to remember events prior to the illness.

anaphoric reference Referring to a previously named person, persons, thing or things by the appropriate noun (e.g. mentioning 'the man' and then in the next sentence citing the same character as 'he').

anatomical age *Biological age,* measured through relatively gross state of body (e.g. bone structure, body build, etc) rather than through *physiological age.* See *carpal age.*

anger at prospect of dying stage See *Kubler-Ross's stages of dying.*

anniversary reaction Negative feelings engendered by it being the anniversary (or general time of year) of an event distressing to a subject (e.g. death of a close friend or relative).

Anomalous Sentences Repetition Test (ASRT) Commercial test designed to identify patients in early stages of *dementia* from those with *pseudodementia.* Subjects are required to repeat sentences spoken by the tester.

anomia A failure to name objects.

antediluvian ageing myth Myth that at some distant time (antediluvian = 'before the flood'), a (usually virtuous and pious) race of people existed, who had incredibly long lifespans. See *hyperborean ageing myth.*

anticholinergic Anything which blocks the action of the cholinergic system. This can lead to severe memory loss, and this information is one of the cornerstones of the *cholinergic hypothesis.*

anticipatory grief Preparing for the death of a loved one.

apathetic (personality) See *passive–dependent personality.*

aphasia A failure of language. See *Broca's aphasia* and *Wernicke's aphasia.*

Aphasia Screening Test Sub-test of the *Halstead-Reitan Neuropsychological Battery,* used to assess for signs of *aphasia.*

apnoea Temporary suspension of breathing, usually in sleep. Commoner in the very young and the very old. Several possible causes.

apportioned grandmother See *Robertson's taxonomy of grandmothers*.

apraxia An inability to recognise objects by touch.

armoured approach personality *Defensiveness personality*.

armoured-defensive personality *Personality* type found in Neugarten et al.'s (1961,1968) studies. Possessors of this type were either ***holding on*** (maintaining a high level of activity to 'defeat' ageing); or ***constricted*** (dwelling on what they had lost through ageing).

arteriosclerotic dementia *Dementia* resulting from cardiovascular causes (e.g. *stroke* and *multi-infarct dementia*).

articulatory loop Previous term for the *phonological loop*.

ASRT *Anomalous Sentences Repetition Test.*

assessment of daily living (ADL) Any method of measuring daily activities, usually with the purpose of identifying memory slips, ability to cope independently, etc.

attention The ability to concentrate on a target item(s) despite distracting stimuli. See *divided attention, selective attention*, and *sustained attention*.

autobiographical memory Memory for events peculiar to one's own life, as opposed to past events which everyone has experienced (i.e., events which have been 'in the news', such as general elections, train crashes). See *flashbulb memory* and *observer memory*.

autoimmune theory of ageing Theory that the ageing body's autoimmune system falters, and begins to attack the body's own cells as if they were infections. See *disposable soma theory of ageing, free radical theory of ageing, Hayflick phenomenon*, and *somatic mutation theory of ageing*.

autonomic (neuron) Carrying signals from the *central nervous system* to bodily systems over which there is little conscious control (e.g. glands, smooth and cardiac muscle).

awareness of dying The degree to which a person is aware s/he has a fatal illness.

baby boom generation *Age cohort* of people born between the mid-1940s and 1960s, when there was an appreciable increase in the birth rate in the USA and other westernised nations.

backward masking A method used in *iconic memory* experiments. A *to-be-remembered* item is presented for a brief period of time on a display screen, and is immediately supplanted by a different image (a 'mask') which has the potential (depending upon its appearance, intensity, etc) to destroy the memory of the to-be-remembered item. This process of disrupting the *memory trace* is called backward masking.

backward span A *short term memory* task in which a list of items is presented to the subject, who must repeat them back in reverse order of presentation – a more sadistic form of the *ordered recall* task.

Baltes's theory of lifespan development A rich and complex theory, devised by psychologist P. Baltes. Argues that development is determined by three factors – purely environmental, purely biological, and mixtures of biological and environmental. These influences express themselves through three strands of development. (1) *normative age-graded development* is the basic developmental pattern one would expect to find in any normal individual (e.g. in terms of *biological ageing*, the onset of puberty, in term of *social ageing*, the effects of retirement on behaviour and attitudes). (2) *normative history-graded development* charts the effects of historical events which would be normally experienced by the whole of the *age cohort* (e.g. experience of food rationing would be normal for most English people in their sixties, but would be unusual for people in their twenties). (3) *non-normative life development* measures the effects of major events unique to an individual's life.

bargaining at prospect of dying stage See *Kubler-Ross's stages of dying.*

BDI *Beck Depression Inventory.*

BDS *Blessed Dementia Scale*

Beck Depression Inventory (BDI) A multiple choice questionnaire, where the subject is required to indicate which of a choice of responses best describes him/herself in relation of a range of potentially depressive attributes.

Behaviour Rating Scale (BRS) See *Clifton Assessment Procedure for the Elderly.*

benign senescent forgetfulness *Age associated memory impairment.*

beta waves A pattern of electrical activity detected by EEG with a frequency above 12 Hz.

Binswanger's disease *Dementia* whose origins are disputed, but whose symptoms are akin to those of *lacunar dementia* (some commentators have argued that they are the same condition).

biographical approach The analysis of the lives of pre-eminent members of professions, etc, to see if there are any common factors to explain their greatness. Has been widely used in *creativity* research.

biological age The body's state of physical development/degeneration. This is gauged against the state of an average person of the same *chronological age.* See *anatomical age, physiological age.*

birth cohort A group of people born in the same period of time. See *cohort.*

Blessed Dementia Scale (BDS) A simple test of intellectual impairment and functioning, usually employed in the assessment of *demented* patients. The test requires the patient to answer some simple memory questions (e.g. 'what is your name?', 'who is the current Prime Minister?') and to perform some simple intellectual tasks (e.g. 'count backwards in steps of three'). Details of how capable the patient is of looking after him- or herself are collected from a *caregiver*. The test provides a useful 'ready reckoner' of how intellectually impaired a patient is, and how much professional nursing care and assistance is required. The Blessed Dementia Scale (named after its author, Dr Blessed) is a British test. The American equivalent is the *Mental Status Questionnaire*, which has nearly the same format.

blood-brain barrier A physiological mechanism which prevents potentially damaging chemicals in the bloodstream from entering the brain.

body transcendence versus body preoccupation In Peck's theory, realising that in old age, bodily fitness and health can no longer be a prime cause of self-esteem.

bovine spongiform encephalopathy (BSE) Degenerative disease of the nervous system in cattle, colloquially known as *mad cow disease*. The cause is unknown – the most popular theory is that it is due to cattle eating feed infected with scrapie, a sheep disease. Some (as yet unproven) suggestions that the disease may be transferrable to humans, and/or may be related to one of the *dementias*.

bradykinesia Very slow movement. A common feature of *Parkinsonism*.

bradylexia Very slow (but not necessarily inaccurate) reading.

brain stem Section of the brain which is the meeting place between the spinal cord and the brain. Besides acting as a relay station between the spinal cord and other areas of the brain, the brain stem controls many life support mechanisms (e.g. blood pressure, respiration).

brick test Semi-serious term for a *creativity* test in which the subject must think of novel uses for an everyday object (often a house brick, hence the name).

Brinley plot A graph of the average response times of old people plotted against those of young people performing the same task.

Broca's aphasia A specific problem with producing speech, resulting from brain damage.

Brown-Peterson task Named after its inventors, the task presents subjects with a list of *to-be-remembered* items, then gives them a distracting task (usually counting backwards in units of 2 or 3), before asking subjects to recall the to-be-remembered items. The task thus assesses *concurrent processing*.

BRS *Behaviour Rating Scale*.

BSE *Bovine spongiform encephalopathy*.

bulimia The urge to eat vast quantities of food.

CAMDEX Cambridge Mental Disorders of the Elderly Examination – a test battery of measures for assessing elderly people for *dementia* and other aspects of mental health and psychological wellbeing.

CAPE *Clifton Assessment Procedure for the Elderly.*

caregiver A person who looks after a patient or child. In the context of this book, the term usually refers to the relative of an elderly patient who is principally responsible for the latter's welfare.

Caregiver Strain Index (CSI) Measure of stress and strain in *caregivers* (usually caregivers of elderly patients).

caretaker (1) *Caregiver* (2) For the benefit of American readers – 'caretaker' is commonly used in British English to denote a janitor, particularly of a school.

carpal age *Chronological age* calculated through state of wrist (carpal) bones.

CAS *Cognitive Assessment Scale.*

cascade model of ageing Model of ageing which argues that changes begin in a relatively slight fashion, and then gather momentum and accelerate in severity.

cataracts A progressive opaqueness of the lens, ultimately causing blindness.

catastrophe theory *error catastrophe theory.*

CBS *Chronic brain syndrome.*

CDR *Clinical Dementia Rating.*

cellular garbage theory Model of ageing which argues that the decline of the elderly body is attributable to the accumulation of 'waste products' from the cells' metabolic processes.

central executive The section of the *working memory* model which controls and oversees the specialist *slave systems*. The central executive is itself a memory store (though of limited capacity).

central nervous system (CNS) The collective term for *neurons* forming the brain and the spinal cord.

cerebellum Area of the brain primarily responsible for balance and co-ordinating movement.

cerebral cortex Usually known by its abbreviated name of *cortex*. The cerebral cortex is the characteristic wrinkled surface of the brain. It is divided into two linked *hemispheres* and can be divided into four regions or lobes which display different functions. The cerebral cortex is responsible for the majority of higher intellectual functioning.

cerebral haemorrhage Bleeding in the brain. See *subdural haematoma.*

cerebrospinal fluid Fluid which cushions and in part supplies the brain with nutrients.

CFQ *Cognitive Failures Questionnaire.*

changing environment effect *Cohort effect.*

choice reaction time The time taken for a subject to make the correct response when there is more than one stimulus, and each stimulus requires a different response. Compare with *simple reaction time.*

cholinergic hypothesis Theory that much of the memory loss in *dementia of the Alzheimer type* can be attributed to depletion of the *cholinergic system.* See *ganglioside, ondansetron,* and *tacrine.*

cholinergic system Shorthand for the network of *neurons* which use the chemical *acetylcholine* as their *neurotransmitter.* About 90 per cent of neurons in the brain are cholinergic.

chronic brain syndrome (CBS) Long-term degeneration of brain tissue, resulting in severe impairment of personality and/or intellectual functioning. Largely synonymous with *dementia.*

chronic living-dying phase (of dying) See *Pattison's stages of dying.*

chronological age The length of time a person has been alive.

chunking A *mnemonic* strategy for making long lists of items easier to remember. Items are grouped ('chunked') into sub-groups of 3 or 4 instead of being treated as a continuous list. Thus, the sequence *1789675401* might be 'chunked' into *178 967 5401.*

circumlocution Talking round the topic in question because the appropriate word cannot be recalled (found to spectacular effect in some *demented* patients).

CJD Creutzfeldt-Jakob Disease.

Clifton Assessment Procedure for the Elderly (CAPE) Test battery consisting of two 'sub-batteries' – the *Cognitive Assessment Scale (CAS)* and the *Behaviour Rating Scale (BRS),* measuring intellectual skills and personality respectively, in elderly subjects (particularly hospital patients and the institutionalised elderly).

Clinical Dementia Rating (CDR) A 'checklist' for assessing the level of functioning a patient suspected of *dementia* is capable of on various tasks. From this, his/her level of impairment, and hence the severity of the dementia can be calculated.

C.N.S. *Central nervous system.*

cognition The study of thought processes (including memory and problem solving).

cognitive Pertaining to *cognition.*

Cognitive Assessment Scale (CAS) See *Clifton Assessment Procedure for the Elderly.*

Cognitive Failures Questionnaire (CFQ) A test, devised by the psychologist Donald Broadbent, which asks subjects to report instances of memory failure in recent everyday life (e.g. forgetting to buy items when shopping).

cohort A group of people raised in the same environment and/or period of time.

cohort effect A difference between age groups which is better attributed to differences in the ways they were raised and educated than to their ages per se.

cohort sequential design *overlapping longitudinal study.*

compensation General and often ill-defined theory that the elderly can compensate for failings in one (usually *fluid intelligence*-based) skill by increasing their reliance on another (usually *crystallised intelligence*-based). See *molar equivalence (ME)*.

complexity effect *Age x complexity effect.*

component efficiency hypothesis Hypothesis that the decline in a skill is due to a decline in one or more of the 'basic' sub-skills governing it.

computed tomography A method of electronically scanning the body (in the context of this book, the brain) and taking the equivalent of X-rays of narrow slices of tissue.

conceptual organisation The ability to treat items at an abstract level in order to uncover basic rules and principles.

concurrent processing Holding items in *working memory* while performing a potentially distracting task at the same time (a common everyday experience is remembering a telephone number while dialling). By changing the nature and/or level of difficulty of the distracting task, the degree of memory loss can be affected. A technique frequently used to test how well subjects can retain information in memory and thus how efficient their intellectual and *mnemonic* skills are. In the working memory model, concurrent processing is held to be controlled by the *central executive.*

confabulating A polite euphemism for 'lying'. Can also imply a deliberate strategy to cover up shortcomings in intellectual performance (e.g. seen in some patients in the early stages of dementia).

constraint seeking strategy In solving a problem (e.g. in a 'twenty questions' game), seeking answers which progressively reduce the set size of all possible answers.

constricted (personality) See *armoured-defensive* personality.

constructiveness *Personality* type discovered by Reichard et al. (1962). Elderly people possessing this *personality trait* had come to terms with their lives, and were prepared to help others.

contextual perspective The belief that ageing effects are in a large part attributable to social and environmental effects rather to a biological process.

contrast sensitivity function (CSF) A measure of the changing ability to focus clearly on a fine pattern of dark and light parallel lines when the relative darkness and lightness of the lines is altered.

corpus callosum The principal link between the left and right *hemispheres* of the brain.

correlation A statistical term which, technically speaking, means how much of the variance in one variable can be predicted by variance in another. In layperson's terms, a correlation describes the strength of the relationship between two variables, and the extent to which a change in one is met by a change in the other. Correlations are represented by the symbol *r*. Correlations can be positive (i.e., as one variable increases, so does the other) or negative (i.e., as one variable increases, the other decreases). Correlations also vary in strength – a value of 0 means that no relationship exists between the variables, a value of 1 indicates a perfect positive correlation (i.e., for every increase in one variable, there is exactly the same increase in the other) and a value of -1 indicates a perfect negative correlation (i.e., every rise in one variable is met with exactly the same fall in the other). In 'real life', correlations fall somewhere between these extremes. The closer the figure is to 1 or -1, the stronger the correlation (typically, a value of .3 or better is taken to be a good indicator). 'Correlation' is not synonymous with 'causation'. There is no method of deciding whether one variable is causing the other to alter. It should also be considered if both might not be governed by a third party (see *partial correlation*). A correlation can only show that two variables are associated with each other. For the mathematically minded: the percentage of the variance in one variable which the other predicts can be easily calculated by squaring *r* and multiplying the result by 100 (e.g. variables A and B correlate at .6; A predicts 36% of B's variance).

Corsi blocks task A test of *visuo-spatial memory*. Subjects are shown an array of blocks positioned on a table. The experimenter taps on some of these blocks in a sequence which the subject is asked to copy. The experimenter gradually increases the length of sequence until the subject's *memory span* is discovered.

cortex See *cerebral cortex*.

cortical Pertaining to the *cerebral cortex*.

cortical dementias *Dementias* whose principal focus of damage is in the *cerebral cortex*.

creativity The ability to produce novel and appropriate ideas and solutions.

Creutzfeldt-Jakob Disease (CJD) A very rare *dementia*, contracted through contact with diseased nervous tissue. In addition to archetypal *demented* symptoms, there are severe disturbances of gait and movement.

critical loss Pertaining to the *terminal drop model*, the theory that a decline in some intellectual abilities can be endured, but that a fall in others constitutes a 'critical loss' which heralds death.

cross-linking theory of ageing Theory that the physical decline of the elderly body can be attributed to a loss of elasticity of tissues (skin, muscles, etc).

cross-sectional research/samples/study This refers to the experimental method where age differences are measured by testing different age groups in the same test period. Contrast with *longitudinal research/samples/study*, and see *overlapping longitudinal study*.

CRT *Choice reaction time.*

crystallised intelligence The amount of factual (as opposed to autobiographical) knowledge a person has acquired during a lifetime – roughly corresponds to the lay term 'general knowledge'.

CSI *Caregiver Strain Index.*

CT/CT scan See *computed tomography.*

cued recall Experimental technique for assessing memory in which the subject is given information about the item s/he is supposed to recall (i.e., s/he is given a 'hint', such as the first letter of a to-be-remembered word).

CV Cardiovascular (i.e., pertaining to the heart and blood vessels).

cytologic theory Theory of ageing that the bodily decline can be attributed to 'poisoning' by toxins (including the waste products of metabolic processes). Compare with *wear and tear theory.*

DAT *Dementia of the Alzheimer type.*

death preparation Preparing for the psychological and practical impact of the death of oneself or of a loved one. Usually helps to lessen the negative effects of the event. To some extent, 'passive' death preparation increases with age, as the probability of dying increases.

defensiveness personality *Personality* type discovered by Reichard et al. (1962). Elderly people possessing this *personality trait* had a strong urge to carry on working to 'prove' they were still young.

delirium See *acute confusional state.*

Delirium Rating Scale (DRS) A test assessing the likelihood that a patient's symptoms indicate *delirium (acute confusional state)* rather than an illness with which it can be easily confused (e.g. *dementia*).

delta waves A pattern of electrical activity detected by *EEG* with a frequency between 0 and 4Hz.

demented Describing the state associated with *dementia.*

demented dyslexia A condition found in some *demented* patients, where they can read aloud perfectly normally, and yet have no understanding of what they are reading.

dementia A global deterioration of intellectual function, resulting from atrophy of the *central nervous system.* The illness takes many forms: the commonest are *dementia of the Alzheimer type* and *multi-infarct dementia.* In some (older) textbooks, 'dementia' refers purely to those cases arising in pre-*senile* patients, and 'senile dementia' to cases in senile patients. This distinction is now largely disregarded.

dementia of the Alzheimer type Form of *dementia* whose symptoms have a characteristic pattern, first described by Alois Alzheimer in the 1900s.

dementia praecox Now outmoded term (invented by Emil Kraeplin 1883) for the illness now known as schizophrenia (the term 'schizophrenia' was invented by Bleuler 1911). The term means 'pre-senile dementia', but should not be confused with the condition now graced with that name.

dementia pugilistica *Pugilistic dementia.*

dementia syndrome of depression (DSD) *Pseudodementia.*

denial of dying stage See *Kubler-Ross's stages of dying.*

dental age Calculation of *chronological age* from the state of the subject's teeth. Useful for dead humans and live horses.

dependency ratio The ratio of working to non-working members of the population.

dependent personality *Personality* type discovered by Reichard et al. (1962). Elderly people possessing this *personality trait* had some life satisfaction, but relied on others to help them.

depression at prospect of dying stage See *Kubler-Ross's stages of dying.*

depression with cognitive impairment *Pseudodementia.*

depressive pseudodementia *Pseudodementia.*

deterioration quotient (DQ) Measure of rate of intellectual decline associated with ageing, first devised by Wechsler. Sections of the WAIS (or indeed many other intelligence test batteries) can be divided into those measuring *crystallised intelligence* (held to be unaffected by ageing), and those measuring *fluid intelligence* (held to decline with ageing). These can also be referred to as ***hold tests*** and ***don't hold tests*** respectively. The DQ is calculated as {[(score on hold tests) − (score on don't hold tests)]/(score on hold tests)} x 100. A phenomenon of the WAIS is that hold and don't hold scores are equal in early adulthood. Hence, the bigger the gap in an old person's hold and don't hold test scores, the greater the deterioration. The DQ expresses this change as a percentage. See *efficiency quotient.*

Dewey's paradox of ageing John Dewey, philosopher, argued that 'we are... in the unpleasant and illogical condition of extolling maturity and depreciating age' (Dewey 1939).

Diagnostic and Statistical Manual of Mental Disorders Usually known by its abbreviation of DSM, followed by the suffix of the edition in question. At the time of writing, the current edition is the 3rd, which has been revised, and is therefore known as *DSM III-R* (American Psychiatric Association 1987). The DSM is the American Psychiatric Association's classification of all mental illnesses and handicaps. It is a hugely influential publication, not only in the USA, but also worldwide. The DSM lists the major symptoms which characterise and distinguish between different mental illnesses and handicaps. It also takes note of life events and physical illnesses which may exacerbate or ameliorate the condition a patient is suffering from. The DSM can be criticised for paying too much attention to the disease and not enough to the patient, but as an objective taxonomy, it is still the best available.

dichotic listening task A measure of divided attention. Subjects hear (via stereo headphones) different messages in either ear, and must then report what they have heard in either ear.

diencephalon Also called the *interbrain*. A collective term for a number of key segments of the brain 'sandwiched' between the *brain stem, cerebellum* and *cortex*. More important areas include the *thalamus, hypothalamus* and *hippocampus*.

differential preservation The theory that some intellectual skills may be preserved better than others in ageing. However, see *preserved differentiation*. See *age x treatment interaction*.

digit span *Memory span* for numbers.

digit-symbol test A member of the *Wechsler Adult Intelligence Test* battery, which assesses the ability to learn an arbitrary matching of abstract symbols and numbers.

disease cohort A group of people suffering from the same disease. See *cohort, patient cohort*.

disengaged (personality) See *integrated personality*.

disengagement theory The theory that elderly people seek to lose much of their contact with the outside world, in preparation for death. See *activity theory*.

disorganised personalities *Personality* type found in Neugarten et al.'s (1961,1968) studies. Possessors of this type were not capable of normal functional behaviour.

disposable soma theory of ageing The theory that the body 'sacrifices' replacing all somatic (non-reproduction) cells lost through natural 'wear and tear' to concentrate on reproductive fitness. This, it is argued, is the evolutionary force which 'causes' ageing. See *autoimmune theory of ageing, free radical theory of ageing, Hayflick phenomenon*, and *somatic mutation theory of ageing*.

distal ageing effects Ageing changes attributable to relatively distant events (e.g. poor self-image in old age because of childhood bullying) or events which are only felt through several intermediaries. See *proximal ageing effects*.

distracters See *target*.

disuse theories of ageing Theories which argue that intellectual skills worsen in old age because they are not practised frequently enough.

divergent thinking Usually associated with *creativity*. The ability to create ideas and solutions stemming from a simple proposition or problem.

divided attention The ability to attend to and process information from more than one source simultaneously.

don't hold tests See *deterioration quotient (DQ)*.

dopamine Type of *neurotransmitter*.

double ABCX model An attempt to account for the stress induced in a family by a major crisis befalling one of its older members. The letters refer to variables expressing the seriousness of the crisis, the amount of available help, etc.

double jeopardy Term denoting the problem faced by elderly members of an ethnic minority who face not only *ageism* but racism as well.

DRS *Delirium Rating Scale.*

DSD *dementia syndrome of depression.*

DSM III-R *Diagnostic and Statistical Manual of Mental Disorders*, 3rd Edition, Revised.

Duke Longitudinal Study 20 years *longitudinal study* of community residents aged 50+ years in Raleigh-Durnham, North Carolina, USA.

dying trajectory (1) The speed with which a person is likely to die. (2) The emotional and intellectual states associated with dying.

dysarthria Disorder of muscular control of speech (and often of skills associated with the same muscles, such as eating and drinking).

dyscalculia A profound problem with arithmetical skills. Can be developmental or acquired as the result of brain damage in adulthood.

dyslexia A profound reading problem (though note there is evidence of some reading ability). The syndrome can be inherited (developmental dyslexia) or can be acquired through brain damage (acquired dyslexia).

dyslogia Poor spoken articulation.

dysphasia A profound spelling problem.

dysphonia Disorder of voice production.

E *Extroversion–introversion.*

echolalia Abnormal repetition of what has just been said.

ecogenic An event not tied to a particular historical epoch. See *epogenic.*

ecological validity The degree to which a study's findings bear any relevance to everyday life.

EEG See *electroencephalograph.*

efferent (neurons) Carrying signals from the *central nervous system* to the *peripheral nervous system.*

efficiency quotient (EQ) Measure of an old person's intellectual abilities relative to the performance of young adults, who are assumed to be at the peak of their abilities. Basically, it is the IQ which the young adult would be recorded as possessing, if s/he had the same raw score as an elderly subject. E.g. an elderly man has a raw test score of 95, which is good for his age group, and gives him an IQ of 130. However, a score of 95 would be a poor score for a young adult, and would give him/her an IQ of 70. The old person's EQ is therefore classed as 70. By comparing EQ with IQ, a measure of the extent of a person's age-related decline in intelligence can be calculated. However, a more useful single measure is probably the *deterioration quotient*.

ego In Freudian theory, a person's rational self. See also *id* and *superego*.

ego differentiation versus work-role preoccupation In Peck's theory, coming to terms with retirement, and realising that status is no longer conferred by one's employment.

ego integration See *integrity versus despair*.

ego transcendence versus ego preoccupation In Peck's theory, coming to terms with the fact that one is inevitably going to die.

elder abuse Abuse of the elderly, particularly those who are mentally enfeebled. The abuse can be physical, but also psychological or financial (e.g. extorting money). See *granny bashing*.

eldering Ageing in terms of *social age*.

elderspeak The use of patronising 'baby talk' by younger people talking to the elderly.

electroencephalograph Often (understandably) shortened to *EEG*, this is a device which measures the pattern of electrical activity on the scalp and by extrapolation, of the *cerebral cortex* underneath. The rate of activity and where on the scalp it occurs can give some insight into how active and healthy an individual's brain is.

encoding The process of creating a *memory trace*.

encopresis Faecal incontinence. See *enuresis*.

enuresis Urinary incontinence. See *encopresis*.

episodic memory A term devised by Tulving (1972) to denote memory for events from a person's own life. Compare with *semantic memory* and *autobiographical memory*.

epogenic An event unique to a particular historical epoch. See *ecogenic*.

EPQ *Eysenck Personality Questionnaire*.

EQ *efficiency quotient*.

error catastrophe theory Model of ageing which attributes bodily decline in old age to faulty replication of proteins.

ethnogerontology The study of ageing in different ethnic/cultural groups.

etiology See *aetiology*.

excitatory (neurons) An excitatory *neuron* either: (a) causes (almost invariably in combination with other excitatory neurons) another neuron to become active and/or (b) makes a neuron already active to send signals at a faster rate.

explicit memory Memory which is consciously retrieved/searched for. Contrast with *implicit memory*, which is the recall of items or the use of memorised information which the subject is unaware of recalling or even possessing.

extroversion See *extroversion–introversion*.

extroversion–introversion A *personality trait* from *Eysenck's personality model*, measuring the degree to which a person is outgoing and self-confident (*extroverted*) or shy and retiring (*introverted*).

extrovert Person possessing *extroversion*.

extroverted Adjective of *extroversion*.

Eysenck Personality Questionnaire A test to assess the degree to which a person possesses the *personality traits* of *Eysenck's personality model*.

Eysenck's personality model A model of *personality* which argues that personality is composed of a mix of three *personality traits* – *extroversion–introversion, neuroticism* and *psychoticism*.

Famous Names Test (FNT) A measure of *remote memory*. Subjects are presented with a list of names of people famous for brief periods of time since the 1920s, and are asked to identify those names which they can remember being 'in the news' at some point in the past. Included in the list are some fictitious names, to prevent subjects *confabulating* and saying 'yes' to every name on the list. The test also includes a set of very famous names (Margaret Thatcher, Winston Churchill, etc) who have been famous for appreciable periods of time. These names are always recognised by normal individuals, but may cause problems for some patients suffering from certain types of *amnesia* or *dementia*.

FAST model Model by Reisberg et al. (1989) which describes 7 stages of progressively worsening intellectual deterioration found in patients suffering from *dementia of the Alzheimer type*.

feeling of knowing (FOK) A person's understanding of his or her own level of knowledge (i.e., how good he or she feels his or her knowledge is).

flashbulb memory Term devised by R. Brown to denote an *autobiographical* memory of a key event in one's life, which is perceived as being unusually vivid (like a photo taken with a flashbulb). There is considerable debate over whether such memories are qualitatively different from others, or whether they have simply been recalled many more times, therefore making them appear unusually vivid.

fluid intelligence The ability to solve problems for which there are no solutions derivable from formal training or cultural practices. There is usually an added assumption that to have a high level of fluid intelligence, a person must solve the said problems quickly. Fluid intelligence roughly corresponds to layperson's concepts of 'wit'.

FNT *Famous Names Test.*

focused (personality) See *integrated personality*.

FOK *Feeling of Knowing*.

formal operations In Piaget's theory of cognitive development, the period from 11 years + when the child begins to think in genuinely abstract terms.

fourth age Period of old age (usually during terminal illness, *dementia*, etc) when the person is dependent on others for basic welfare provision. See *third age*.

free radical theory of ageing Free radicals are ions (charged atomic particles) which are produced in chemical reactions in the body. The theory argues that the free radicals damage the cells and their *chromosomes*, thereby causing physical degeneration. Some theorists argue that consuming extra daily quantities of vitamin C will offset these effects. See *autoimmune theory of ageing, disposable soma theory of ageing, Hayflick phenomenon*, and *somatic mutation theory of ageing*.

free recall A memory task in which items can be recalled in any order (i.e., the order in which they were originally presented does not have to be reproduced). Compare with *ordered recall*.

frontal lobes The front section of the *cerebral cortex* extending back to the temples. Primarily involved in planning and controlling actions and thoughts (e.g. by getting words in the right order when speaking, producing socially appropriate behaviour).

functional age The average age at which a particular set of abilities are found (i.e. it measures how well an individual performs relative to his/her age group).

g General intellectual capacity – a term devised by Spearman to describe a general intellectual ability which, he felt, underpinned all intellectual skills. Today often used more loosely to denote subjects' general level of intelligence.

ganglioside Drug whose effects include the enhanced release of acetylcholine (a key neurotransmitter in the brain – see *cholinergic hypothesis*). Has been cited as a possible treatment for patients suffering from *dementia*. See *ondansetron* and *tacrine*.

Gc/gc Symbol for *crystallised intelligence*.

GDS *Geriatric Depression Scale*.

general slowing hypothesis *speed hypothesis*.

Geriatric Depression Scale (GDS) A 'yes–no' questionnaire measuring the level of depression in the respondent. The questions are geared to match the symptoms and lifestyles typically found in depressed elderly people.

Geriatric Mental State (GMS) A standardised interview package for assessing the mental state of elderly patients.

geriatrics Medical treatment and study of ageing. See *gerontology*.

geronting Ageing in terms of *psychological ageing*.

gerontologists Practitioners of *gerontology*.

gerontology The study of old age. The term is usually restricted to psychological and sociological aspects of ageing.

Gf/gf Symbol for *fluid intelligence.*

Gibson Spiral Maze A test of *psychomotor* skill, in which the subject is required to trace a pencil line around a spiral shaped path as quickly as possible.

glaucoma An excess accumulation of fluid in the eyeball, increasing pressure on retinal cells, leading to their (permanent) destruction.

GMS *Geriatric Mental State.*

Gorham Proverb Interpretation Test Commercial measure of intelligence through ability to interpret proverbs. See *proverb interpretation.*

graceful degradation The phenomenon that the cell loss which accompanies ageing is reflected in a gentle loss of memories and level of skill (rather than a wholesale and absolute loss).

granny bashing Slang term for physical *elder abuse.*

granny dumping Slang term for the process whereby caregivers (usually sons and/or daughters), who cannot cope with looking after an elderly relative, abandon him/her to the local authorities (sometimes literally leaving him/her on the doorstep of the local hospital/social services office).

granulovacuolar degenerations Malformed (and usually dead) *neurons* which (under a microscope) look like dense granules.

greying population Term describing the increasing proportion of elderly people in industrialised nations.

Hachinski Ischaemic Score (IS) A diagnostic technique for distinguishing *dementias* of cardiovascular origin, and specifically, *multi infarct dementia.* Patients are scored on the number of symptoms they display (and some, more indicative, symptoms are weighted). A score of seven or more is taken to indicate multi-infarct dementia.

Halstead-Reitan Neuropsychological Battery (HRNB) A battery of neuropsychological tests, assessing abstract reasoning, linguistic, sensory, visuo-spatial, and motor skills.

Hayflick limit See *Hayflick phenomenon.*

Hayflick phenomenon Named after its discoverer, L. Hayflick. Living cells taken from a body can be reared in a laboratory, and will reduplicate a limited number of times (the *Hayflick limit*). The older the animal from which the cells are taken, the lower this number is. This implies that the upper limit of life expectancy may be due to the simple fact that the body's cells can only reduplicate a limited number of times. See *autoimmune theory of ageing, disposable soma theory of ageing, free radical theory of ageing,* and *somatic mutation theory of ageing.*

integrated personality *Personality* type found in Neugarten et al.'s (1961,1968) studies. Possessors of this type were of three kinds: *reorganisers* (finding new things to do as old ones became impractical); *focused* (activities were restricted to a small scope, but were rewarding); or *disengaged* (deliberately avoiding responsibility).

integrity versus despair In Erickson's theory, a conflict which has to be resolved in old age – whether to come to terms with one's past (*ego integration*) or to feel that past events cannot be amended.

intellectual realism Term (first used by G.H. Luquet 1927) describing drawings or pictures in which the 'true' state of the objects is represented, rather than drawing what can actually be seen ('perceptual realism'). The term is used particularly of young children's drawings. A common example is that in drawing two objects, one placed slightly behind the other so that not all of it can be seen, the children draw both objects in their entirety.

intelligence quotient Often (erroneously) used as a synonym for 'intelligence'. The intelligence quotient is used to denote how intelligent a person is, in comparison with the rest of his or her age cohort. Traditionally, a score of 100 has denoted a person of average intelligence for his/her age cohort – i.e. 50 per cent of the group are cleverer, 50 per cent are less clever then this person. A score of more than 130 indicates someone who is exceptionally bright for the group (i.e., there are few people in the age group with better scores) and a score of 70 or below indicates someone who is unusually stupid. What is often overlooked is that the intelligence quotient is a relative scale. It is known that test scores decrease in old age. Thus, an old person may score 25 per cent less than when s/he was younger. However, his/her *intelligence quotient* may remain the same, because the rest of the subject's age group is also in decline and thus, the subject's relative position within the age cohort remains the same. Hence, intelligent quotients may remain fairly stable across age because they adjust to what in absolute terms is a large decline in ability.

interbrain See *diencephalon*.

introversion See *extroversion–introversion*.

introvert Person possessing *introversion*.

introverted Adjective of *introversion*.

intrusions When referring to linguistic errors in *demented* patients – an inappropriate response which is the repeat of a reply to an earlier question.

IQ *Intelligence quotient.*

irregular spelling A word has an irregular spelling if its pronunciation by normal rules (i,e, how one might try to pronounce the word if one had never seen it before) is different from the way it is supposed to be pronounced. Examples of irregular spelling abound in English – 'quay', 'misled', etc. It follows that the only way to pronounce irregular spellings is to learn them – working from logical first principles is not an effective strategy.

IS *Hachinski Ischaemic Score.*

Ischaemic Rating Scale *Hachinski Ischaemic Score.*

Kendrick Battery for the Detection of Dementia in the Elderly Early version (1972) of the *Kendrick Cognitive Tests for the Elderly.*

Kendrick Cognitive Tests for the Elderly Test battery for identifying dementia in subjects aged 55 year +. Consists of two tests. The ***Kendrick Object Learning Test (KOLT)*** is a memory test for arrays of pictures which vary in number of pictures per array, and the time over which the memories must be retained. The ***Kendrick Digit Copying Test (KDCT)*** measures the speed at which the subject copies a set of 100 numbers.

Kendrick Digit Copying Test (KDCT) See *Kendrick Cognitive Tests for the Elderly.*

Kendrick Object Learning Test (KOLT) See *Kendrick Cognitive Tests for the Elderly.*

Kluver-Bucy syndrome A collection of abnormal behaviours, including *hyperorality, bulimia, visual agnosia, hypermatamorphosis,* and loss of *affect.*

Korsakoff's syndrome (KS) Severe amnesia (particularly for new information), resulting from long term alcohol abuse coupled with vitamin deficiency through poor diet. Damage is particularly centred in the hippocampus. Korsakoff patients are commonly used as a control group in studies of *dementia.*

Kreutzfeld-Jakob Disease *Creutzfeldt-Jakob Disease.*

KS *Korsakoff's syndrome.*

Kubler-Ross's stages of dying Psychological stages exhibited by dying people, identified by E. Kubler-Ross. Consist of *denial* of the possibility of death, followed by *anger. Bargaining* follows (pleas to the deity, fate, etc), followed by *depression,* and finally, *acceptance.* See *Pattison's stages of dying.*

lacunar deficits The phenomenon, sometimes encountered in brain-damaged patients, where some intellectual functions are almost completely destroyed, while others remain relatively intact.

lacunar dementia (LD) Some (though not all) commentators argue that patients suffering from *multi-infarct dementia,* and who exhibit *lacunar deficits,* should be reclassified as suffering from lacunar dementia. See *Binswanger's disease.*

late adult transition The period surrounding retirement.

late paraphrenia Mental disorder of the elderly, whose symptoms are principally feelings of persecution, and elaborate fantasies of the same. Commoner in women. Can have a variety of causes, including circulation problems and previous episodes of mental illness.

LD *Lacunar dementia.*

letter strings Groups of letters which may or may not form real words.

Lewy body A form of damage found in the brain cells of some *demented* patients (particularly those suffering from *Parkinson's Disease*). Under a microscope, the Lewy body is a round body comprised of a dense packet surrounded by looser filaments.

Lewy body disease A proposed (though as yet not universally accepted) category of *dementia* attributable to the presence of *Lewy bodies.*

lexical decision task A very heavily used psychological experimental method. Subjects are shown *letter strings* and asked to judge as quickly as possible if the strings form real words or not. Note that the subjects do not have to judge what a discovered real word 'says'.

life crisis A set of profoundly negative feelings created by the transition from one *social age* to another (e.g. upon retiring).

life expectancy How much longer an average person can expect to live. More accurately, the age at which 50% of an *age cohort* is predicted to have died. Contrast with *lifespan.*

lifespan The maximum age which a member of a species can be expected to live for. Contrast with *life expectancy.*

living will Signed and witnessed declaration by a person that in the event of becoming so ill as to be placed on a 'life support' system, that such apparatus be switched off if there is no prospect of a satisfactory recovery.

long term memory The brain's permanent store of information, as opposed to the transitory *short term memory / working memory* stores. Long term memory is often defined (though not entirely accurately) as memory for events which occurred longer than a few minutes ago. Long term memory is often classified according to the nature of the subject matter being recalled – see entries for *autobiographical, episodic, prospective, remote,* and *semantic memory.*

longitudinal research/samples/study The experimental method of testing the same group of people at different ages. Contrast with *cross-sectional research / samples / study.* See *overlapping longitudinal study,* and *sequential research design.* See *time-lag comparison.*

loudness recruitment Sounds in a particular frequency band (usually high) are (mis)interpreted as being louder then usual, sometimes to the point of being painful.

LTM *Long term memory.*

macular degeneration The degeneration and ultimate loss of the eye's 'yellow spot' or macula, which is responsible for the highest resolution of focusing in the eye.

mad cow disease *Bovine spongiform encephalopathy.*

matching (subjects) Groups of test subjects are especially chosen because they have identical scores on some vital parameter(s). Such groups are said to be *matched* for the parameter(s) in question, and any difference between them on tests cannot be attributed to the said parameter(s). This narrows down the range of explanations for a group difference, if one is found. For example, two groups might be selected so that they have the same level of education. If it is then discovered that the two groups differ in intelligence level, this cannot be attributed to educational level. This leaves the experimenter free to search for other explanations.

ME *Molar equivalence.*

ME-MD strategy See *molar equivalence (ME).*

memory span The longest list of items which a subject can reliably remember. Researchers vary in their interpretation of 'reliably' – some hold that the memory span is the longest list which can be consistently remembered, while others take it to be the list length which is correctly remembered on 50 per cent of occasions. 'Span' usually has a prefix denoting the type of items remembered – see *digit span, verbal span,* and *word span.*

memory trace The storage of a memory.

mental capacity The limit on how much information a mind can process at any one time, and/or how quickly it can process information. The term is a useful conceptual notion, but producing an objective, accurate measure of it is often impossible. It can be estimated, however, and it is known that it differs between individuals (generally, young adults can process more information at a faster rate than e.g. children and elderly people), and within individuals across time (e.g. capacity often declines in old age).

Mental Status Questionnaire Devised by Kahn et al. (1960), a simple assessment of a (usually demented) patient's intellectual status and degree of functional independence. See *Blessed Dementia Scale.*

metaknowledge See *Feeling of Knowing.*

metamemory A person's knowledge about their own *mnemonic* abilities – their strengths and weaknesses, their capacity, methods of making *to-be-remembered* items more memorable, etc.

method of loci A technique for improving *long term memory.* First devised by the Ancient Greeks, the technique involves juxtaposing the *to-be-remembered* items into mental pictures of familiar scenes (e.g. familiar street scenes). By taking an imaginary 'walk' through these scenes, the to-be-remembered items should be readily 'visible' to the mind's eye.

MID *Multi-infarct dementia.*

Mill Hill Vocabulary Test A measure of vocabulary, the test requires subjects to provide definitions of words, whose obscurity increases as the test progresses (there is no time limit). Commonly used as a measure of *crystallised intelligence.*

Mini Mental State Examination (MMSE) A quickly-administered assessment of the general intellectual state of a patient. Questions include measures of orientation for time and place, basic tests of short term memory, ability to name common objects, etc. The test is scored out of 30, with a score of 23 or less taken as indicative of sub-normal functioning.

Minnesota Multiphasic Personality Inventory (MMPI) Personality test, yielding scores on a ten scales, which are indices of (principally abnormal) personality traits.

mitochondria Sub-cellular particles which generate energy within a cell.

MMPI *Minnesota Multiphasic Personality Inventory.*

MMSE *Mini Mental State Examination.*

mnemonic Pertaining to memory.

molar equivalence (ME) A *molar skill* is one which can be decomposed into a number of sub-skills (*molecular decomposition (MD)*). E.g. playing croquet is a molar skill, since it can be decomposed into sub-skills (e.g. planning of future moves; aiming of mallet; strategic knowledge based on past experience, etc). If a molar skill is performed equally well by groups of widely differing ages, then 'molar equivalence' is said to have occurred. If molar equivalence occurs even though some of the sub-skills can be shown to be worse in one of the age groups (e.g. old croquet players are less good at aiming the mallet) then a *ME-MD strategy* (or *compensation*) is said to have occurred (e.g. because the older players have a better strategic skill which compensates for other shortcomings).

molar skill See *molar equivalence.*

molecular decomposition (MD) See *molar equivalence.*

morphology Strictly speaking, the science of form. Used in *dementia* research to denote an awareness of word meanings and word structure.

motor (neurons) Carrying signals from the *central nervous system* to skeletal muscle. Sometimes inaccurately used to denote all signals emanating from the central nervous system (however, see *autonomic*).

motor skills Ability to move and control bodily movements. 'Fine motor skills' describes control of relatively delicate movements (e.g. manual dexterity, holding and manipulating small objects).

MSQ *Mental Status Questionnaire.*

multi-infarct dementia A form of *dementia*, caused by the brain suffering a large number of *infarcts*. Patients typically suffer a stepwise rather than gradual pattern of decline.

N *Neuroticism.*

naming latency The speed with which a subject can read a word aloud.

NART *National Adult Reading Test.*

National Adult Reading Test (NART) A list of words, most with very *irregular spellings*, which the subjects are required to read out loud (i.e. pronounce). The more words correctly pronounced, the higher the test score.

negative correlation A value of *r* falling below zero and greater than or equal to -1. See *correlation.*

neural noise Concept that neural signals lose some of their fidelity because of interfering signals from neighbouring neurons, and a general failure of insulation of neurons. This is assumed to make mental processing less efficient. Neural noise is held to be inversely related to intelligence (i.e., the brighter the person, the less the noise), and to worsen in old age (due to a general worsening in the 'quality' of nervous tissue).

neuritic plaque *Senile plaque.*

neurofibrillary tangles (NFT) Clumps of dead central nervous system *neurons* which (under a microscope) look like knotted string. Caused by abnormal protein metabolism.

neuronal Adjective derived from *neuron*, hence a term describing anything pertaining to the nervous system.

neuron/neurone An individual 'nerve' or 'nerve cell' (strictly speaking, a 'nerve' is a collection of neurons forming a common path for sending messages; usually the term is reserved for neuronal structures not in the brain, and the term 'tract' is used for such structures within the brain).

neuroticism As used in this book, *a personality trait* from *Eysenck's personality model.* Neuroticism measures how anxious and emotionally unstable a person is.

neurotransmitters Chemicals transmitted between *neurons* at *synapses*. The means by which neurons communicate with each other.

NFT Neurofibrillary tangle.

NINCDS-ADRDA criteria A set of criteria for evaluating the probability that a patients is suffering from *dementia of the Alzheimer type*. The initials refer to the 'National Institute of Neurological and Communicative Disorders and Stroke' and the 'Alzheimer's Disease and Related Disorders Association of America', the two bodies who jointly devised the scheme. It provides a diagnosis of 'probable', 'possible' or 'definite'.

'noise' in nervous system *Neural noise.*

non-normative life development See *Baltes's theory of lifespan development.*

noradrenalin *A neurotransmitter.*

noradrenergic system Shorthand for network of neurons using *noradrenalin* as their *neurotransmitter*. Primarily used in the control of smooth muscle.

normal distribution A distribution of scores which has a characteristic curve with one peak above the horizontal axis, and whose left and right halves are symmetrical. It also has the property that the statistical measures of the mean (the average), the median (the point at which half the sample have lower scores and half higher) and the mode (the commonest single score) are equal. Because the distributions of a great many 'natural' variables (e.g. height, weight, IQ) assume this pattern, it has been accepted as the norm (hence its name). However, this does not mean that other shapes of distributions are somehow 'aberrant'.

normal pressure hydrocephalus Caused by the failure of *cerebrospinal fluid* to drain away, leading to a destructive pressure on *brain tissue*. The complaint can lead to *demented* symptoms.

normative age-graded development See *Baltes's theory of lifespan development.*

normative history-graded development See *Baltes's theory of lifespan development.*

Object Memory Evaluation (OME) Measure of memory for objects. The subject is presented with a set of everyday objects, and is asked to recall them at short (30 or 6- seconds) and long (5 minutes) intervals. Five learning trials are given, and measures are taken of which items are recalled on which trial (and which are not).

observer memory The phenomenon that one's distant *autobiographical memories* are usually recalled as if one was a bystander.

obsolescence effect Theory that some of the 'deterioration' in old age may be because older people's mental strategies are no longer in tune with the modern world (i.e. are obsolescent), rather than decayed per se. I.e., ageing changes may be due to qualitative changes in mental strategies.

occipital lobes The region of the *cerebral cortex* roughly in the region of the back of the head. Their principal function is in visual perception.

old age dependency ratio The number of people aged 60 and over divided by the number aged 20–64 in a given population. This gives an indication of how many people are working and hence helping to support pensions and other welfare provisions for the elderly.

old elderly Most commonly defined as those individuals aged over 75 years (though some commentators differ over this figure). See also *young elderly.*

OME *Object Memory Evaluation.*

ondansetron Drug whose effects include the enhanced release of acetylcholine (a key neurotransmitter in the brain – see *cholinergic hypothesis*). Has been cited as a possible treatment for patients suffering from *dementia.* See *ganglioside* and *tacrine.*

ordered recall A memory task in which items have to be recalled in exactly the order they were originally presented in. Compare with *free recall.*

overlapping longitudinal study An attempt to overcome the pitfalls of the *cross-sectional research* and *longitudinal research* methods. Different age groups of subjects are tested and compared, and then retested some time (usually years) later. At each testing, the different age groups can be compared, as in a cross-sectional study (e.g. a group of 40-year-old subjects can be compared with a group of 60-year-old subjects). Also, however, the same *age cohort's* scores can be compared across test periods (e.g. an the scores of a group of subjects who were 40 on the first test session and 60 on the next can be compared). This enables researchers to keep a check on possible *cohort effects*. E.g. suppose that on retesting, the 40-year-old subjects have scores 20 per cent higher than the 60-year-old subjects. This might seem to indicate an age decline. However, suppose it is found that the scores of the 60-year-old group, when they were 40, were only 5 per cent higher. This indicates that a principal cause of the difference is not ageing per se, but rather that the two age groups have been reared differently.

P *Psychoticism.*

paired associate learning Remembering which item was previously presented with (paired with) which (e.g. the subject sees the words *cat* and *briefcase* presented together; later, the subject is shown the word *cat* and is asked which word appeared with it).

parietal lobes The region of the *cerebral cortex* which occupies an area contiguous with an Alice band across the head. Their role is hard to concisely define, but they can be said to be involved in maintaining an awareness of the body's state and location, and in interpreting symbols (e.g. object recognition and some aspects of reading).

Parkinsonian dementia Any *dementia* in which symptoms of *Parkinsonism* are present.

Parkinsonism A set of symptoms, including a shuffling gait and trembling hands, *bradykinesia*, and *hypokinesia*, typically found in *Parkinson's Disease* (hence its name), but also in other illnesses (e.g. *dementia of the Alzheimer type*).

Parkinson's Disease (PD) Illness, caused by a decline in the substantia nigra, an area of the brain responsible for producing *dopamine*. The characteristic symptoms of the illness have the group description of *Parkinsonism*.

partial correlation A statistical technique for assessing how much of the *correlation* between two variables is due to the co-incidental effect of a third variable.

partialled out The process whereby the coincidental effect of a third variable is mathematically removed from the correlation between two variables. See *partial correlation* and *correlation*.

passive-dependent personality *Personality* type found in Neugarten et al.'s (1961,1968) studies. Possessors of this type relied on others to help them (*succourant seeking*) or withdrew from human interaction as much as possible (*apathetic*).

passive euthanasia Allowing someone to die by not administering life-saving or life-prolonging treatment.

patient cohort A group of people with not only illness in common, but also a set of attitudes (e.g. feeling 'unhealthy'). Compare with *cohort* and *disease cohort*.

Pattison's stages of dying Psychological stages which a dying person passes through, identified by E.M. Pattison (1977) (1) *acute crisis phase* – great anxiety upon realising that death is imminent. (2) *chronic living-dying phase* – a period of mourning for what is being lost. (3) *terminal phase* – an inward withdrawal and resignation/acceptance. See *Kubler-Ross's stages of dying*.

PD *Parkinson's Disease.*

peg board task There are several variants of this test of *psychomotor* skill, but the central feature of all of them is that the subject is required to put pegs into holes as quickly as possible.

peripheral nervous system (PNS) Neurons connecting the *central nervous system* to the rest of the body.

perseverations When referring to linguistic errors in *demented* subjects – the inappropriate and immediate repetition of a phrase.

personality 'The individual characteristics and ways of behaving that, in their organization or patterning, account for an individual's unique adjustments, to his or her total environment' (Hilgard, Atkinson & Atkinson 1979).

personality trait An enduring characteristic of *personality* which is hypothesised to underpin behaviour.

PET/PET scan See positron emission tomography.

PHI *Profound hearing impairment.*

phoneme The smallest unit of speech whose substitution or removal from a word causes a change in the word's sound. More loosely, the basic sounds which make up words (and even more loosely, the verbal equivalent of letters).

phonological Pertaining to *phonemes*.

phonological loop *Slave system* in the *working memory* model. A temporary memory store of any information capable of being stored *phonologically* (i.e. words, letters, and numbers).

phonology Strictly speaking, the study of phonetics. Term used in *dementia* research to denote an awareness of phonological structure.

physiological age *Biological age* expressed through the state of the body's physiological processes (e.g. metabolic rate). See *anatomical age*.

Piagetian conservation tasks A series of tests (named after their inventor, Piaget) intended to demonstrate the illogicality of children's thought processes.

Piaget's 'kidnapping' Anecdote by Piaget's (the famous developmental psychologist) which demonstrates the fallibility of *autobiographical memory*. Piaget had a distinct memory of a kidnap attempt on himself when he was aged two years, which his nurse successfully repulsed. As an adolescent, Piaget discovered that the nurse had made up the whole episode, and accordingly, his memory was an elaboration of her story, rather than of a real event.

Pick's bodies Damaged *neurons*, found in the brains of *Pick's Disease* patients, which under a microscope, have a characteristic swollen appearance.

Pick's Disease Named after its discoverer, a form of *dementia* characterised by a progressive deterioration of brain tissue commencing in the *frontal lobes* and progressing backwards. Psychologically, there are often disturbances in personality before any intellectual changes manifest themselves.

PMA See *Primary Mental Abilities Test.*

PNS *Peripheral nervous system.*

positive correlation A value of *r* greater than 0 and less than or equal to 1. See *correlation.*

positron emission tomography An electronic scanning method which measures how a section of the body (in the context of this book, the brain) metabolises a dose of (mildly radioactive) glucose. This gives an indication of how active (and by implication, healthy) different areas of the brain are.

post-developmental A phrase by some *gerontologists* (e.g. Bromley) to denote that changes in old age are detrimental rather than developmental or beneficial.

postformal thought Theory that in adulthood, subjects develop the ability to combine subjective and objective criteria in resolving a problem. The term refers to the fact that it is felt to develop after *formal operations* (though it is not intended to imply that it is automatically 'superior').

potential lifespan *Lifespan.*

pragmatics The understanding of the intent of an utterance, which may lie beyond a literal interpretation of what has been said or written.

pre-morbid IQ The *IQ* level (usually estimated) of a person before the onset of an illness (usually one which has affected the intellect – e.g. *dementia*).

pre-senile dementia *Dementia* whose onset occurs before the patient's sixtieth birthday. Was once felt to be qualitatively distinct from *senile dementia*, but this division is now disputed.

presbycusis Hearing loss characterised by a relatively greater difficulty in perceiving high frequency sounds.

presbyopia An inability to focus on near objects.

preserved differentiation The theory that some intellectual skills are relatively better preserved than others in old age, because they have always been better (i.e., the same difference would have been found in youth, though the absolute size of the scores might have been higher). The argument is implausible when discussing the general population, but has some attractiveness in discussing certain specific samples of the populace where the preserved skills were essential to their livelihood. E.g. a group of professional musicians may have a better preserved level of manual dexterity. This could be due to practice enabling them to maintain this (*differential preservation*), or because they have always had better manual dexterity (preserved differentiation). See *age x treatment interaction*.

primary ageing Age changes to the body (e.g. wrinkling skin, brittler bones, etc). See *secondary ageing*, and *universal ageing*.

primary memory Another term for *short term memory*.

Primary Mental Abilities Test An intelligence *test battery* devised by Thurstone.

primary vascular dementia *Multi infarct dementia.*

priming When referring to memory experiments (as in this book), 'priming' refers to providing hints about items a subject is trying to *recall*. See *initial letter priming*.

probabilistic ageing Aspects of ageing likely to affect most (but by no means all) who reach old age (e.g. arthritis). Similar to *secondary ageing*. See *universal ageing*.

processing resources theory of ageing Any theory which argues that changes in ageing intellectual skills are attributable to a lowered capacity for mental calculations (e.g. of *working memory*), lowered speed of processing, etc.

profound hearing impairment (PHI) *Hearing impairment* of >90dB.

progeria Disease in which the patients from being babies appear to age at an abnormally fast rate, usually dying in their teens. Though sharing many of the features of normal ageing, the illness is not simply accelerated normal ageing. Compare with *Werner syndrome*.

programmed senescence The belief that the body is genetically programmed to age.

progressive supranuclear palsy (PSP) An illness characterised by disturbances of motor function and mild to moderate *dementia*.

prospective memory The ability to remember to do something in the future.

proverb interpretation Specialist tests, such as the *Gorham Proverb Interpretation Test*, and several other studies, have tested subjects' abilities to provide meanings of proverbs. Patients in the early stages of *dementia* may give very literal interpretations of well-known proverbs (e.g. 'people in glass houses...' may be literally interpreted as advice to greenhouse owners). However, on less well-known or unfamiliar proverbs, normal elderly people may provide relatively concrete interpretations relative to younger subjects' more abstract ones.

proximal ageing effects Ageing changes directly attributable to changes in another process (e.g. a *stroke*, due to an ageing cardiovascular system). See *distal ageing effects*.

pseudodementia This is a side-effect of depression in some elderly people – a lowering in intellectual abilities, which in turn masquerades as *dementia*.

PSP *Progressive supranuclear palsy*.

psychological age A person's psychological state compared to that of an average person of the same *chronological age*.

psychometrics Strictly speaking, the measurement of psychological traits and skills. More generally used to denote the study of psychological differences between people.

psychomotor skill A physical skill in which there is a strong component of intellectual prowess or vice versa.

psychosis with cerebral arteriosclerosis *multi-infarct dementia*.

psychotherapy Any treatment regime which is based on an integrated theory of mind.

psychoticism As used in this book, a *personality trait* in *Eysenck's personality model*. Psychoticism measures the degree of emotional 'coldness' a person possesses.

pugilistic dementia *Dementia*-type symptoms resulting from blows to the head. The precise symptoms vary, but usually include disturbances of movement as well as intellectual impairment. The symptoms are permanent, unlike the colloquial notion of being 'punch drunk', which can be relatively short-lived. Most often encountered in boxers (hence the name), but also can occur as a result of other violent activities or accidents.

pyramidal society Society in which there are far more young than old people. The population can be envisioned as a pyramid with the youngest age groups at the bottom, supporting increasingly small blocks of older age groups. See *rectangular society*.

quality ratio In studies of creativity, the ratio of good to indifferent works produced by a person during a particular period. The quality ratio tends to remain constant throughout life.

r Symbol for *correlation*.

RAGS *Relatives' Assessment of Global Symptomatology*.

Raven's Progressive Matrices A popular commercial test of fluid intelligence. Subjects are given a series of problems (against the clock) which have the common theme of a logically-governed sequence, from which one member is missing. The subjects' task is to provide the missing member, using a multiple-choice test design.

re-engagement theory *Activity theory*.

reaction time The time taken for a person to respond to the appearance of a stimulus.

recall The ability to remember items in memory without any prompting. See *ordered recall* and *free recall*.

recognition The ability to identify which items have been previously encountered when given a list of alternatives to choose from.

rectangular society (1) Future society in which the *age cohorts'* survival rates would follow *rectangular survival curves*. (2) Society in which there are roughly equal numbers of people alive in each age decade (i.e., equal numbers of 0–9 year olds, 10–19 year olds, etc). A histogram plotting numbers against age decade would appear like a rectangle. See *pyramidal society*.

rectangular survival curve Hypothesised graph of percentage of *survivors* in an *age cohort* in a future of very effective medical care. By this reckoning, very few people will die until in their *lifespan* is reached, when most will die within a few years of each other. A graph of the percentage of the age cohort alive at different ages (with percentage on the vertical axis, and age on the horizontal) would thus look rectangular – a practically horizontal line going from left to right, joined to a practically vertical line going downwards when the lifespan mark is reached on the horizontal axis.

reflex arc A simple connection between *afferent* and *efferent neurons* in the spinal cord. This mechanism is responsible for a number of reflexes (e.g. the knee jerk reflex).

regression hypothesis Theory that the elderly's linguistic skills revert to the qualitative state of a child's.

rehearsal (memory) The process of repeating *to-be-remembered* items 'in the head' in an effort to remember them better.

Relatives' Assessment of Global Symptomatology (RAGS) Questionnaire measure of symptoms of the patient observed by his/her *caregivers*.

reminiscence peak The phenomenon that the bulk of *autobiographical memories* stem from when people were aged 10–30 years.

remote grandmother See *Robertson's taxonomy of grandmothers*.

remote memory Memory for non-autobiographical events which have occurred during a subject's lifetime. A frequent proviso is that these events must not include very famous ones, which are seen as part of common general knowledge, and thus more properly classified as part of *semantic memory*.

reorganisers See *integrated personality*.

reversible dementia An illness which produces *dementia*-like symptoms which can be cured (and hence reverse the dementing symptoms).

Ribot's hypothesis The theory that in damaged or decaying minds, memories for recent events should be worse than memories for remote ones.

Rivermead Behavioural Memory Test A set of memory tasks analogous to everyday situations where memory is required (e.g. face recognition, remembering a route set out by the experimenter). The test is intended for adults of all ages with memory problems, and it is often used for assessing *demented* patients.

Robertson's taxonomy of grandmothers J.F. Robertson (1977) categorised grandmothers into four types. (1) *apportioned grandmother* – has both a social and a personal set of expectations for her grandchildren; (2) *symbolic grandmother* – has a social set of expectations; (3) *individualised grandmother* – has a set of personal expectations; (4) *remote grandmother* – relatively detached from the whole idea of being a grandmother.

rocking chair personality See *dependent personality*.

RT Abbreviation of *reaction time*.

SATSA *Swedish Adoption/Twin Study on Aging*.

schema A collection of memories about an event or item which enable one to plan responses and to interpret information surrounding the said event or item. For example, if one is asked to dinner at an expensive restaurant, one's schema for expensive restaurants will indicate that turning up in jeans and a T-shirt would not be a good idea.

Seattle Longitudinal Aging Study *Longitudinal study* of psychological ageing, run by K.W. Schaie. Subjects were first tested in 1956, and have been retested every seven years.

secondary ageing Age changes which are associated with, but not necessarily an inevitable consequence of ageing (e.g. arthritis, cataracts). See *primary ageing*, and *probabilistic ageing*.

selective attention The ability to attend to one stimulus set against a range of distracting stimuli.

self-hatred personality *Personality* type discovered by Reichard et al. (1962). Elderly people possessing this *personality trait* (unrealistically) blame themselves for all their misfortunes.

semantic Meaning.

semantic deficit hypothesis Model of ageing which argue that age-related deficits in intellectual functioning are attributable to a failure to adequately process incoming information (e.g. to-be-remembered items) for the information they contain.

semantic facilitation A phenomenon whereby the meaning of previously-encountered words or phrases enables one to identify subsequent words or phrases faster if they have similar meanings than if they do not. For example, the word *butter* will be identified faster if one has just seen the word *bread* than if one had just seen the word *lizard*.

semantic memory A term devised by Tulving (1972) to denote memories for facts. Compare with *episodic memory*.

semantic priming *Semantic facilitation*.

senescence Old age, usually with the implication of normal ageing.

senescing Ageing in terms of *biological age*.

senile Medical term for 'old'. NEVER to be used as a synonym for *demented*.

senile dementia See *dementia*.

senile Dementia of the Alzheimer type. See *dementia of the Alzheimer type*.

senile plaques (SP) Amorphous clumps of dead *neurons*, found in all elderly people, but particularly prevalent in *demented* individuals.

senile psychosis Misleading synonym for *dementia*. Although some *demented* patients do have feelings of persecution in the early stages of the illness, this is far from universal.

sentential grouping An (usually) inefficient and illogical classification of objects on the basis that they can be included in the same sentence or short story.

sequential research design *Longitudinal study* in which different *age cohorts* are tested at intervals over several years. In addition, age cross-sections of the population are also tested in tandem with the longitudinal test panel, to gain an insight into possible *cohort effects*.

SETOF *Speed-error-tradeoff-function*.

short term memory A temporary memory for events which have occurred in the past few seconds to (at most) the past couple of minutes (commentators differ over the length of time to be included in the definition). The characteristics of short term memory are that it has a limited capacity (typically, and depending on the individual, between 5 and 9 items), is easily disrupted, and items in short term memory are quickly forgotten unless a conscious effort is made to *rehearse* them. See also *primary memory* and *working memory*.

simple reaction time The time taken for a subject to respond when there is only one type of stimulus and one type of response. Compare with *choice reaction time*.

slave systems A term derived from computing to denote systems (usually capable of one type of operation only) which can only operate under the direct command of a master controller. In the case of the *working memory* model, the slave systems under the command of the *central executive* include the *phonological loop* and the *visuo-spatial sketchpad*.

SOA *Stimulus onset asynchrony*.

social age A set of behaviours and attitudes considered to be socially appropriate for the *chronological age* of the individual (i.e., what is colloquially known as 'acting one's age').

social clock A hypothesised mechanism which an individual 'consults' to determine the most appropriate behaviour for his/her *social age*.

somatic When pertaining to the *peripheral nervous system*, information from joints, skin and skeletal muscle transmitted to the *central nervous system*.

somatic mutation theory of ageing Theory that as cells are lost through natural 'wear and tear' they are replaced by cells which are increasingly likely to contain genetic 'errors' (i.e., are mutations), and are less likely to function efficiently. Accordingly, the body progressively deteriorates. See *autoimmune theory of ageing, disposable soma theory of ageing, free radical theory of ageing,* and *Hayflick phenomenon.*

SP *Senile plaque.*

span Abbreviation of *memory span.*

Spearman's g See *g.*

speed-error-tradeoff-function A measure of the degree to which an individual is prepared to 'trade' speed at performing a task (i.e., slow down) in order to reduce the number of errors made. A measure often used in *reaction time* experiments.

speed hypothesis Theory that intellectual ageing can be explained in terms of a general slowing of intellectual functions (particularly as measured by *reaction times*).

spinal cord The principle meeting point between *peripheral* and *central nervous system neurons.*

SRT *Simple reaction time.*

standard deviation Statistical measure used, inter alia, to indicate the range of scores in a sample. A useful rule of thumb is that for a *normal distribution,* the range of scores between the mean minus two standard deviations and the mean plus two standard deviations accounts for approximately 95% of the sample's scores.

stimulus onset asynchrony In a *backward masking* experiment, the difference between the length of time the to-be-remembered item has to be presented alone and the length of time it has to be presented when it is followed by a mask in order for it to be correctly recognised.

STM *Short term memory.*

stroke Damage to brain tissue caused by the cessation its blood supply. The psychological effect of the stroke very much depends upon the location of the injury. The term is usually reserved for a relatively large scale haemorrhage, to contrast with the *infarct.*

sub-cortical Pertaining to areas of the brain other than the *cerebral cortex.*

sub-cortical dementias *Dementias* whose principal focus of damage is not in the *cerebral cortex*.

subdural haematoma Blood clot in the brain. See *cerebral haemorrhage*.

succourant-seeking See *passive-dependent personality*.

sundown syndrome The phenomenon observed in some *demented* patients, who get up during the night and wander about, without apparent regard for the propriety of the time or place.

superego In Freudian theory, a person's set of (often overly harsh) moral dictums. See also *ego* and *id*.

supraspan learning Learning lists of items whose number exceeds one's *memory span*.

survival curve Graph plotting the numbers of survivors in an *age cohort* against their *chronological age*.

survivors Term sometimes used to describe members of an *age cohort* who have lived past a particular age (usually 60 or 65 years, in ageing research).

sustained attention The ability to concentrate on a set task without being distracted.

Swedish Adoption/Twin Study on Aging An ongoing study, begun in 1979, of both identical and non-identical twins, reared apart or reared together. By studying individuals with different strengths of genetic linkage and different amounts of shared upbringing in common, it is hoped to trace the differential effects of genetics and environment on personality changes in later life.

symbolic grandmother See *Robertson's taxonomy of grandmothers*.

synapse The junction between two *neurons*.

syntactic Pertaining to *syntax*.

syntax Grammar.

tacrine Drug whose effects include the enhanced release of acetylcholine (a key neurotransmitter in the brain – see *cholinergic hypothesis*). Has been cited as a possible treatment for patients suffering from *dementia*. See *ondansetron* and *ganglioside*.

target This has two meanings in the context of this book. (1) In *recognition* memory tasks, a target is an item which has been previously encountered, and which must be chosen instead of alternative items (*distracters*) which have not been encountered before. (2) In *attention* tasks, a target is an item which must be located from among a range of other items (*distracters*).

TBR *To-be-remembered.*

temporal lobes Section of the *cerebral cortex* occupying, roughly speaking, the area of the left and right temples. Their chief function is interpreting information – in most individuals the left temporal lobe is essential in comprehending and producing speech and writing. They are also strongly involved in the storage of memories.

terminal drop model A theory that elderly individuals maintain the same level of intellectual functioning until a sudden decline a few months/years before their death.

terminal phase (of dying) See *Pattison's stages of dying.*

tertiary ageing A phase of rapid deterioration during dying.

tertiary memory *Remote memory.*

test battery A group of tests designed to assess the same skill (usually intelligence, or memory, or personality).

thalamus Co-ordinates and channels information and execution of motor movements. Damage of this area leads to *Parkinsonism.*

thanatology The study of death and dying.

theta waves A pattern of electrical activity detected by *EEG* with a frequency between 4 and 8Hz.

third age Active and independent old age. Compare with *fourth* age.

threshold age In the context of this book, the *chronological age* which (arbitrarily) denotes the onset of old age.

threshold model of dementia The theory that individuals have a genetically-fixed predisposition to develop *dementia*, but that it requires an environmental cause to push the person past a particular point so that the onset of the illness becomes inevitable. In people with a low predisposition, a large environmental input is required, and vice versa.

time-lag comparison Comparing different *age cohorts'* performance at the same age in a *longitudinal study.*

time-lag effect *Cohort effect.*

time-sequential design A curious 'extended' *cross-sectional study* design now no longer practised. Two or more age groups are compared at one time period, and then several years later, different subjects are tested, who are the same ages as the subjects were in the first experiment when they were tested. E.g., a group of 30-year-olds and a group of 40-year-olds are tested in 1970, and then new groups of 30- and 40-year-olds are tested in 1985.

tinnitus A hearing complaint in which the sufferer is afflicted by a (usually permanent) irritating noise (sometimes painful) which interferes with normal hearing. The noise can take many forms, but one of the commonest is a high pitched 'ringing in the ears' and hence its lay term.

tip of the tongue (TOT) The phenomenon of recalling an item from memory in which features of the item can be recalled (e.g. number of syllables, words which sound like it) but the word itself eludes one. A tip of the tongue state can often be induced in the laboratory by providing subjects with the definition of an obscure word and then asking them for the word being described.

to-be-remembered (items) Items in a memory task which the subject must remember.

TOT *Tip of the tongue.*

Trail Making test Sub-test of the *Halstead-Reitan Neuropsychological Battery.* used to assess ability to follow sequences. The subject must make a pencil trail between particular numbers (or in another version, alternate between numbers and letters) printed on a sheet of paper.

trajectory, dying *Dying trajectory.*

transient ischaemic attack *Stroke* whose effects are relatively trivial, and are gone within 24 hours.

triple jeopardy Term devised to reinforce the point that elderly people facing the *double jeopardy* face a third problem in that they often do not receive the help they need and deserve because of prejudice and/or communication problems.

Type A personality A *personality* type prone to being competitive, hard-edged, etc. See *Type B personality.*

Type B personality A *personality* type prone to being easy going and relaxed. See *Type A personality.*

Ulverscroft large print series Series of reprints of popular books in large point size, for the visually handicapped. Traditional market is elderly patrons of public libraries.

universal ageing Aspects of ageing held to affect everyone who reaches old age (e.g. wrinkling skin). Similar to *primary ageing.* See *probabilistic ageing.*

vascular dementia *Multi infarct dementia.*

verbal span *Memory span* for words or letters.

view from the bridge Title of an Arthur Miller play. Also, in Levinson's theory, the desired state in old age where the elderly have come to terms with their past.

viscera The intestines.

visceral Pertaining to the intestines.

visual agnosia An inability to recognise objects by sight.

visual search task A test of *selective attention.* The subject must find a *target* item which is located in an array of distracter items.

visuo-spatial Pertaining to visual shapes and figures.

visuo-spatial memory The ability to remember visual and/or spatial information.

visuo-spatial sketchpad A *slave system* of the *working memory* model; a temporary memory store of visuo-spatial information (further divided into separate stores of visual and spatial information).

visuo-spatial skills/intelligence The ability to interpret visual and/or spatial information.

WAIS See *Wechsler Adult Intelligence Scale.*

wear and tear theory Theory of ageing which argues that parts of the body gradually 'wear out' with use. Compare with *cytologic theory.*

Wechsler Adult Intelligence Scale An intelligence *test battery* covering all commonly assessed areas of intelligence; perhaps the most widely-used commercial intelligence test.

Wechsler Memory Scale The memory tests from the *Wechsler Adult Intelligence Scale* battery, which in themselves form a (memory) test battery.

Werner syndrome An illness akin to *progeria* in its effects, but whose onset is in the late teens, rather than birth. Patients display signs of ageing at a faster rate than normal, and usually die in their forties.

Wernicke-Korsakoff syndrome *Korsakoff's syndrome.*

Wernicke's aphasia A specific failure to understand speech, resulting from brain damage.

Wisconsin Card Sorting Task Measure of hypothesis formation and the ability to reject or not persevere with an invalid one. Subjects must discover the correct rule for matching up cards of differing patterns and colours (e.g. a yellow card must always be matched with a red card). Once they have discovered the correct rule, the experimenter changes the rule, and how quickly the subject stops using the old rule and searches for the new one is measured, as well as how quickly s/he solves the new problem. The test is used with normal subjects and patients of all ages, but is of considerable use in research on the elderly.

word completion task Task in which the subject is required to complete a word, given the first letter(s) (e.g. 'complete AARD - - - -').

word span *Memory span* for words.

working memory Currently the most popular model of short term memory, first described by Baddeley & Hitch (1974). The model argues that short term memory is controlled by the *central executive*, which delegates memory tasks to specialist sub-units or *slave systems*. Principal amongst these are the *phonological loop* and the *visuo-spatial sketchpad*. The model also explains how memories can be kept in a temporary store while *concurrent processing* is performed.

Yngve depth An analytical technique which gives a 'score' for the syntactic complexity of a sentence or phrase.

young elderly The commonest definition is the age group between 60 and 75 years (though some leeway in these boundaries is not unknown). See *old elderly*.

young-old plot Plotting on a graph the performance of young subjects on one axis versus the performance of old subjects on the same task on the other axis. The slope of the line gives an indication of how disadvantaged the old are relative to the young.

zeitgeist Spirit of the (historical) age.

References

Adams, C. (1991) Qualitative age differences in memory for text: A life-span developmental perspective. *Psychology and Aging, 6,* 323–336

Adams, R.D. (1980). The morphological aspects of aging in the human nervous system. In J.E. Birren & R.B. Sloane (eds), *Handbook of Mental Health and Aging.* Englewood Cliffs, N.J.: Prentice-Hall, 149–162.

Adams-Price, C (1992) Eyewitness memory and aging: Predictors of accuracy in recall and person recognition. *Psychology and Aging, 7,* 602–608

Aiken, L.R. (1989) *Later Life Hillsdale.* New Jersey: Lawrence Erlbaum Associates.

Alafuzoff, I., Iqbal, K., Friden, H. *et al.* (1989) Histopathological classification of dementias by multivariate data analysis. In K. Iqbal, H.M. Wisniewski & B. Winblad (eds), *Alzheimer's Disease and Related Disorders.* New York: Alan R. Liss

Albert, M.S. (1988) Cognitive function. In M.S. Albert & M.B. Moss (eds), *Geriatric Neuropsychology.* New York: Guilford.

Albert, M.S., Duffy, F.H. & Naeser, M.A. (1987) Nonlinear changes in cognition and their non-psychological correlation. *Canadian Journal of Psychology, 41,* 141–157.

Albert, M.S. & Stafford, J.L. (1988). Computed tomography studies. In M.S. Albert & M.B. Moss (eds), *Geriatric Neuropsychology.* New York: Guilford Press.

Alpaugh, P.K. & Birren, J.E. (1977). Variables affecting creative contributions across the adult life span. *Human Development, 20,* 240–248.

Alzheimer, A. (1907) About a peculiar disease of the cerebral cortex, (trans. L. Jarvik & H. Greenson), *Alzheimer's Disease & Associated Disorders, 1,* 7–8.

American Psychiatric Association (1987) *Diagnostic and Statistical Manual of Mental Disorders (3rd edition, rev) (DSM-III-R).* Washington, DC: American Psychiatric Association.

Anderson, B & Palmore, E (1974) Longitudinal evaluation of ocular function. In E. Palmore (ed), *Normal Aging.* Durham, N.C.: Duke University Press, 24–32.

Anderson, K (1974) Science probes ways to prolong life. *Science Digest, 76,* 36–41.

Appell, J., Kertesz, A. & Fisman, M. (1982) A study of language functioning in Alzheimer patients, *Brain and Language, 17,* 73–91

Arenberg, D. (1982) Changes with age in problem solving. In F.M. Craik, A.S. Trehub (eds) *Aging and Cognitive Processes.* New York: Plenum.

Auden, W.H. (1979) Oxford. *Selected Poems.* London: Faber.

Baddeley, A.D. (1983) *Your Memory: A User's Guide.* London: Pelican.

Baddeley, A.D. (1986) *Working Memory.* Oxford: Oxford Science Publications.

Baddeley, A.D. (1990) *Human Memory: Theory and Practice.* Exeter: Lawrence Erlbaum Associates.

Baddeley, A.D. & Hitch, G. (1974) Working Memory. In G.H.Bower (ed) *Attention and Performance VI*. New York: Academic Press.

Baddeley, A.D., Logie, R., Bressi, S., Della Sala, S. & Spinnler H. (1986) Dementia and working memory. *Quarterly Journal of Experimental Psychology, 38A,* 603–618.

Backman, L., Josephsson, S., Herlitz, A. *et al.* (1991) The generalizability of training gains in dementia: Effects of an imagery-based mnemonic on face-name retention duration. *Psychology and Aging, 6,* 489–492

Baltes, P. & Reese, H.W. (1984) The lifespan perspective in developmental psychology. In M.H. Boornstein & M.E. Lamb (eds), *Developmental Psychology*. Hillsdale, New Jersey: Lawrence Erlbaum.

Baltes, P. & Willis, S.L. (1982) Plasticity and enhancement of intellectual functioning in old age. In F.M. Craik & A.S. Trehub (eds) *Aging and Cognitive Processes.* New York: Plenum.

Barefoot, J.C. (1992) Developments in the measurement of hostility. In H. Friedman (ed) *Hostility, Coping and Health.* Washington, DC: American Psychological Association, 13–31

Barefoot, J.C., Beckham, J.C., Haney, T.L. *et al.* (1993) Age differences in hostility among middle-aged and older adults. *Psychology and Aging, 8,* 3–9

Bartlett, F.C. (1932) *Remembering.* Cambridge: Cambridge University Press.

Bayles, K.A. (1985a) Verbal perseveration of dementia patients. *Brain and Language 25,* 102–116.

Bayles, K.A. (1985b) Communication in dementia. In H.K. Ulatowska (ed) *The Aging Brain: Communication in the Elderly.* San Diego: College-Hill Press.

Bayles, K.A. & Tomoeda, C.K. (1983) Confrontation naming impairment in dementia. *Brain and Language, 19,* 98–114.

Bayley, N (1968) Behavioral correlates of mental growth: Birth to thirty-six years. *American Psychologist, 23,* 1–17.

de Beauvoir, S. (1970) *Old Age.* London: Penguin Books.

Becker, J.T., Boller, F., Saxton, J. & McGonigle-Gibson, K.L. (1987) Normal rates of forgetting of verbal and non-verbal material in Alzheimer's Disease. *Cortex, 23,* 59–72.

Bell, L.J. (1980) *The large print book and its user.* London: Library Association.

Belmont, J.M., Freeseman, L.J. & Mitchell, D.W. (1988) Memory and problem solving: the cases of young and elderly adults. In M.M. Gruneberg, P.E. Morris & R.N. Sykes (eds) *Practical Aspects of Memory.* Volume 2.

Bengtson, U.L. & Kuypers, J. (1986) The family support cycle: psychosocial issues in the aging family. In J.M.A. Munnichs, P. Mussen & E. Olbrich (eds) *Life Span and Change in a Gerontological Perspective.* New York: Academic Press.

Bengtson, U.L. & Treas, J. (1980) The changing family context of mental health and aging. In J.E. Birren & B. Sloane (eds) *Handbook of Mental Health and Aging.* New Jersey: Prentice Hall.

Berg, C.A. & Sternberg, R.J. (1992) Adults' conceptions of intelligence across the adult life span. *Psychology and Aging, 7,* 221–231.

Berg, L. (1988) Mild senile dementia of the Alzheimer type: Diagnostic criteria and natural history. *Mount Sinai Journal of Medicine, 55,* 87–96.

Berg, L., Danzinger, W.L., Storandt, M. *et al.* (1984) Predictive features in mild senile dementia of the Alzheimer type. *Neurology, 34,* 563–569.

Bergman, M., Blumenfeld, V.G., Casardo, D. *et al.* (1976). Age-related decrement in hearing for speech: Sampling and longitudinal studies. *Journal of Gerontology, 31,* 533–538.

Bernlef, J. (1988) *Out of Mind* London: Faber & Faber. English translation by Adrienne Dixon.

Bilash, I. & Zubeck, J.P. (1960) The effects of age on factorially 'pure' mental abilities. *Journal of Gerontology, 15,* 175–182.

Binstock, R.H. & George, L.K. (eds) (1990) *Handbook of Aging and the Social Sciences.* London: Academic Press.

Birren, J.E. (1964). *The Psychology of Aging.* Englewoof Cliffs, N.J.: Prentice–Hall.

Birren, J.E., Butler, R.N., Greenhouse, S.W., Sokoloff, L. & Yarrow, M.R. (1963) *Human Aging.* Washington: Public Health Service Publication No. 986.

Birren, J.E. & Schaie, K.W. (eds) (1990) *Handbook of the Psychology of Aging.* San Diego: Academic Press.

Birren, J.E., Woods, A.M. & Williams, M.V. (1980). Behavioral slowing with age: Causes, organization and consequences. In L.W. Poon (ed) *Aging in the 1980s: Psychological issues.* Washington, D.C.: American Psychological Association.

Blackburn, J.A. & Papalia, D.E. (1992) The study of adult cognition from a Piagetian perspective. In R.J. Sternberg & C.A. Berg (eds) *Intellectual Development.* Cambridge: Cambridge University Press.

Blessed, G., Tomlinson, B.E. & Roth, M. (1968) The association between quantitative measures of dementia and of senile changes in the cerebral grey matter of elderly subjects. *British Journal of Psychiatry, 114,* 797–811.

Blum, J.E., Clark, E.T. & Jarvik, L.F. (1973). The N.Y.S. Psychiatric Institute Study of aging twins. In L.F. Jarvik, C. Eisdorfer & J.E. Blum (eds) *Intellectual functioning in adults.* New York: Springer.

Bosman, E.A. (1993) Age-related differences in the motoric aspects of transcription typing skill. *Psychology and Aging, 8,* 87–102.

Botwinick, J. (1967) *Cognitive Processes in Maturity and Old Age.* New York: Springer.

Botwinick, J. (1973) *Aging and Behaviour.* New York: Springer.

Botwinick, J (1977) Intellectual abilities. In J.E. Birren & K.W. Schaie (eds) *Handbook of the Psychology of Aging.* New York: Van Nostrand Reinhold.

Botwinick, J. & Storandt, M. (1974) Vocabulary ability in later life. *Journal of Genetic Psychology, 125,* 303–308.

Botwinick, J., Robbin, J.S. & Brinley, J.F. (1960) Age differences in card sorting performance in relation to task difficulty, task set and practice. *Journal of Experimental Psychology, 59,* 10–18.

Botwinick, J., West, R. & Storandt, M. (1978) Predicting death from behavioral performance. *Journal of Gerontology, 33,* 755–762.

Bouma, H., Legein, C.P., Melotte, H.E. & Zabel, L. (1982) Is large print easy to read? Oral reading rate and word recognition of elderly subjects. *IPO Annual Progress Report, 17, 84–90.*

Bowles, N.L. & Poon, L.W. (1981) The effect of age on speed of lexical access. *Experimental Aging Research, 7, 417–425.*

Branconnier, R.J., Cole, J.D., Spera, K.F. & DeVitt, D.R. (1982) Recall and recognition as diagnostic indices of malignant memory loss in senile dementia: a Bayesian analysis. *Experimental Aging Research, 8, 189–193.*

Brayne, C. & Beardsall, L. (1990) Estimation of verbal intelligence in an elderly community: an epidemiological study using NART. *British Journal of Clinical Psychology, 29, 217–224.*

Breen, A.R., Larson, E.B., Reifler B.V., Vitaliano, P.P. & Lawrence, G.L. (1984) Cognitive performance and functional competence in coexisting dementia and depression. *J. Am. Geriatr. Soc., 32, 132–137.*

Brinkman, S.D., Largen, J.W., Gerganoff, S. & Pomara, N. (1983) Russelli Revised Wechsler Memory Scale in the evaluation of dementia. *Journal of Clinical Psychology, 39, 989–993.*

Brody, J.A. (1988) Changing health needs of the ageing population. *Research and the ageing population.* Ciba Foundation Symposium 134. Chichester: Wiley 208–220.

Bromley, D.B. (1958) Some effects of age on short-term learning and memory. *Journal of Gerontology, 13, 398–406.*

Bromley, D.B. (1988) *Human Ageing. An introduction to gerontology.* 3rd. Edition. Bungay: Penguin Books.

Bromley, D.B. (1991) Aspects of written language production over adult life. *Psychology and Aging, 6, 296–308.*

Brouwers, P. (1984) Differential perceptual-spatial impairment in Huntington's and Alzheimer's dementias. *Archives of Neurology, 41, 1073–1076.*

Brown, R. & McNeill, D. (1966) The 'tip-of-the-tongue' phenomenon. *Journal of Verbal Learning and Verbal Behavior, 5, 325–337.*

Bucht, G. & Adolfsson, R. (1983) The Comprehensive Psychopathological Rating Scale in patients with dementia of Alzheimer type and multi-infarct dementia. *Acta Psychiatrica Scandanavica, 68, 263–270.*

Burke, D.M., White, H. & Diaz, D.L. (1987) Semantic priming in young and old adults: Evidence for age constancy in automatic and attentional processes. *Journal of Experimnetal Psychology: Human Perception and Performance, 13, 79–88.*

Burke, D. Worthley, J. & Martin, J. (1988) I'll never forget what's-her-name: aging and tip of the tongue experiences in everyday life. In M.M. Gruneberg, P.E. Morris & R.N. Sykes (eds) *Practical Aspects of Memory: Current Research and Issues.* Chichester: Wiley.

Burke, D. & Yee, P. (1984) Semantic priming during sentence processing by young and older adults. *Developmental Psychology, 20, 903–910.*

Burns, R (1988) A Two-way T.V. system operated by senior citizens. *American Behavioral Scientist, 31, 576–587.*

Burnside, I.M., Ebersole, P. & Monea, H.E. (eds) (1979) *Psychosocial Caring Throughout the Lifespan.* New York: McGraw Hill.

Butler, R.N. (1967) *Creativity in Old Age.* New York: Plenum.

Butler, R.W., Dickinson, W.A., Katholi, C. & Halsey, J.H. (1983) The comparative effects of organic brain disease on cerebral blood flow and measured intelligence. *Annals of Neurology, 13,* 155–159.

Burnside, I.M. (1976) The special sense and sensory deprivation. In I.M. Burnside (ed) *Nursing and the Aged.* New York: McGraw-Hill, 380–397.

Butcher, J.N., Aldwin, C.M., Levenson, M.R. *et al.* (1991) Personality and aging: A study of the MMPI-2 among older men. *Psychology and Aging, 6,* 361–370.

Byrd, M. (1985) Age differences in the ability to recall and summarise textual information. *Experimental Aging Research, 11,* 87–91.

Byrd, M. (1986) The use of organisational strategies to improve memory for prose passages. *International Journal of Aging and Human Development, 23,* 257–265.

Camp, C.J. (1988) Utilisation of world knowledge systems. In L.W. Poon, D.G. Rubin & B.A. Wilson (eds) *Everyday Cognition in Adulthood and Later Life.* Cambridge: Cambridge University Press.

Cantone, G, Orsini, A, Grossi, D & DeMichele, G (1978) Verbal and spatial memory span in dementia: an experimental study of 185 subjects. *Acta Neurologica, 33,* 175–183.

Carey, R.G. (1979) Weathering widowhood: problems and adjustment of the widowed during the first year. *Omega, 10,* 263–274.

Carter, J.H. (1982) The effects of aging on selected visual functions: color vision, glare sensitivity, field of vision, and accommodation. In R. Sekuler, D. Kline & K. Dismukes (eds) *Aging and Human Visual Function.* New York: Alan R. Liss, 121–130.

Caspi, A. & Elder, G.H. (1986) Life satisfaction in old age: linking social psychology and history. *Journal of Psychology and Aging, 1,* 18–26.

Cattell, R.B. (1971) *Abilities: Their structure, growth and action.* Boston: Houghton Mifflin.

Cavanagh, J.C. & Murphy, N.Z. (1986) Personality and metamemory correlates of memory performance in younger and older adults. *Educational Gerontology, 12,* 385–394.

Cerella, J. (1990) Aging and information-processing rate In J.E. Birren & K.W. Schaie (eds) *Handbook of the Psychology of Aging* 3rd edition San Diego: Academic Press.

Cerella, J. & Fozard, J.L. (1984) Lexical access and age. *Developmental Psychology, 20,* 235–243.

Chamberlain, W (1970) Restriction in upward gaze with advancing age. *Transactions of the American Ophthalmological Society, 68,* 234–244.

Charness, N. (1979) Components of skill in bridge. *Canadian Journal of Psychology, 133,* 1–16.

Charness, N. (1981) Aging and skilled problem solving. *Journal of Experimental Psychology: General, 110,* 21–38.

Cicirelli, V.G. (1976) Categorization behavior in aging subjects. *Journal of Gerontology, 31,* 676–690.

Cicirelli, V.G. (1993) Attachment and obligation as daughters' motives for caregiving behavior and subsequent effect on subjective burden. *Psychology and Aging, 8,* 144–155.

Clayton, V.P. & Birren, J.E. (1980) The development of wisdom across the life span: A reexamination of an ancient topic. In P.B. Baltes & O.G. Brim (eds) *Life-Span Development and Behavior, 3,* New York: Academic Press.

Cockburn, J. & Smith P.T. (1988) Effects of age and intelligence on everyday memory tasks. In M.M. Gruneberg, P.E. Morris & R.N. Sykes (eds) *Practical Aspects of Memory: Current Research and Issues.* Chichester: Wiley.

Cohen, D. & Dunner, D. (1980) The assessment of cognitive dysfunction in dementing illness. In J.O. Cole & J.E. Barrett (eds) *Psychopathology in the Aged.* New York: Raven.

Cohen, G. (1981) Inferential reasoning in old age. *Cognition, 9,* 59–72.

Cohen, G. (1988) Age differences in memory for texts: production deficiency or processing limitations? In D.M. Burke & L.L. Light (eds) *Language, Memory and Aging.* New York: Cambridge University Press.

Cohen, G. (1989) *Memory in the Real World.* Hove: Lawrence Erlbaum Associates.

Cohen, G. & Faulkner, D. (1984) Memory for text: some age differences in the nature of the information that is retained after listening to texts. In H. Bouma & D. Bouwhuis (eds) *Attention and Performance X: Control of Language Processes.* Hillsdale: Lawrence Erlbaum.

Cohen, G. & Faulkner, D. (1986) Memory for proper names: age differences in retrieval. *British Journal Developmental Psychology, 4,* 187–197.

Cohen, G. & Faulkner, D. (1988) Life span changes in autobiographical memory. In M.M. Gruneberg, P.E. Morris & R.N. Sykes (eds) *Practical Aspects of Memory: Current Research and Issues.* Chichester: Wiley.

Cohen, G. & Faulkner, D. (1989) The effects of aging on perceived and generated memories Motivation and aging. In Poon, L.W., Rubin, D.C. & Wilson, B.A. (eds) *Everyday Cognition in Adulthood and Late Life.* Cambridge: Cambridge University Press.

Connelly, S.L., Hasher, L. & Zacks, R. (1991) Age and reading: The impact of distraction. *Psychology and Aging, 6,* 533–541.

Cook, A.S., & Oltjenbruns, K.A. (1989) *Dying and Grieving.* New York: Holt, Rinehart and Winston.

Coppel, D.B., Burton, C., Becker, J. & Fiore, J. (1985) Relationships of cognition associated with coping reactions to depression in spousal caregivers of Alzheimer's disease patients. *Cognitive Therapy and Research, 9,* 253–266.

Corkin, S., Growden, J.H., Nissen, M.J., Huff, F.J., Freed, D.M. & Sagar, H.J. (1984) Recent advances in the neuropsychological study of Alzheimer's disease. In R.J. Wurtman, S. Corkin & J.H. Growden (eds) *Alzheimer's Disease: Advances in Basic Research and Therapies.* Center for Brain Science and Metabolism Trust: Cambridge, Mass.

Corsi, P.M. (1980) Human memory and the medial temporal region of the brain. Unpub. PhD Thesis, McGill University. In B. Kolb & I.Q. Winshaw (eds) *Fundamentals of Human Neuropsychology.* San Francisco: W.H. Freeman.

Corso, J.F. (1981) *Aging Sensory Systems and Perception.* New York: Praeger.

Corso, J.F. (1987) Sensory-perceptual processes and aging. *Annual Review of Gerontology and Geriatrics, 7.* New York: Springer.

Costa, P.T., Jr., & McCrae, R.R. (1985) Hypochondriasis, neuroticism and aging: When are somatic complaints unfounded? *American Psychologist, 40,* 19–28.

Cowgill, D. (1970) The demography of aging. In A.M. Hoffman (ed) *The Daily Needs and Interests of Older People.* Springfield. Illinois: C.C. Thomas.

Coyne, A.C., Liss, L. & Geckler, C. (1984) The relationship between cognitive status and visual information processing. *Journal of Gerontology, 39,* 711–717.

Craik, F.M. (1977) Age differences in human memory. In J.E. Birren & K.W. Schaie (eds) *Handbook of the Psychology of Aging.* New York: Van Nostrand Reinhold.

Craik, F.I.M. & Jennings, J.M. (1992) Human memory. In F.I.M. Craik & T.A. Salthouse (eds) *The Handbook of Aging and Cognition Hillsdale,* New Jersey: Lawrence Erlbaum.

Craik, F.M. & Rabinowitz, J.C. (1984) Age differences in the acquisition and use of verbal information. In H. Bouma & D. Bouwhuis (eds) *Attention and Performance X: Control of Language Processes.* Hillsdale: Erlbaum, 471–499.

Crandall, R.C. (1980) *Gerontology. A behavioral science approach.* Reading, Mass: Addison-Wesley.

Crawford, J.R., Stewart, L.E., Garthwaite, P.H., Parker, D.M. & Bessan, J.A.O. (1988) The relationship between demographic variables and NART performance in normal subjects. *British Journal of Clinical Psychology, 27,* 181–182.

Crook, T.H. & West, R.L. (1990) Name recall performance across the adult life span. *British Journal of Psychology, 81,* 335–349.

Crosson, C.W. & Robertson-Tchabo, E.A. (1983) Age and preference for complexity among manifestly creative women. *Human Development, 26,* 149–155.

Cumming, E. & Henry, W.E. (1961) *Growing Old.* New York: Basic Books.

Cunningham, W.R. (1987) Intellectual abilities and age. In K.W. Schaie (ed) *Annual Review of Gerontology and Geriatrics, 7.* New York: Springer.

Cunningham, W.R. & Brookbank, J.W. (1988) *Gerontology: The Psychology, Biology and Sociology of Aging.* New York: Harper & Row.

Cunningham, W.R., Clayton, V. & Overton, W. (1975) Fluid and crystallised intelligence in young adulthood and old age. *Journal of Gerontology, 30,* 53–55.

Cunningham, W.R. & Owens, W.A. (1983). The Iowa State study of the adult development of intellectual abilities. In K.W. Schaie (ed) *Longitudinal studies of adult psychological development.* New York: Guilford Press, 20–39.

Dannefer, D. & Perlmutter, M. (1990) Development as a multidimensional process: Individual and social constituents. *Human Development, 33,* 108–137.

Davis, D.R. (1987) Personality Test. In: R.L. Gregory (ed) *The Oxford Companion to the Mind.* Oxford: Oxford University Press.

Davis, P.E. & Mumford, S.J. (1984) Cued recall and the nature of the memory disorder in dementia. *British Journal of Psychiatry, 144,* 383–386.

Dawkins, R. (1976) *The Selfish Gene.* Oxford: Oxford University Press.

Decker, D.L. (1980) *Social gerontology. An introduction to the dynamics of aging.* Boston: Little, Brown & Company.

Denney, N.W. (1974) Evidence for developmental changes in categorization criteria for children and adults. *Human Development, 17,* 41–53.

Denney, D.R. & Denney, N.W. (1973) The use of classification for problem solving: a comparison of middle and old age. *Developmental Psychology, 9,* 275–278.

Denney, N.W. & Denney, D.R. (1974) Modelling effects on the questioning strategies of the elderly. *Developmental Psychology, 10,* 458.

DeVries, H.A. (1975) Physiology of exercise and aging. In D.S. Woodruff & J.E. Birren (eds) *Aging: Scientific Perspectives and Social Issues.* New York: Van Nostrand Reinhold.

Dewey, J. (1939) Introduction. In E.V. Cowdry *Problems of Ageing.* Baltimore: Williams & Wilkins.

Diesfeldt, H.F. (1984) The importance of encoding instruction and retrieval cues in the assessment of memory in senile dementia. *Archives of Gerontology and Geriatrics, 3,* 51–57.

Dixon, R.A., Hultsch, D.F., Simon, E.W. & van Eye, A. (1984) Verbal ability and text structure effects on adult age differences in text recall. *Journal of Verbal Learning and Verbal Behaviour, 23,* 569–578.

Domey, R.G., McFarland, R.A. & Chadwick, E. (1960) Dark adaptation as a function of age and time: II. A derivation. *Journal of Gerontology, 15,* 267–279.

Dubno, J.R., Dirk, D.D. & Morgan, D.E. (1984) Effects of age and mild hearing loss on speech recognition in noise. *Journal of Acoustical Society of America, 76,* 87–96.

Duffy, F.H. & McAnulty, G. (1988) Electrophysiological studies. In M.S. Albert & M.B. Moss (eds) *Geriatric Neuropsychology.* New York: Guilford Press.

Dura, J.R., Stukenberg, K.W. & Kiecolt-Glaser, J.K. (1991) Anxiety and depressive disorders in adult children caring for demented parents. *Psychology and Aging, 6,* 467–473.

Eaves, L.J., Eysenck, H.J. & Martin, N.G. (1989) *Genes, Culture and Personality.* London: Academic Press.

Eisdorfer, C. & Wilkie, F. (1977) Stress, disease, aging and behaviour. In J.E. Birren & K.W. Schaie (eds) *Handbook of the Psychology of Aging.* New York: Academic Press.

Elias, M.F., Elias, J.W. & Elias, P. (1990) Biological and health influences on behavior. In J.E. Birren & K.W. Schaie (eds) *Handbook of the Psychology of Aging, 3rd edition.* San Diego: Academic Press.

Elias, M.F., Elias, P.K. & Elias, J.W. (1977) *Basic processes in adult developmental psychology.* St. Louis: C.V. Mosby.

Ellis, A.W. (1984) *Reading, Writing and Dyslexia. A Cognitive Approach.* London: Erlbaum.

Engen, T (1977) Taste and smell. In J.E. Birren & K.W. Schaie (eds) *Handbook of the psychology of aging.* New York: Van Nostrand Reinhold.

Erikson, E.H. (1963) *Childhood and Society.* New York: Norton.

Erikson, E.H. (1982) *The Life Cycle Completed: a Review.* New York: Norton.

Eysenck, H.J. (1952) The effects of psychotherapy: an evaluation. *Journal of Consulting Psychology, 16,* 319–324.

Eysenck, H.J. (1985) The theory of intelligence and the psychophysiology of cognition. In R.J. Steinberg (ed) *Advances in Research in Intelligence, 3,* Hillsdale, New Jersey: Lawrence Erlbaum.

Eysenck, H.J. (1987) Personality and Ageing: an Exploratory Analysis. *Journal of Social Behavior and Personality, 3,* 11–21.

Eysenck, H.J. & Eysenck, M.W. (1985) *Personality and Individual Differences: A Natural Science Approach.* New York: Plenum.

Eysenck, H.J. & Eysenck, S.B.G. (1969) *Personality, Structure and Measurement.* London.

Eysenck, H.J. & Kamin, L. (1981) *The Intelligence Controversy.* New York: Wiley.

Feher, E., Largen, J.W., Barr, D.L. & Smith, R.C. (1984) Relationships between cerebral atrophy imaged by CT scanning and neurophysiological test results in Alzheimer's disease. *International Journal of Neuroscience, 24,* 315–317.

Ferguson, S.A., Hastroudi, S. & Johnson. M.K. (1992) Age difference in using source-relevant cues. *Psychology and Ageing, 7,* 443–452.

Field, D. (1981) Retrospective reports by healthy intelligent people of personal events of their adult lives. *International Journal of Behavioral Development, 4,* 77–79.

Fozard, J.L. (1980) The time for remembering. In L.C. Poon (ed) *Aging in the 1980's: Psychological Issues.* Washington D.C.: American Psychological Association.

Fozard, J.L., Wolf, E., Bell, B., McFarland, R.A. & Podolsky, S. (1979) Visual perception and communication. In J.E. Birren & K.W. Schaie (eds), *Handbook of the Psychology of Aging.* New York: Van Nostrand Reinhold.

Fredericksen, J.R. (1978) Assessment of perceptual, decoding and lexical skills and their relation to reading proficiency. In A.M. Lesgold, J.W. Pellegrino, S.D. Fokkema & R. Glaser (eds) *Cognitive Psychology and Instruction.* New York: Plenum.

Freed, D.M., Corkin, S., Growden, J.H. & Nissen, M.J. (1989) Selective attention in Alzheimer's Disease: Characterizing cognitive subgroups of Alzheimer's Disease. *Neuropsychologia, 27,* 325–339.

Friedman, D., Hamberger, M., & Ritter, W. (1993) Event-related potentials as indicators of repetition priming in young and older adults: Amplitude, duration, and scalp distribution. *Psychology and Aging, 8,* 120–125.

Fries, J.F. & Crapo, L.M. (1981) Vitality and Aging: Implications of the Rectangular Curve. San Francisco: Freeman.

Fry, P.S. (1986) *Depression Stress and Adaptations in the Elderly.* Rockville: Aspen Publications.

Fuld, P.A. (1984) Test profile of cholinergic dysfunctions and of Alzheimer-type dementia. *Journal of Clinical Neuropsychology, 6,* 380–392.

Funkenstein, H.H. (1988) Cerebrovascular disorders. In M.S. Albert & M.B. Moss (eds) *Geriatric Neuropsychology.* New York: Guilford.

Gatz, M., Bengtson, V.L. & Blum, M.J. (1990) Caregiving families. In J.E. Birren & K.W. Schaie (eds) *Handbook of the Psychology of Aging,* 3rd. edition. San Diego: Academic Press.

Gibson, A.J. (1981) A further analysis of memory loss in dementia and depression in the elderly. *British Journal of Clinical Psychology, 20,* 179–185.

Gibson, H.B. (1992) *The Emotional and Sexual Lives of Older People.* London: Chapman & Hall.

Gilleard, C.J. (1979) Psychomotor performance of elderly psychiatric patients on the Gibson Spiral Maze test. *Perception and Motor Skills, 48,* 678.

Gilleard, C.J. (1984) Aging, dementia and Gibson Spiral Maze performance: a brief note. *Perception and Motor Skills, 58,* 889–90.

Gilmore, G.C., Tobias, T.R. & Royer, F.L. (1985) Aging and similarity grouping in visual search. *Journal of Gerontology, 40,* 586–592.

Gould, O.N. & Dixon, R.A. (1993) How we spent our vacation: Collaborative storytelling by young and old adults. *Psychology and Aging, 8,* 10–17.

Graf, P. & Schachter, D.L. (1985) Implicit and explicit memory for new associations in normal and amnesic subjects. *Journal of Experimental Psychology: Learning, Memory and Cognition, 11,* 501–518.

Graham, I.D. & Baker, P.M. (1989) Status, age and gender: perceptions of old and young people. *Canadian Journal on Aging, 8,* 255–267.

Grossi, D & Orsini, A (1978) The visual crosses test in dementia: an experimental study of 110 subjects. *Acta Neurologica, 33,* 170–174.

Grossi, D, Orsini, A & Ridente, G (1977) Preliminary remarks about a neuropsychological study of organic dementia. *Acta Neurologica, 32,* 682–696.

Gruman, G.J. (1966) *A history of ideas about the prolongation of life: the evolution of prolongivity hypothesis to 1800.* Philadelphia: American Philosophical Society.

Gurland, B & Toner, J (1983) Differentiating dementia from nondementing conditions. In R Mayeux & W.G. Rosen (eds) *The Dementias.* New York: Raven.

Haan, N. (1972) Personality development from adolescence to adulthood in the Oakland growth and guidance studies. *Seminars in Psychiatry, 4,* 399–414.

Haase, E.R. (1977) Diseases presenting as dementia. In C.E. Wells (ed) *Dementia.* Philadelphia: Davis.

Hachinski, V.C., Iliff, L.D., Zilkha, E. *et al.* (1975) Cerebral blood flow in dementia. *Archives of Neurology, 32,* 632–637.

Hachinski, V.C., Lassen, N.A. & Marshall, J (1974) Multi-infarct dementia, a cause of mental deterioration in the elderly. *Lancet, 1978,* 207–210.

Hamm, V.P. & Hasher, L. (1992) Age and the availability of inferences. *Psychology and Aging, 7,* 56–64.

Harkins, S.W., Price, D.D. & Martelli, M. (1986) *Special senses in aging: A current biological assessment.* Ann Arbor, MI: The Institute on Gerontology at the University of Michigan.

Harrington, D.L. & Haaland, K.Y. (1992) Skill learning in the elderly: Diminished implicit and explicit memory for a motor sequence. *Psychology and Aging, 7,* 425–435.

Hart, S. & Semple, J.M. (1990) *Neuropsychology and the Dementias.* London: Taylor & Francis.

Hartley, J.T. (1988) Aging and individual differences in memory for written discourse. In L.L. Light & D. Burke (eds) *Language, Memory and Aging.* New York: Cambridge University Press.

Hasher, L. & Zacks, R.T. (1979) Automatic and effortful processes in memory. *Journal of Experimental Psychology: General, 108,* 356–388.

Havinghurst, R.J., Neugarten, B.L.A. & Tobin, S.S.C. (1968) Disengagement and patterns of aging. In B.L. Neugarten (ed) *Middle Age and Aging.* Chicago: University of Chicago Press.

Hawkins, H.L., Kramer, A.F. & Capaldi, D. (1992) Aging, exercise, and attention. *Psychology and Aging, 7,* 643–653.

Hayflick, L. (1977) The cellular basis for biological aging. In C.E. Finch & L. Hayflick (eds) *Handbook of the Biology of Aging.* New York: Academic Press.

Hayslip, B. & Sterns, H.L. (1979) Age differences in relationships between crystallised and fluid intelligence and problem solving. *Journal of Gerontology, 34,* 404–414.

Hecaen, H & Albert, M.L. (1978) *Human Neuropsychology.* Chichester: John Wiley.

Herbst, K.G. (1982) Social attitudes to hearing loss in the elderly. In F. Glendenning (ed) *Acquired Hearing Loss and Elderly People.* Keele: Beth Johnson Foundation Publications.

Herrmann, D.J. (1984) Questionnaires about memory. In J.E. Harris & P.E. Morris (eds) *Everyday Memory, Actions, and Absentmindedness.* London: Academic Press.

Herrmann, D.J., Rea, A & Andrzejewski, S (1988) The need for a new approach to memory training. In M.M. Gruneberg, P.E. Morris & R.N. Sykes (eds) *Practical Aspects of Memory: Current Research and Issues.* Chichester: Wiley.

Hertzog, C. (1991) Aging, information processing speed, and intelligence. In K.W. Schaie & M.P. Lawton (eds) *Annual Review of Gerontology and Geriatrics, 11,* 55–79.

Herzog, A.R., House, J.S. & Morgan, J.N. (1991) Relation of work and retirement to health and well-being in older age. *Psychology and Aging, 6,* 202–211.

Heston, L.L., Mastri, A.R., Anderson, V.E. & White, J. (1981) Dementia of the Alzheimer type. Animal genetics, natural history and associated conditions. *Arch. Gen. Psychiat., 38,* 1085–1090.

Hilgard, E.R., Atkinson, R.L. & Atkinson, R.C. (1979) *Introduction to Psychology, 7th Edition.* New York: Harcourt Brace Jovanovich.

Holland, C. & Rabbitt, P. (1989) Subjective and objective measures of vision and hearing loss in elderly drivers and pedestrians. Talk at ESRC/General Accident Insurance Company Symposium on Road Traffic Accidents. University of Reading, 5th July. Cited: Rabbitt (1990).

Holland, C.A. & Rabbitt, P.M.A. (1990) Autobiographical and text recall in the elderly: an investigation of a processing resource deficit. *Quarterly Journal of Experimental Psychology, 42A,* 441–470.

Holliday, S.G. & Chandler, M.J. (1986) *Wisdom: Exploratios in adult competence. Contributions to human development, 17, Basel: Karger.* Cited: Perlmutter, M. & Hall, E. (1992) *Adult Development and Aging.* New York: John Wiley, p 269.

Horn, J.L. (1978) Human ability systems. In P.B. Baltes (ed) *Life-span development and behaviour Vol. I.* New York: Academic Press, 211–256.

Horn (1982) The theory of fluid and crystallised intelligence in relation to concepts of cognitive psychology and aging in adulthood. In F.I.M. Craik & S. Trehub (eds) *Aging and Cognitive Processes.* New York: Plenum.

Horn, J.L. & Cattell, R.B. (1967) Age differences in fluid and crystallised intelligence. *Acta Psychologia, 26,* 107–129.

Howard, D.V. (1988) Aging and memory activation: the priming of semantic and episodic memories. In L.L. Light & D.M. Burke (eds) *Language, Memory and Aging.* New York: Cambridge University Press.

238 / THE PSYCHOLOGY OF AGEING

Howard, D.V. & Howard, J.H. (1992) Adult age differences in the rate of learning serial patterns: evidence from direct and indirect tests. *Psychology and Aging, 7,* 232–241.

Hudson, L. (1987). Creativity. In R.L. Gregory & O.L. Zangwill (eds) *The Oxford Companion to the Mind.* Oxford: Oxford University Press.

Huff, F.J., Corkin, S. & Growdon, J.M. (1986) Semantic impairment & anomia in Alzheimer's disease. *Brain & Language, 28,* 235–249.

Hultsch, D.F., Hertzog, C., Small, B.J. *et al.* (1992) Short-term longitudinal change in cognitive performance in later life. *Psychology and Aging, 7,* 571–584.

Hunziker, O., Abdel'Al, S., Frey, H., Veteau, M.-J. & Meier-Ruge, W. (1978) Quantitative studies in the cerebral cortex of aging humans. *Gerontology, 24,* 27–31.

Hutchinson, K.M. (1989) Influence of sentence context on speech perception in young and older adults. *Journal of Gerontology: Psychological Sciences, 44,* 36–44.

Hybertson, E.D., Perdue, J., & Hybertson, D. (1982) Age differences in information acquisition strategies. *Experimental Aging Research, 8,* 109–113.

Jackson, J.L., Bogers, H & Kersholt, J (1988) Do memory aids aid the elderly in their day to day remembering? In M.M. Gruneberg, P.E. Morris & R.N. Sykes (eds) *Practical Aspects of Memory: Current Research and Issues.* Chichester: Wiley.

Jackson, J.S., Antonucci, T.C. & Gibson, R.C. (1990) Cultural, racial, and ethnic minority influences on aging. In J.E. Birren & K.W. Schaie (eds) *Handbook of the Psychology of Aging, 3rd edition.* San Diego: Academic Press.

Jaffe, G.J., Alvarado, J.A., & Juster, R.P. (1986) Age-related changes of the normal visual field. *Archives of Ophthalmology, 104,* 1021–1025.

James, C. (1983) *Falling Towards England.* London: Jonathan Cape.

Jarvik, L.F. (1983) Age is in – is the wit out? In D. Samuel, S. Algeri, S. Gershon, V.E. Grimm & G. Toffanl (eds) *Aging of the Brain.* New York: Raven Press, 1–7.

Jarvik, L.F. & Falek, A. (1963) Intellectual stability and survival in the aged. *Journal of Gerontology, 18,* 173–176.

Jeffreys, M. (ed) (1989) *Growing Old in the Twentieth Century.* London: Routledge.

Jenike, M (1988) Depression and other psychiatric disorders. In M.S. Albert & M.B. Moss (eds) *Geriatric Neuropsychology.* New York: Guilford.

Jennings, J.M. & Jacoby, L.L. (1993) Automatic versus intentional uses of memory: Aging, attention, and control. *Psychology and Aging, 8,* 283–293.

Johnson, P. & Falkingham, J. (1992) *Ageing and Economic Welfare.* London: Sage.

Kahn, R.L., Goldfarb, A.I., Pollack, M. & Peck, A (1960) Brief objective measures for determination of mental status in the aged. *American Journal of Psychiatry, 117,* 326–328.

Kail, R. & Pelligrino, J.W. (1985) *Human Intelligence: Perspective and prospects.* San Francisco: Freeman.

Kart, C.S. (1981) *The Realities of Aging.* Boston: Allyn & Bacon.

Kart, C.S. Metress, E.S. & Metress, J.F. (1978) *Aging and Health: Biologic and Social Perspectives.* Menlo Park, Calif: Addison-Wesley.

Katzman, R., Lasker, B. & Bernstein, N. (1988) Advances in the diagnosis of dementia: Accuracy of diagnosis and consequences of misdiagnosis of disorders causing dementia. In R.D. Terry (ed) *Aging and the Brain*. New York: Raven.

Kausler, D.H. (1982) *Experimental Psychology and Human Aging*. New York: John Wiley.

Kemper, S. (1986) Limitation of complex syntactic construction by elderly adults. *Applied Psycholinguistics, 7*, 277–287.

Kemper, S. (1987a) Adults' diaries: changes to written narratives across the life span. *Conference on Social Psychology and Language, July 20–24, 1987*.

Kemper, S. (1987b) Life-span changes in syntactic complexity. *Journal of Gerontology, 42*, 323–328.

Kemper, S. (1988) Geriatric psycholinguistics: syntactic limitation of oral and written language. In L.L. Light & D.M. Burke (eds) *Language, Memory and Aging*. New York: Cambridge University Press.

Kemper, S. (1992) Language and aging In F.I.M. Craik & T.A. Salthouse (eds) *The Handbook of Aging and Cognition*. Hillsdale, New Jersey: Lawrence Erlbaum.

Kemper, S. & Rash, S.J. (1988) Speech and writing across the life span. In P.E. Morris, M.M. Gruneberg & R.N. Sykes (eds) *Practical Aspects of Memory*. Chichester: Wiley.

Kennedy, S, Kiecolt-Glaser, J.K., & Glaser, R (1988). Immunological consequences of acute and chronic stressors: mediating role of interpersonal relationships. *British Journal of Medical Psychology, 61*, 77–85.

Kermis, M.D. (1983) *The Psychology of Human Aging. Theory, Research and Practice*. Boston: Allyn and Bacon.

Kermis, M.D. (1986) *Mental Health in Late Life. The Adaptive Process*. Boston: Jones & Bartlett.

Kidson & Chen (1986) DNA damage, DNA repair and the genetic basis of Alzheimer's disease. In D.F. Swaab *et al.* (eds) *Progress in Brain Research, 70*. Amsterdam: Elsevier.

Kirkwood, T.B.L. (1988) The nature and causes of ageing. In *Research and the Ageing Population*. CIBA Foundation Symposium 134. Chichester: Wiley. 193–207.

Kite, M.E., Deaux, K. & Miele, M. (1993) Stereotypes of young and old: Does age outweigh gender? *Psychology and Aging, 8*, 19–27.

Kleemeier, R.W. (1962) Intellectual changes in the senium. *Proceedings of the Social Statistics Section of the American Statistical Association, 1*, 290–295.

Kogan, N (1990) Personality and Aging. In J.E. Birren & K.W. Schaie (eds) *Handbook of the Psychology of Aging, 3rd. edition*. San Diego: Academic Press.

Kopelman, M.D. (1985) Rates of forgetting in Alzheimer-type dementia and Korsakoff's syndrome. *Neuropsychologia, 23*, 623–638.

Krause, N., Jay, G. & Liang, J. (1991) Financial strain and psychological well-being among the American and Japanese elderly. *Psychology and Aging, 6*, 170–181.

Krmpotic-Nemanic, J. (1969) Presbycusis and retrocochlear structures. *International Audiology, 8*, 210–220.

Kvavilashvili, L (1987) Remembering intention as a distinct form of memory. *British Journal of Psychology, 78*, 507–518.

Kuypers, J.A. & Bengtson, U.L. (1973) Social breakdown and competence. *Human Development, 16*, 181–201.

Kynette, D. & Kemper, S. (1986) Aging and the loss of grammatical form: a cross-sectional study of language performance. *Language and Communication, 6,* 65–72.

La Rue, A. (1992) *Aging and Neuropsychological Assessment.* New York: Plenum.

Labouvie-Vief, G. (1992) A neo-Piagetian perspective on adult cognitive development In R.J. Sternberg & C.A. Berg (eds) *Intellectual Development.* Cambridge: Cambridge University Press.

Labouvie-Vief, G & Gonda, J.N. (1976) Cognitive strategy training and intellectual performance in the elderly. *Journal of Gerontology, 31,* 327–332.

Larrabee, G.J. & Crook, T.H. (1993) Do men show more rapid age-associated decline in simulated everyday verbal memory than do women? *Psychology and Aging, 8,* 68–71.

Larson, R. (1978) Thirty years of research on the subjective well-being of older Americans. *Journal of Gerontology, 33,* 109–125.

Laslett, P. (1976) Societal development and aging. In R.H. Binstock & E. Shanas (eds) *Handbook of Aging and the Social Sciences.* New York: Reinhold.

Laurence, M.W. & Arrowood, A.J. (1982) Classification style differences in the elderly. In F.I.M. Craik & S. Trehub (eds) *Aging and Cognitive Processes.* New York: Plenum.

Laver, G.D. & Burke, D.M. (1993) Why do semantic priming effects increase in old age? A Meta-analysis. *Psychology and Aging, 8,* 34–43.

Leli, D.A. & Scott, L.H. (1982) Cross-validation of the two indexes of intellectual deterioration on patients with Alzheimer's disease. *Journal of Consulting and Clinical Psychology, 50,* 468.

Lennox, G., Lowe, J.S., Godwin-Austen, M.L. & Mayer, R.J. (1989) Diffuse Lewy body disease: An important differential diagnosis in dementia with extrapyramidal features. In K. Iqbal, H.M. Wisniewski & B. Winblad (eds) *Alzheimer's Disease and Related Disorders.* New York: Alan R. Liss.

Levenson, R.W. Cartensen, L.L. & Gottman, J.M. (1993) Long-term marriage: Age, gender, and satisfaction. *Psychology and Aging, 8,* 310–313.

Levinson, D. (1978) *The Season of a Man's Life.* New York: Ballantine.

Levinson, D. (1980) Conception of the adult life course. In N. Smelser & E. Erikson (eds) *Themes of Work and Love in Adulthood.* Cambridge, Mass.: Harvard University Press.

Light, L.L. (1992) The organization of memory in old age In F.I.M. Craik & T.A. Salthouse (eds) *The Handbook of Aging and Cognition.* Hillsdale, New Jersey: Lawrence Erlbaum.

Light, L.L. & Albertson, S.A. (1988) Comprehension of pragmatic implications in young and older adults. In L.L. Light & D.M. Burke (eds) *Language, Memory and Aging.* New York: Cambridge University Press.

Light, L.L. & Albertson, S.A. (1989) Direct and indirect tests of memory for category exemplars in young and older adults. *Psychology and Aging, 4,* 487–492.

Light, L.L. & Anderson P.A. (1985) Working-memory capacity, age and memory for discourse. *Journal of Gerontology, 40,* 737–747.

Lima, S.D., Hale, S. & Myerson, J. (1991) How general is general slowing? Evidence from the lexical domain. *Psychology and Aging, 6,* 416–425.

Lindenberger, U., Kliegl, R. & Baltes, P.B. (1992) Professional expertise does not eliminate age differences in imagery-based memory performance during adulthood. *Psychology and Aging, 7,* 585–593.

Lindenberger, U., Mayr, U. & Kliegl, R. (1993) Speed and intelligence in old age. *Psychology and Aging, 8,* 207–220.

Lopata, H. (1973) *Widowhood in an American City.* Cambridge: Schenkman.

Luquet, G.H. (1927) *Le Dessin Enfant.* Paris: Alcan.

Maas, M.S. & Kuypers, J.A. (1974) *From Thirty to Seventy.* San Francisco: Jossey-Bass.

Maddox, G.I. (1970a) Persistence of life style among the elderly. In E. Palmore (ed) *Normal Aging.* Durham: Duke University Press.

Maddox, G.L. (1970b) Themes and issues in sociological theories of human aging. *Human Development, 13,* 17–27.

Mandel, R.G. & Johnson, N.S. (1984) A developmental analysis of story recall and comprehension in adulthood. *Journal of Verbal Learning and Verbal Behaviour, 23,* 643–659.

Marsden, C.D. & Harrison, M.J.G. (1972) Outcome of investigation of patients with presenile dementia. *British Medical Journal, 2,* 249–252.

Marsh, G.A. (1980) Perceptual changes with aging. In E.W. Busse & D.G. Blazer (eds)I Handbook of Geriatric Psychiatry. New York: Van Nostrand Reinhold.

Marsh, G.R. & Watson, W.E. (1980) Psychophysiological studies of aging effects on cognitive processes. In D.G. Stein (ed) *The Psychobiology of Aging. Problems and Perspectives.* New York: Elsevier North-Holland.

Marshall, L. (1981) Auditory processing in ageing listeners. *Journal of Speech and Hearing Disorders, 43,* 226–240.

Martin, A., Brouwers, P., Cox, C., & Fedio, P. (1985) On the nature of verbal memory deficit in Alzheimer's disease. *Brain & Language, 25,* 323–342.

Martin, A. & Fedio, P. (1983) Word production and comprehension in Alzheimer's disease: the breakdown of semantic knowledge. *Brain & Language, 19,* 124–141.

Martin, C.E. (1981) Factors affecting sexual functioning in 60–79 year old married males. *Archives of Sexual Behavior, 10,* 339–420.

Martone, M., Butlers, N., Payne, M. *et al.* (1984) Dissociation between skill learning and verbal recognition in amnesia and dementia. *Arch. Neurol., 41,* 965–970.

Masoro, E.J. (1988) Food restriction in rodents: An evaluation of its role in the study of aging. *Journal of Gerontology, 43,* 59–64.

Masters, W.H. & Johnson, V.E. (1966) *Human Sexual Response.* Boston: Little, Brown.

Maylor, E.A. (1990a) Age and prospective memory. *Quarterly Journal of Experimental Psychology, 42A,* 471–493.

Maylor, E.A. (1990b) Age, blocking and the tip of the tongue state. *British Journal of Psychology, 81,* 123–134.

McCrae, R.R., Arenberg, D. & Costa, P.T. (1987) Declines in divergent thinking with age: Cross-sectional, longitudinal, and cross-sequential analyses. *Psychology and Aging, 2,* 130–137.

McCubbin, H.I., & Patterson, J.M. (1982) Family adaptation to crises. In H.I. McCubbin, A.E. Cauble, & J.M. Patterson (eds) *Family Stress, Coping and Social Support.* Springfield: Thomas.

McDowd, J.M. & Filion, D.L. (1992) Aging, selective attention and inhibitory processes: A psychophysiological approach. *Psychology and Aging, 7,* 65–71.

McEvoy, C.L., Nelson, D.L., Holley, P.E. & Stelnicki, G.S. (1992) Implicit processing in the cued recall of young and old adults. *Psychology and Aging, 7,* 401–408.

McHale, M.C., McHale, J. & Streatfield, G.J. (1979) *Children in the World.* Washington, D.C.: Population Reference Bureau.

McFarland, R.A. & Fisher, M.B. (1955) Alterations in dark adaptation as a function of age. *Journal of Gerontology, 10,* 424–428.

Meacham, J.A. (1990) The loss of wisdom In R.J. Sternberg (ed) *Wisdom: Its Natuer, Origins, and Development.* Cambridge: Cambridge University Press.

Medawar, P.B. (1952) *An Unsolved Problem of Biology.* London: H.K. Lewis.

Meier-Ruge, W., Gygax, P. & Wiernsperger, N. (1980) A synoptic view of pathophysiology and experimental pharmacology in gerontological brain research. In C. Eisdorfer & W.E. Fann (eds) *Psychopharmacology of Aging.* New York: S.P. Medical and Scientific Books, 65–98.

Meier-Ruge, W., Hunziker, O., Iwangoff, P., Reichlmeier, K. & Schultz, U. (1980) Effect of age on morphological and biochemical parameters of the human brain. In D.G. Stein (ed) *The Psychobiology of Aging. Problems and Perspectives.* New York: Elsevier North-Holland.

Merriman, A. (1984) Social customs affecting the role of elderly women in Indian society. In D.B. Bromley (ed) *Gerontology: Social and Behavioural Perspectives.* London: Croom Helm.

Metter, E.J. (1988) Positron emission tomography and cerebral blood flow studies. In M.S. Albert & M.B. Moss (eds) *Geriatric Neuropsychology.* New York: Guilford Press.

Meyer, B.J.F. (1987) Reading comprehension and aging. In K.W. Schaie (ed) *Annual Review of Gerontology and Geriatrics, 7.* New York: Springer.

Midwinter, E (1991) *The British Gas Report on Attitudes to Ageing 1991.* British Gas.

Miller, E. (1973) Short and long-term memory in patients with presenile dementia (Alzheimer's disease). *Psy. Medicine, 3,* 221–224.

Miller, E. (1974) Psychomotor performance in presenile dementia. *Psy. Medicine, 4,* 65–69.

Miller, E. (1975) Impaired recall and the memory disturbance in presenile dementia. *British Journal of Social and Clinical Psychology, 14,* 73–79.

Miller, E. & Lewis, P. (1977) Recognition memory in elderly patients with depression and dementia: a signal detection analysis. *Journal of Abnormal Psychology, 86,* 84–86.

Miller, M. (1979) *Suicide After Sixty: The Final Alternative.* New York: Springer.

Morris, R.G. (1984) Dementia and the functioning of the articulatory loop system. *Cognitive Neuropsychology, 1,* 143–157.

Morris, R.G. (1986) Short-term forgetting in senile dementia of the Alzheimer's type. *Cognitive Neuropsychology, 3,* 77–97.

Morris, R.G., Craik, F.I.M. & Gick, M.L. (1990) Age differences in working memory tasks. The role of secondary memory and the central executive system. *Quarterly Journal of Experimental Psychology, 42A,* 67–86.

Morris, R.G., Gick, M.L. & Craik, F.I.M. (1988) Processing resources and age differences in working memory. *Memory and Cognition, 16,* 362–366.

Morris, R.G. & Kopelman, M.D. (1986) The memory deficit in Alzheimer-type dementia: a review. *Quarterly Journal of Experimental Psychology, 38A,* 575–602.

Morrissey, E., Becker, J. & Rubert, M.P. (1990) Coping resources and depression in the caregiving spouses of Alzheimers patients. *British Journal of Medical Psychology, 63,* 161–171.

Morrow, D.G., Von Leirer, O. & Altieri, P.A. (1992) Aging, expertise, and narrative processing. *Psychology and Aging, 7,* 376–388.

Morse, C.K. (1993) Does variability increase with age? An archival study of cognitive measures. *Psychology and Aging, 8,* 156–164.

Moscovitch, M. (1982) A neurophysiological approach to memory and perception in normal and pathological aging. In F.I.M. Craik & S. Trehub (eds) *Aging and Cognitive Processes.* New York: Plenum.

Moss, M.B. & Albert, M.S. (1988) Alzheimer's disease and other dementing disorders. In M.S. Albert & M.B. Moss (eds) *Geriatric Neuropsychology.* New York: Guilford.

Murphy, C. (1985) Cognitive and chemosensory influences on age-related changes in the ability to identify blended foods. *Journal of Gerontology, 40,* 217–222.

Murphy, E.A. (1978) Genetics of longetivity in man. In E.L. Schneider (ed) *The Genetics of Aging.* New York: Plenum Press.

Myerson, J., Ferraro, F.R., Hale, S. & Lima, S.D. (1992) General slowing in smenatic priming and word recognition. *Psychology and Aging, 7,* 257–270.

National Council on Aging (1975) *The Myth and Reality of Aging in America.* Washington, D.C.

Nebes, R.D. (1992) Cognitive dysfunction in Alzheimer's Disease. In F.I.M. Craik & T.A. Salthouse (eds) *The Handbook of Aging and Cognition.* Hillsdale, New Jersey: Lawrence Erlbaum.

Nebes, R.D. & Brady, C.B. (1990) Preserved organization of semantic attributes in Alzheimer's Disease. *Psychology and Aging, 5,* 574–579.

Nelson, H.E. & McKenna, P. (1973) The use of current reading ability in the assessment of dementia. *British Journal of Social and Clinical Psychology, 14,* 259–267.

Nelson, H.E. & O'Connell, A. (1978) Dementia: the estimation of premorbid intelligence levels using the New Adult Reading Test. *Cortex, 14,* 234–244.

Neugarten, B.L. (1977) Personality and aging. In J.E. Birren & K.W. Schaie (eds) *Handbook of the Psychology of Aging.* New York: Reinhold.

Neugarten, B.L., Havinghurst, R.J. & Tobin, S.S. (1961) The measurement of life satisfaction. *Journal of Gerontology, 16,* 134–143.

Neugarten, B.L., Havinghurst, R.J. & Tobin, S.S. (1968) Personality and pattern of aging. In B.L. Neugarten (ed) *Middle Age and Aging.* Chicago University Press.

Nielsen, J., Homma, A. & Bjorn-Hendriksen, T. (1977) Follow-up 15 years after a geronto-psychiatric prevalence study: Conditions concerning death, and life expectancy in relation to psychiatric diagnosis. *Journal of Gerontology, 32,* 554–561.

Nigro, G. & Neisser, U (1983) Point of view in personal memories. *Cognitive Psychology, 15,* 465–482.

Nissen, M.J. & Corkin, S. (1985) Effectiveness of attentional cueing in older and younger adults. *Journal of Gerontology, 40,* 185–191.

Nissen, M.J., Corkin, S., Buonanno, F.S. *et al.* (1985) Spatial vision in Alzheimer's disease. *Archives of Neurology, 42,* 667–671.

Norman, A. (1985) *Triple Jeopardy: Growing Old in a Second Homeland.* London: Centre for Policy on Ageing.

Norris, M.L. & Cunningham, D.R. (1981) Social impact of hearing loss in the aged. *Journal of Gerontology, 36,* 727–729.

Norris, M.P. & West, R.L. (1993) Activity memory and ageing: The role of motor retrieval and strategic processing. *Psychology and Aging, 8,* 81–86.

O'Carroll, R.E., Baikie, E.M. & Whittick, J.E. (1987) Does the National Adult Reading Test hold in dementia? *British Journal of Clinical Psychology, 26,* 315–316.

O'Carroll, R.E. & Gilleard, C.J. (1986) Estimation of premorbid intelligence in dementia. *British Journal of Clinical Psychology, 25,* 157–158.

OECD (1988) *Ageing Populations: The Social Policy Implications.* Paris: OECD.

Olsen, D.R., Torrance, N. & Hildyard, A. (eds) (1985) *Literacy, Language and Learning.* Cambridge: Cambridge University Press.

OPCS (1991) *National Population Projections 1989 Based.* Series PP2 No. 17. London: HMSO.

Owens, W.A. (1959) Is age kinder to the initially more able? *Journal of Gerontology, 14,* 334–337.

Owsley, C., Sekuler, R. & Boldt, C. (1981) Aging and low-contrast vision: Face perception. *Invest. Ophthalmol. Vis. Sci., 21,* 362–365.

Oyer, H.J. & Deal, L.V. (1989) Temporal aspects of speech and the aging process. *Folia-Phoniatrica, 37,* 109–112.

Palmore, E. & Cleveland, W. (1976). Aging, terminal decline and terminal drop. *Journal of Gerontology, 31,* 76–81.

Papalia, D.E. (1972) The status of several conservation abilities across the life-span. *Human Development, 15,* 229–243.

Park, D.C. & Shaw, R.J. (1992) Effect of environmental support on implicit and explicit memory in younger and older adults. *Psychology and Aging, 7,* 632–642.

Parkin, A.J. & Walter, B.M. (1992) Recollective experience, normal aging, and frontal dysfunction. *Psychology and Aging, 7,* 290–298.

Parnes, H. (1981) *Work and Retirement: A Longitudinal Study of Men.* Cambridge, Mass.: MIT Press.

Pattison, E.M. (1977) *The Experience of Dying.* New York: Prentice Hall.

Peck, R.C. (1968) Psychological developments in the second half of life. In B.L. Neugarten (ed) *Middle Age and Aging: A Reader in Social Psychology.* Chicago: University of Chicago Press.

Peretz, J.A. & Cummings, J.L. (1988) Subcortical dementia In U. Holden (ed) *Neuropsychology and Ageing.* London: Croom Helm.

Perez, F.I., Rivera, V.M., Meyer, J.S. *et al.* (1975) Analysis of intellectual and cognitive performance in patients with multi-infarct dementia, vertobrobasilar insufficiency with dementia and Alzheimer's disease. *Journal of Neurology, Neurosurgery & Psychiatry, 38,* 533–540.

Perfect, T.J. (in press) What can Brinley plots tell us about cognitive aging? *Journal of Gerontology: Psychological Sciences.*

Perlmutter, M (1978) What is memory aging the aging of? *Developmental Psychology, 14,* 330–345.

Perlmutter, M. & Hall, E. (1992) *Adult Development and Aging.* New York: John Wiley.

Perlmutter, M. & Mitchell, D.B. (1982) The appearance and disappearance of age differences in adult memory. In F.I.M. Craik & S. Trehub (eds) *Aging and cognitive processes.* New York: Plenum.

Perlmutter, L.C. & Monty, R.A. (1989) Motivation and aging. In Poon, L.W., Rubin, D.C. & Wilson, B.A. (eds) *Everyday Cognition in Adulthood and Late Life.* Cambridge: Cambridge University Press.

Perlmutter, M., Adams, C., Berry, S., Kaplan, M. & Person, D. (1987) Aging and memory. In K.W. Schaie (ed) *Annual Review of Gerontology and Geriatrics, 7,* 57–92. New York: Springer.

Petit, T.L. (1982) Neuroanatomical and clinical neuropsychological changes in aging and senile dementia. In F.I.M. Craik & S. Trehub (eds) *Aging and Cognitive Processes.* New York: Plenum.

Petros, T., Tabar, L., Cooney, T. & Chabot, R.J. (1983) Adult age differences in sensitivity to semantic structure of prose. *Developmental Psychology, 19,* 907–914.

Pitts, D.G. (1982) The effects of aging on selected visual functions: dark adaptation, visual acuity, stereopsis, and brightness contrast. In R. Sekuler, D. Kline & K. Dismukes (eds) *Aging and Human Visual Function.* New York: Alan R. Liss, 121–130.

Poon, L.W., Fozard, J.L., Paushock, D.R. & Thomas, J.C. (1979) A questionnaire assessment of age differences in retention of recent and remote events. *Experimental Age Research, 5,* 401–411.

Poon, L.W. & Schaffer, G. (1982) Prospective memory in young and elderly adults. *Paper presented at meeting of American Psychological Association,* Washington D.C. Cited West (1988).

Post, F. (1982) Functional disorders. In R. Levy & F. Post (eds) *The Psychiatry of Later Life.* Oxford: Blackwell.

Powell, R.R. (1974) Psychological effects of exercise therapy upon institutionalized geriatric mental patients. *Journal of Gerontology, 29,* 157–161.

Pratt, M.W., Diessner, R., Hunsberger, B. *et al.* (1991) Four pathways in the analysis of adult development and aging: comparing analyses of reasoning about personal-life dilemmas. *Psychology and Aging, 6,* 666–675.

Pruchno, R. & Kleban, M.H. (1993) Caring for an institutionalized parent: The role of coping strategies. *Psychology and Aging, 8,* 18–25.

Qureshi, H. & Wlaker, A. (1989) *The Caring Relationship: Elderly People and Their Families.* London: Macmillan.

Rabbitt, P.M.A. (1979) Some experiments and a model for changes in attentional selectivity with old age. In F. Hoffmeister & C. Muller (eds) *Bayer Symposium VII. Evaluation of Change.* Bonn: Springer.

Rabbitt, P.M.A. (1980) A fresh look at reaction times in old age. In D.G. Stein (ed), The Psychobiology of Aging: Problems and Perspectives. New York: Elsevier.

Rabbitt, P.M.A. (1982) How do the old know what to do next? In F.I.M. Craik & S. Trehub (eds) *Aging and Cognitive Processes.* New York: Plenum.

Rabbitt, P.M.A. (1984) Memory impairment in the elderly. In P.E. Bebbington & R. Jacoby (eds) *Psychiatric Disorders in the Elderly.* London: Mental Health Foundation, 101–119.

Rabbitt, P.M.A. (1988a) The faster the better? Some comments on the use of information processing rate as an index of change and individual differences in performance. In I. Hindmarch, B. Aufdembrinke & H. Ott (eds) *Psychopharmacology and Reaction Time.* London: John Wiley.

Rabbitt, P.M.A. (1988b) Does fast last? Is speed a basic factor determining individual differences in memory? In M.M. Gruneberg, P.E. Morris & R.N. Sykes (eds) *Practical Aspects of Memory.* Volume 2.

Rabbitt, P.M.A. (1988c) Human Intelligence (Critical Notice of R.J. Sternberg's work). *Quarterly Journal of Experimental Psychology, 40A,* 167–187.

Rabbitt, P.M.A. (1989) Secondary central effects on memory and attention of mild hearing loss in the elderly. *Acta Psychologica Scandanavica.*

Rabbitt, P.M.A. (1990) Applied cognitive gerontology: some problems, methodologies and data. *Applied Cognitive Psychology, 4,* 225–246.

Rabbitt, P. (1993) Does it all go together when it goes? *Quarterly Journal of Experimental Psychology, 46A,* 385–434.

Rabbitt, P.M.A. & Abson, V. (1990) 'Lost and found': some logical and methodological limitations of self-report questionnaires as tools to study cognitive ageing. *British Journal of Psychology, 81,* 1–16.

Rabbitt, P.M.A. & Goward, L. (1986) Effects of age and raw IQ test scores on mean correct and mean error reaction times in serial choice tasks: A reply to Smith and Brewer. *British Journal of Psychology, 77,* 69–73.

Rabbitt, P.M.A. & Winthorpe, C. (1988) What do old people remember? The Galton paradigm reconsidered. In M.M. Gruneberg, P.E. Morris & R.N. Sykes (eds) *Practical Aspects of Memory.* Volume 2.

Raskin, A. (1979) Signs and symptoms of psychopathology in the elderly. In A. Raskin & L.F. Jarvik (eds) *Psychiatric Symptoms and Cognitive Loss in the Elderly.* Washington, D.C.: Hemisphere.

Rebok, G.W. (1987) *Life-Span Cognitive Development.* New York: Holt, Rinehart & Winston.

Reding, M., Haycox, J. & Blass, J. (1985) Depression in patients referred to a dementia clinic: A three-year prospective study. *Archives of Neurology, 42,* 894–896.

Reichard, S Livson, F. & Peterson, P.G. (1962) *Aging and Personality: A Study of 87 Older Men.* New York: Wiley.

Reimanis, G. & Green, R.F. (1971) Imminence of death and intellectual decrement in the aged. *Developmental Psychology, 5,* 270–272.

Reisberg, B., Ferris, S.H., de Leon, M.J. *et al.* (1989) The stage specific temporal course of Alzheimer's Disease: Functional and behavioural concomitants based upon cross-sectional and longitudinal observation. In K. Iqbal, H.M. Wisniewski & B. Winblad (eds) *Alzheimer's Disease and Related Disorders.* New York: Alan R. Liss.

Reisberg, B., Ferris, S.H., Franssen, E. *et al.* (1989) Clinical features of a neuropathologically verified familial Alzheimer's cohort with onset in the fourth decade: Comparison with senile onset Alzheimer's Disease and etiopathogenic implications. In K. Iqbal, H.M. Wisniewski & B. Winblad (eds) *Alzheimer's Disease and Related Disorders.* New York: Alan R. Liss.

Ribot, T. (1882) *Diseases of memory.* London: Kegan, Paul, Tench & Co.

Ribovich, J.K. & Erikson, L. (1980) A study of lifelong reading with implications for instructional programs. *Journal of Reading, 24,* 20–26.

Rice, G.E. (1986a) The everyday activities of adults: implications for prose recall. Part I. *Educational Gerontology, 12,* 173–186.

Rice, G.E. (1986b) The everyday activities of adults: implications for prose recall. Part II. *Educational Gerontology, 12,* 187–198.

Rice, G.E. & Meyer, B.J.F. (1986) Prose recall: effects of aging, verbal ability and reading behaviour. *Journal of Gerontology, 41,* 469–480.

Rice, G.E., Meyer, B.J.F. & Miller, D.C. (1988) Relation of everyday activities of adults to their prose recall performance. *Educational Gerontology, 14,* 147–158.

Riegel, K.F. & Riegel, R.M. (1972) Development, drop, and death. *Developmental Psychology, 6,* 306–319.

Rivera, P.A., Rose, J.M., Futterman, A. *et al.* (1991) Dimensions of perceived social support in clinically depressed and nondepressed female caregivers. *Psychology and Aging, 6,* 323–237.

Robertson, J.F. (1977) Grandmotherhood: A study of role concepts. *Journal of Marriage & the Family, 39,* 165–174.

Rodgers, B. (1984) The trend of reading standards re-assessed. *Educational Research, 26,* 153–166.

Rosen, W.G., Mohs, R.C. & Davis, K.L. (1984) A new rating scale for Alzheimer's disease. *American Journal of Psychiatry, 14,* 1356–1364.

Rosenthal, C.J. (1986) Family supports in later life: does ethnicity make a difference? *The Gerontologist, 26,* 19–24.

Rossor, M. & Iversen, L.L. (1986) Non-cholinergic neurotransmitter abnormalities in Alzheimer's disease. *British Medical Bulletin, 42,* 70–74.

Roth, M. (1979) The early diagnosis of Alzheimer's disease: an introduction. In A.I.M. Glen & L. Whalley (eds) *Alzheimer's Disease: Early Recognition of Potentially Reversible Deficits.* Edinburgh: Churchill Livingstone.

Roth, S. & Cohen, L.J. (1986) Approach avoidance, and coping with stress. *American Psychologist, 41,* 813–819.

Rubens, A & Benson, D.F. (1971) Associative visual agnosia. *Archives of Neurology, 24*, 305–316.

Russell, D.W. & Catrona, C.E. (1991) Social support, stress, and depressive symptoms among the elderly: test of a process model. *Psychology and Aging, 6*, 190–201.

Ryan, W.J. (1972) Acoustic aspects of the aging voice. *Journal of Gerontology, 27*, 265–268.

Ryff, C.D. (1991) Possible selves in adulthood and old age: A tale of shifting horizons. *Psychology and Aging, 6*, 286–295.

Salthouse, T. (1982) *Adult Cognition.* New York: Springer.

Salthouse, T.A. (1984) Effects of age and skill in typing. *Journal of Experimental Psychology: General, 13*, 345–371.

Salthouse, T (1985) *A Theory of Cognitive Aging.* Amsterdam: North-Holland.

Salthouse, T.A. (1991a) Mediation of age differences in cognition by reductions in working memory and speed of processing. *Psychological Science, 2*, 179–183.

Salthouse, T.A. (1991b) *Theoretical Perspectives on Cognitive Aging.* Hillsdale, New Jersey: Lawrence Erlbaum.

Salthouse, T.A. (1992a) Reasoning and spatial abilities. In F.I.M. Craik & T.A. Salthouse (eds) *The Handbook of Aging and Cognition.* Hillsdale, New Jersey: Lawrence Erlbaum.

Salthouse, T.A. (1992b) *Mechanisms of Age-Cognition Relations in Adulthood.* Hillsdale, New Jersey: Lawrence Erlbaum.

Sanadi, D.R. (1977) Metabolic changes and their significance in aging. In C.E. Finch & L. Hayflick (eds) *Handbook of the Biology of Aging.* New York: Van Nostrand Reinhold.

Schaie, K.W. (1977) Toward a stage theory of adult cognitive development. *Aging and Human Development, 8*, 129–138.

Schaie, K.W. (1979) The primary mental abilities in adulthood: an exploration in the development of psychometric intelligence. In P.B. Baltes & O.G. Brim (eds) *Life-Span Development and Behavior Vol. 2.* New York: Academic Press, 67–115.

Schaie, K.W. (1983) The Seattle Longitudinal Study: a 21-year exploration of psychometric intelligence in adulthood. In K.W. Schaie (ed) *Longitudinal Studies of Adult Psychological Development.* New York: Guilford Press, 64–135.

Schaie, K.W. (1989) Perceptual speed in adulthood: Cross-sectional studies and longitudinal studies. *Psychology and Aging, 4*, 443–453.

Schaie, K.W. & Hertzog, C. (1986) Toward a comprehensive model of adult intellectual development: Contributions of the Seattle Longitudinal Study. In R.J. Sternberg (ed) *Advances in Human Intelligence, 3.* Hillsdale, New Jersey: Erlbaum. 79–118.

Schaie, K.W. & Willis, S.L. (1991) *Adult Development and Aging.* New York: HarperCollins.

Schiffman, S (1977) Food recognition by the elderly. *Journal of Gerontology, 32*, 586–592.

Schlotterer, G., Moscovitch, M., Crapper, M & McLachlan, D (1984) Visual processing deficits as assessed by spatial frequency contrast sensitivity and backward masking in normal ageing and Alzheimer's disease. *Brain, 107*, 309–325.

Schultz, R. & Williamson, G.M. (1991) A 2-year longitudinal study of depression among Alzheimer's caregivers. *Psychology and Aging, 6,* 569–578.

Schwartz, M.F., Marin, O.S.M. & Saffran, E.M. (1979) Dissociation of language function in dementia: a case study. *Brain and Language, 7,* 277–306.

Schweber, M.S. (1989a) Down Syndrome and the measurement of chromosome 21 DNA amounts in Alzheimer's Disease. In G. Miner, L. Miner, R. Richter *et al.* (eds) *Familial Alzheimer's Disease: Molecular Genetics and Clinical Prospects.* New York: Marcel Dekker.

Schweber, M.S. (1989b) Alzheimer's Disease and Down Syndrome. In K. Iqbal, H.M. Wisniewski & B. Winblad (eds) *Alzheimer's Disease and Related Disorders.* New York: Alan R. Liss.

Sekuler, R. & Blake, R. (1985) *Perception.* New York: Random House.

Sekuler, R., Hutman, L.P. & Owsley, C. (1980) Human aging and vision. *Science, 209,* 1255–1256.

Sekuler, R. & Owsley, C. (1982) The spatial vision of older humans. In R. Sekuler, D. Kline & K. Dismukes (eds) *Aging and Human Visual Function.* New York: Alan R. Liss, 121–130.

Sekuler, R., Owsley, C. & Hutman, L. (1982) Assessing spatial vision of older people. *American Journal of Optometry and Physiological Optics, 59,* 961–968.

Selkoe, D.J. (1992) Aging brain, aging mind. *Scientific American, 267,* 97–103.

Seltzer, B. & Sherwin, I. (1983) A comparison of clinical features in early- and late-onset primary degenerative dementia: one entity or two? *Archives of Neurology, 40,* 143–146.

Shindler, A.G., Caplan, L.R. & Hier, D.B. (1984) Intrusion and perseverations. *Brain & Language, 23,* 148–158.

Shock, N.W. (1977) Biological theories of aging. In J.E. Birren & K.W. Schaie (eds) *Handbook of the Psychology of Aging.* 1st edition. New York: Van Nostrand Reinhold.

Siegler, I.C., McCarty, S.M. & Logue, P.E. (1982) Wechsler Memory Scale scores, selective attention, and distance from death. *Journal of Gerontology, 37,* 176–181.

Simonton, D.K. (1990) Creativity and wisdom in aging. In J.E. Birren & K.W. Schaie (eds) *Handbook of the Psychology of Aging 3rd edition.* San Diego: Academic Press.

Smith, J., Heckhausen, J., Kliegl, R. & Baltes, P.B. (1984) Cognitive reserve capacity, expertise, and aging: Plasticity of digit span performance. *Meeting of Gerontological Society of America, San Antonio.* Cited Rebok (1987).

Smith, S.W. *et al.* (1989) Adult age differences in the use of story structure in delayed free recall. *Experimental Aging Research, 9,* 191–195.

Spencer, R.P. (1976) Change in weight and of the human lens with age. *Annals of Ophthalmology, 8,* 440–441.

Spirduso, W.W. & MacRae, P.G. (1990) Motor Performance and Aging. In J.E. Birren & K.W. Schaie (eds) *Handbook of the Psychology of Aging, 3rd edition.* San Diego: Academic Press.

St. George-Hyslop, P.H., Tanzi, R.E., Polinsky, R.J. *et al.* (1987) The genetic defect causing familial Alzheimer's Disease maps on chromosome 21. *Science, 325,* 885–890.

Stephens, S.D.G. (1982) Rehabilitation and service needs. In M.E. Lutman & M.P. Haggard (eds) *Hearing science and hearing disorders.* London: Academic Press.

Stevens, M (1979) Famous personality test. A test for measuring remote memory. *Bulletin of the British Psychological Society, 32,* 211.

Stine, E.L., Wingfield, A. & Poon L.W. (1986) How much and how fast: rapid processing of spoken language in later adulthood. *Psychology and Aging, 1,* 303–311.

Stine, E.L., Wingfield, A. & Poon, L.W. (1989) Speech comprehension and memory through adulthood: The roles of time and strategy. In Poon, L.W., Rubin, D.C. & Wilson, B.A. (eds) *Everyday Cognition in Adulthood and Late Life.* Cambridge: Cambridge University Press.

Stocker, F.W. & Moore, L.W. Jr. (1975) Detecting changes in the cornea that come with age. *Geriatrics, 30,* 57–69.

Stokes, G. (1992) *On Being Old. The Psychology of Later Life.* London: The Falmer Press.

Storandt, M. (1976) Speed and coding effects in relation to age and ability level. *Developmental Psychology, 12,* 177–178.

Storandt, M. (1977) Age, ability level and scoring the WAIS. *Journal of Gerontology, 32,* 175–178.

Storandt, M. & Futterman, A. (1982) Stimulus size and performance on two subtests of the Wechsler Adult Intelligence Scale by younger and older adults. *Journal of Gerontology, 37,* 602–603.

Strube, M.J., Berry, J.M., Goza, B.K. & Fennimore, D. (1985) Type A behavior, age and psychological well-being. *Journal of Personality and Social Psychology, 49,* 203–218.

Stuart-Hamilton, I.A. (1986) The role of phonemic awareness in the reading style of beginning readers. *British Journal of Educational Psychology, 56,* 271–285

Stuart-Hamilton, I.A. (in press) Intellectual realism in the drawings of elderly people. To appear in: *Journal of Educational Gerontology, 8,* 110–114.

Stuart-Hamilton, I.A., Perfect, T. & Rabbitt, P. (1988) Remembering who was who. In M.M. Gruneberg, P.E. Morris & R.N. Sykes (eds) *Practical Aspects of Memory.* Volume 2.

Stuart-Hamilton, I.A., Rabbitt, P.M.A. & Huddy, A. (1988) The role of selective attention in the visuo-spatial memory of patients suffering from dementia of the Alzheimer type. *Comprehensive Gerontology B, 2,* 129–134.

Sulkava, R. (1982) Alzheimer's disease and senile dementia of the Alzheimer type: a comparative study. *Acta Neurologica Scandanavica, 65,* 636–650.

Sulkava, R. & Amberia, K. (1982) Alzheimer's disease and senile dementia of Alzheimer type: a neuropsychological study. *Acta Neurologica Scandanavica, 65,* 651–660.

Sundstrom, G (1986) Intergenerational mobility and the relationship between adults and their aging parents in Sweden. *The Gerontologist, 26,* 367–371.

Swan, G.E., Dame, A. & Carmelli, D. (1991) Involuntary retirement, Type A behavior, and current functioning in elderly men: 27-year follow-up of the Western Collaborative Group Study. *Psychology and Aging, 6,* 384–391.

Taub, H.A. (1979) Comprehension and memory of prose materials by young and old adults. *Experimental Aging Research, 5,* 3–13.

Taub, H.A., Baker, M.T. & Kline, G.E. (1982) Perceived choice of prose materials by young and elderly adults. *Educational Gerontology, 8,* 447–453.

Taub, H.A. & Kline, G. (1978) Recall of prose as a function of age and input modality. *Journal of Gerontology, 33,* 725–730.

Taylor, J.L., Miller, T.P., & Tinklenberg, J.R. (1993) Correlates of memory decline: A 4-year longitudinal study of older adults with memory complaints. *Psychology and Aging, 8,* 185–193.

Tenney, Y.J. (1984) Ageing and the misplacing of objects. *British Journal of Developmental Psychology, 2,* 43–50.

Teri, L. & Wagner, A.W. (1991) Assessment of depression in patients with Alzheimer's Disease: Concordance among informants. *Psychology and Aging, 6,* 280–285.

Thomae, H. (1980) Personality and adjustment to aging. In J.E. Birren & R.B. Sloane (eds) *Handbook of Mental Health and Aging.* New Jersey: Prentice-Hall.

Thompson, I.M. (1988) Communication changes in normal and abnormal ageing. In U. Holden (ed) *Neuropsychology and Aging.* London: Croom Helm.

Thompson, L.W., Gallagher-Thompson, D.G. Futterman, A. *et al.* (1991) The effects of late-life spousal bereavement over a 30-month interval. *Psychology and Aging, 6,* 434–441.

Thompson, L.W., Gong, V., Haskins, E. & Gallagher, D. (1987) Assessment of depression and dementia during the later years. In K.W. Schaie (ed) *Annual Review of Gerontology and Geriatrics, 7,* 295–324.

Thornton, E.W. (1984) *Exercise and Ageing: An Unproven Relationship.* Liverpool: Liverpool University Press.

Thurstone, T.G. (1958) *Manual for the SRA Primary Mental Abilities.* Chicago: Science Research Associates.

Tsai, H.K., Chou, F.S. & Cheng, T.J. (1958) On changes in ear size with age, as found among Taiwanese-Formosans of the Fukienese extraction. *Journal of the Formosan Medical Association, 57,* 105–111.

Tulving, E. (1972) Episodic and semantic memory. In E. Tulving & D.L. Horton (eds) *Verbal Behavior and General Behavior Theory.* New Jersey: Prentice-Hall.

Tun, P.A., Wingfield, A. Stine, E.A. & Mecsas, C. (1992) Rapid speech processing and divided attention: Processing rate versus processing resources as an explanation of age effects. *Psychology and Aging, 7,* 546–550.

Turner, J.S. & Helms, D.B. (1987) *Lifespan Development 3rd Edition.* New York: Holt, Rinehart and Winston.

Uttl, B. & Graf, P. (1993) Episodic spatial memory in adulthood. *Psychology and Aging, 8,* 257–273.

Vanderplas, J.M. & Vanderplas, J.H. (1980) Some factors affecting legibility of printed materials for older adults. *Perceptual and Motor Skills, 50,* 923–932.

Verrillo, R.T. (1982) Effects of aging on the suprathreshold responses to vibration. *Perception and Psychophysics, 32,* 61–68.

Vitaliano, P.P., Breen, A.R., Albert, M.S. *et al.* (1984) Memory, attention, and functional status in community-residing Alzheimer type dementia patients and optimally healthy aged individuals. *Journal of Gerontology, 39,* 58–64.

Vrtunski, P.B., Patterson, M.B., Mack, J.L. & Hill, G.O. (1983) Microbehavioural analysis of the choice reaction time response in senile dementia. *Brain, 106,* 929–947.

Walsh, D.A. (1982) The development of visual information processes in adulthood and old age. In F.I.M. Craik & S. Trehub (eds) *Aging and Cognitive Processes.* New York: Plenum.

Walsh, D.A., Williams, M.V. & Hertzog, C.K. (1979) Age-related differences in two stages of central perceptual processes: The effects of short duration targets and criterion differences. *Journal of Gerontology, 34,* 234–241.

Ward, R. (1977) The impact of subjective age and stigma on older persons. *Journal of Gerontology, 32,* 227–232.

Ward, R.A. (1984) *The Aging Experience.* Cambridge: Harper & Row.

Warrington, E (1975) The selective impairment of semantic memory. *Quarterly Journal of Experimental Psychology, 27,* 635–657.

Wasylenki, D.A. (ed) (1987) *Psychogeriatrics: A Practical Handbook.* London: Jessica Kingsley Publishers.

Waugh, N.C. & Barr, R.A. (1982) Encoding deficits in aging. In F.I.M. Craik & S. Trehub (eds) Aging and Cognitive Processes. New York: Plenum.

Weg, R.B. (1983) Changing physiology of aging: Normal and pathological. In D.S. Woodruff & J.E. Birren (eds) *Aging: Scientific Perspectives and Social Issues.* Monterey, Calif.: Brooks-Cole.

Weiffenbach, J.M., Baum, B.J. & Burghauser, R. (1982) Taste thresholds: Quality specific variation with human aging. *Journal of Gerontology, 37,* 372–377.

Weingartner, H., Kaye, W., Smallberg, S.A. *et al.* (1981) Memory failures in progressive idiopathic dementia. *Journal of Abnormal Psychology, 90,* 187–196.

Weingartner, H., Cohen, R.M., Bunney, W.E. *et al.* (1982) Memory learning impairments in progressive dementia and depression. *American Journal of Psychiatry, 139,* 135–136.

Weinstein, B.E. & Ventry, I.M. (1982) Hearing impairment and social isolation in the elderly. *Journal of speech and hearing research, 25,* 593–599.

Wenger, G.C. (1990) Elderly carers: the need for appropriate intervention. *Ageing and Society, 10,* 197–219.

West, R.L. (1988) Prospective memory and aging. In M.M. Gruneberg, P.E. Morris & R.N. Sykes (eds) *Practical Aspects of Memory.* Volume 2. Chichester: John Wiley.

West, R.L., Crook, T.H., & Barron, K.L. (1992) Everyday memory performance across the life span: Effects of age and noncognitive individual differences. *Psychology and Aging, 7,* 72–82.

Whelihan, W.M., Lesher, E.L., Kleban, M.H. & Granick, S. (1984) Mental status and memory assessment as predictors of dementia. *Journal of Gerontology, 39,* 572–576.

Whitbourne, S.K. (1986) *The Me I Know: A Study of Adult Identity.* New York: Springer.

Whitbourne, S.K. (1987) Personality development in adulthood and old age. In K.W. Schaie (ed) *Annual Review of Gerontology and Geriatrics, 7.* New York: Springer.

White, L.R., Cartwright, W.S., Cornoni-Huntley, J. & Brock, D.B. (1986) Geriatric epidemiology. In C. Eisdorfer (ed) *Annual Review of Gerontology and Geriatrics, 6,* New York: Springer.

White, N & Cunningham, W.R. (1988) Is terminal drop pervasive or specific? *Journal of Gerontology, 43,* 141–144.

Wickens, C.D., Braune, R. & Stokes, A. (1987) Age differences in the speed and capacity of information processing: 1 A dual task approach. *Psychology and Aging, 2,* 70–78.

Wilkins, A. & Baddeley, A. (1978) Remembering to recall in everyday life: an approach to absent-mindedness. In M.M. Gruneberg, P.E. Morris & R.N. Sykes (eds) *Practical Aspects of Memory.* Volume 2. Chichester: Wiley.

Wilkins, R. & Adams, O.B. (1983) Health expectancy in Canada, late 1970s: demographic, regional and social dimensions. *American Journal of Public Health, 73,* 1073–1080.

Williamson, G.M. & Schulz, R. (1992) Physical illness and symptoms of depression among elderly outpatients. *Psychology and Aging, 7,* 343–351.

Wilson, R.S., Bacon, L.D., Fox, J.H., Kaszniak, A.W. (1983) Primary memory and secondary memory in dementia of the Alzheimer type. *Journal of Clinical Neuropsychology, 8,* 337–344.

Wilson, R.S., Kaszniak, A.W., Bacon, L.D., Fox, J.H. & Kelly, M.P. (1982) Facial recognition memory in dementia. *Cortex, 18,* 329–336.

Wilson, R.S. Kaszniak, A.W. & Fox, J.H. (1981) Remote memory in senile dementia. *Cortex, 17,* 41–48.

Winocur, G. (1982) Learning and memory deficits in institutionalized and noninstitutionalized old people. In F.I.M. Craik & S. Trehub (eds) *Aging and Cognitive Processes.* New York: Plenum.

Winthorpe, C. & Rabbitt, P. (1988) Working memory capacity, IQ, age and the ability to recount autobiographical events. In M.M. Gruneberg, P.E. Morris & R.N. Sykes (eds) *Practical Aspects of Memory.* Volume 2.

Wingfield, A. & Stine, E.L. (1986) Organizational strategies in immediate recall of rapid speech by young and elderly adults. *Experimental Aging Research, 12,* 79–83.

Wisniewski, H.M. (1989) Milestones in the history of Alzheimer Disease research. In K. Iqbal, H.M. Wisniewski & B. Winblad (eds) *Alzheimer's Disease and Related Disorders.* New York: Alan R. Liss.

Wisniewski, H.M. & Sturman, J.A. (1988) Neurotoxicity of aluminium. In H. Gitelman (ed) *Aluminium and Health: A Critical Review.* New York: Marcel Dekker.

Woodward, K. (1991) *Aging and its Discontents. Freud and Other Fictions.* Bloomington: Indiana University Press.

Wyndham, J. (1960) *Trouble with Lichen.* London: Michael Joseph.

Zacks, R.T., Hasher, L., Doren, B. *et al.* (1987) Encoding and memory of explicit and implicit information. *Journal of Gerontology, 42,* 418–422.

Zelinski, E.M., Gilewski, M.J. & Schaie, K.W. (1993) Individual differences in cross-sectional and 3-year longitudinal memory performance across the adult life span. *Psychology and Aging, 8,* 176–186.

Zelinski, E.M., Light, L.L. & Gilewski, M.J. (1984) Adult age differences in memory for prose: the question of sensitivity to passage structure. *Developmental Psychology, 20,* 1181–1192.

Index